The Best Ever!

The Best Ever!

PARADES IN NEW ENGLAND, 1788–1940

Jane C. Nylander

BAUHAN PUBLISHING * PETERBOROUGH * NEW HAMPSHIRE
2021

ISBN 978-0-87233-345-1 Paperback edition
ISBN 978-0-87233-347-5 Hardcover edition

Library of Congress Cataloging-in-Publication Data
Names: Nylander, Jane C., 1938- author.
Title: The best ever! : Parades in New England, 1788-1940 / Jane C. Nylander.
Description: First Edition. | Peterborough, New Hampshire ; Sturbridge, MA : Bauhan Publishing : Old Sturbridge Village, 2021. | "The Best Ever! Parades in New England, from 1788-1940 is co-published by Old Sturbridge Village and Bauhan Publishing"—T.p. verso. | Includes bibliographical references and index. |
Identifiers: LCCN 2021038191 | ISBN 9780872333451 (Trade Paperback Edition) | ISBN 9780872333475 (Hardcover Edition)
Subjects: LCSH: Parades—New England--History. | New England—History.
Classification: LCC GT4005 .N95 2021 | DDC 394/.50974--dc23
LC record available at https://lccn.loc.gov/2021038191

All photographs used by permission with credits beginning on page 361.

The Best Ever! Parades in New England, 1788-1940
is co-published by Old Sturbridge Village and Bauhan Publishing

Book design by Henry James and Sarah Bauhan
Cover design by Henry James
Printed by Versa Press

1 OLD STURBRIDGE VILLAGE ROAD
STURBRIDGE, MA 01566

WWW.BAUHANPUBLISHING.COM

printed in the United States of America

Contents

Foreword

Parades in New England enjoy a robust history—as moments of celebration, of community, of civic pride, and of who we are as New Englanders and as Americans. In *The Best Ever! New England Parades, 1788–1940*, Jane Nylander brilliantly captures all the facts and fanfare of this history in a work both celebratory and scholarly.

As Jane herself says, everyone has a parade story! Whether colorful, thrilling processions filled with soldiers, musical bands, and local business displays, or solemn tableaux honoring dignitaries and historical events, parades offer momentary glimpses of the local community and of the world at large. The entries might depict bygone times or present-day innovations, the interests of the young or the contributions of older citizens, but parades always draw people together to witness the activities and events that are of most interest and importance at the time.

From militia musters to broom brigades, from agricultural displays to baby carriage processions, from civic organizations to Uncle Sam, Lady Liberty, and Columbia, *The Best Ever!* brings American history in New England to life. Readers will encounter Revolutionary War and Civil War veterans, political candidates, visiting heads of state, funerals, floral parades, Prohibition supporters, and New England's unique tradition of Antiques and Horribles.

When I came to Old Sturbridge Village as its new President in 2007, the outlook for the museum was dire. Not having a background in museum leadership, I quickly assembled a list of experts who knew the Village and who could serve as key strategic advisors as we wrote the plan for our renaissance. It should come as no surprise that Jane Nylander ranked at the top of the list. Her earlier tenure at Old Sturbridge Village, as Curator of Textiles from 1969 to 1986, was distinguished in a period of tremendous scholarship in the field of New England history, and of keen attention to the collections of the museum and how they might engage the public through our many living exhibits. Small wonder, then, that she has delved into the subject of parades with the same dedicated and careful attention.

For the last fourteen years, Jane has played a key role in helping to invigorate the Board of Directors' commitment to the Village, and in supporting some big, bold, and entrepreneurial steps to put us back on track. This detailed and lavishly illustrated book resonates with both our museum collections and our programs, and with those of historical societies throughout New England.

Old Sturbridge Village is proud to partner with Bauhan Publishing to bring this beautiful book to light as part of our 75th Anniversary celebration in 2021. After a period of historic anxiety and stress in our nation due to the Covid-19 pandemic, we hope that the months ahead provide opportunities for citizens across New England to come together again in the shared spaces of our public and civic experience.

James E. Donahue
President and CEO
Old Sturbridge Village
July 2021

Preface

Ever since I was a little girl, I have been fortunate to spend a part of each summer at a lakeside home in the town of Freedom, New Hampshire. How appropriate to be in a town named Freedom to celebrate the Fourth of July with a family gathering and plenty of loud fireworks echoing from the surrounding mountains and reflecting from the rippling dark water! What better place to enjoy Old Home Week with its garden party, band concert, games, water sports, library book sale, the firefighters' lobster supper, and the wonderful parade? Not just a single Old Home Day, like many New Hampshire towns, but Old Home *Week*! Nine or ten whole days, including *two* weekends devoted to family and community. Away from the screen and the phone, off the grid, doing what we have always done.

A tradition that began in New Hampshire more than a hundred years ago, Old Home Days are still highlights of summertime in dozens of communities throughout New England. In Freedom, people line the streets and their driveways with rows of small American flags. Local children are delighted if they have their own flags to wave as the parade goes by. Larger flags swirl from the bandstand and the town hall. Bunting adorns picket fences and cemetery gates. The post office is kept busy with customers seeking hand cancellations on their outgoing mail. A few families proudly display the same mammoth and moth-eaten old flags every year; some have forty-eight or fewer stars.

Freedom's Old Home Day parade resembles those in small towns across the country with its color guard and bands of musicians, venerable citizens riding in ancient horse-drawn carriages or freshly polished Cadillacs, and a line of antique cars that includes both a Model T and a Stanley Steamer. There are beautifully groomed saddle horses, well-trained oxen, crepe paper-trimmed bicycles and doll carriages, campaigning political candidates distributing candy or favors with their names on them, the Scouts, the Sunday school children, the veterans, the Shriners with their big drums and funny little cars, the Ladies' Aid, and the Friends of the Library. Some large families display old canoes, fishing equipment, or tennis racquets as they walk together with their octogenarians and infants. One big family carries signs from an expanding collection, each identifying their current place of residence—testament to their far-flung modern life and to the strong pull that brings them back to Freedom for the first week in August whenever they can possibly come. There are also children from the summer camps, many from urban homes, and some from countries far away, all of them enjoying a way of life that is different from their own day-to-day experience, yet both wonderful and nurturing, a source of lifelong memories and friendships.

As the end of the line approaches, the scream of fire sirens is heard. Volunteer fire companies from towns all around arrange for coverage through mutual aid, thereby releasing some trucks and crews to participate in the final feature of the Freedom parade. Taxpayers are eager to see the costly new vehicle that provoked such controversy at town meeting time. Obsolete or specialized equipment that has been specially cleaned and polished swells the ranks: both the 1948 forest-firefighting tanker and the 1928 Ford. Veteran firemen compete for the honor of driving the oldest or the newest truck. Before today's stringent safety regulations, children eagerly climbed on firetrucks to ride in parades. Today the children and grandchildren of firefighters ride proudly on laps of family members, throwing candy to spectators, their own classmates among them.

Brave Timothy Nylander, 1979

I have watched Old Home Day parades with family members since 1947 and have even participated in a few. I have taken pictures every year, beginning with my Brownie camera. Snapshots we called them. Although it is always fun to see who has been designated Grand Marshall, the 4-H kids with their heifers, and a '59 Chevy like my own first car, most interesting to me have been the floats. For me, the highlights of any parade are always those creative moving tableaux that illustrate important stories. Sometimes the parade has a comprehensive historical theme with floats that personify abstract ideas, illustrate high points in American history, or highlight significant local traditions. In other years, the topics of the floats are unrelated to each other, reflecting changes in family composition or in national affairs. Over the years I have observed that some topics are repeated again and again no matter what theme has been chosen by the parade committee. The "Log Cabin," the "Quilting Party," the "One-Room Schoolhouse," the "Liberty Bell," New Hampshire's "Old Man of the Mountain," an "Indian Campfire," and jokes about local fishing are perennially popular. In anniversary years there is a tiered cardboard birthday cake with the number of candles equal to that of the year being observed; I think the highest number I have seen so far was 200 for the nation's bicentennial in 1976. Soon we'll see 250.

I remember once turning enthusiastically to my husband, Richard, as the sun beat down on a particularly hot August morning, and saying something like, "This is fabulous. It feels like the whole community has shared its history and defined its priorities. Someone should do a book about Old Home Day parades. Imagine all this creativity in a town of less than 1,500 people. The floats are really folk art in its best possible sense, naïve and narrative at the same time." He agreed, and we turned to appreciate the next float lurching along Elm Street.

Over the course of the next few years the idea of a book kept simmering in my mind. I dragged my family to more than one parade each summer and kept my Instamatic busy. As I talked with friends and colleagues about parades, I realized that, thanks to television broadcasting, most people think first of the Rose Parade, Mardi Gras, the Philadelphia Mummers, and Macy's Thanksgiving Parades as the country's best. Then their memories quickly revert to their own experiences in high school marching bands, escorting high school homecoming Queens and football heroes, carrying lilacs in Memorial Day processions, or the hilarious time they had building a float and creating costumes out of odds and ends for the Fourth of July or Old Home Day. Some laugh out loud as they describe their participation in a distinctly New England phenomenon, a parade of Antiques and Horribles.

I've found that everyone has a parade story. The best are fond memories of people's own participation with a group of family, friends, or neighbors in something that they remember as exciting, colorful, and significant. All American cities and towns have strong parade traditions and most share a common structure and widespread ideas.

Their marching units and creative floats honor various identities and affiliations, promote ideas, candidacies, and products, and at the same time define and strengthen the bonds of community.

I have chosen to focus on New England in order to bring to light the unique stories and rich diversity of the regional parade tradition. I have lived and worked here most of my adult life, so I know it well. My love of the region was inspired not only by summertime visits, but by the careful nurturing of my mother and grandmother, both keepers of old-fashioned traditions who shared a nostalgic view of the New England way of life. During sixteen years in the Curatorial Department of Old Sturbridge Village, I was encouraged to study in the rich collections of New England's local historical societies and libraries. As I began to seek information about parades, I've found that I can go back to any of these places and still meet proud staff and volunteers who are thrilled to share with me the treasured photographs, tattered programs, wrinkled ribbon badges, and crumbling newspaper clippings that document civic occasions that are almost always remembered as "the most magnificent occasion" or "the greatest ever held here." It's an entertaining task that could go on for years, but it is time to draw a line and share the highlights and some of the significance of what I have found.

—Jane C. Nylander
President Emerita
Historic New England
July 2021

Introduction

This study of parades in the years before World War II is centered on New England, a compact and well-defined geographical area that cherishes its rich history and often sees itself as a wellspring of lofty American values. Being locally produced, a parade always reflects the sponsoring community, both what it actually is and what it aspires to be. Much relies on repetition of cherished symbols, myth, and stereotype. The preferred visual narrative blends vivid presentations of selective identities, ideas, behaviors, history, and values that emerge from cultural memory and help to define the present. Even in appearances by New England's unique troops of Antiques and Horribles, past and present are woven together. Further, parades offer a chance for citizens to express differing opinions and lifestyles, innovative ideas, support for reform, and desire for change. Sincerely presented, all this adds up to an authentic and enjoyable experience, illustrating the complex fabric of every city and town.

On parade day, a New England community still reveals itself. Both local residents and out-of-town visitors see what is valued, who is respected, and who has turned out to see and be seen. People join in welcoming distinguished visitors, celebrating the completion of public works, the laying of cornerstones for public buildings, the dedication of statues, and the anniversaries of momentous events. In large cities there is often a celebration of innovation and progress visualized by the appearance of skilled workers and a display of local products. In smaller towns, visitors celebrate the preservation of an iconic landscape with its historic buildings, town common, and tree-lined streets, while mourning the loss of beloved landmarks and complaining about lack of parking. In both cities and towns, elderly residents and returning natives savor shared memories and are reassured that long-honored traditions continue, community values are highlighted and upheld, and priorities are in the right place. Young adults absorb ideas about history and significance, observe both continuity and change, and ponder what might be missing. All are challenged to find a way to illustrate pressing concerns and bring to life additional memories as they plan to participate next year and make it even better.

Children have a vivid civics lesson—witnessing large numbers of people participating in public life, observing who and what is important, what is being questioned, who participates and who just watches, which models to emulate, and which goals to adopt as they see both well-known adults and complete strangers in public roles. They learn through observation and participation how much work it is to be involved in both preparation and cleanup, how much fun it is to share common activity and goals, and how satisfying it is to be part of something bigger than one's self. They may also be prompted to begin considering their own future role in the life of the community.

From the ratification processions of 1788 to the victory celebrations of 1918 and the tercentennial celebrations of the 1920s and 1930s, the impact of parades on the spectators standing street side has multiplied across the country as New England ideas and images spread through print in newspaper descriptions, commercially produced engravings and lithographs, schoolbooks, stereoviews, illustrated magazines, and thousands of postcards. Ideas also spread by word of mouth and personal correspondence as people emigrated, traveled, or spoke on the telephone.

Parade planners have always drawn upon personal experience, fond memories, and favorite stories to create floats displaying memorable scenes of historic events, honoring civic leaders and military heroes, mourning fallen soldiers, or celebrating innovation and progress. The advent of television and now social media have brought faster transmission of ideas and an almost overwhelming variety of images to our rich visual culture. Although many things in parades seem familiar to everyone, some elements reflect the classical education that once gave a widespread basis for understanding allegorical and literary references that may be lost on many in today's audiences. Other presentations offer insight to the less familiar history and traditions of immigrant groups or private associations. Parades themselves are rich sources of ideas about history. Repetition of favorite topics gives them added significance and embeds them in the popular mind.

There is no denying that for a long time the participants displaying their identity in parades were almost exclusively white Protestant men identified as "Citizens on foot or in carriages." Most often the men appeared as elected officials or in groups representing professions, fraternal groups, and the military. Although the Fourteenth Amendment extended citizenship to "all persons born or naturalized in the United States" in 1868, diversity in public processions was still rare. Among the first Black groups to appear were members of the Prince Hall Lodge in Boston. Gradually, self-designated units representing a range of immigrant groups and women's organizations were included, both as marchers and as sponsors of narrative floats. Minutes of parade planning committees make clear that decisions about participation reflected unspoken local customs that excluded people based on race and gender. In many places it is still true that participation depends more on who you know than on who you are.

Undoubtedly women have always worked behind the scenes creating costumes and chaperoning or disciplining children, but for a long time their visible participation was limited to allegorical representations of Columbia, Liberty,

Peace, the colonies, the states, the nation, or the "Queen" of something. Female parade participants were almost always described as "pretty girls." Their prescribed costumes involved low necklines, short sleeves, and soft, clinging fabrics, requirements that expressed sexist tropes. In the same way, racism confined most Black participants to roles as servants, grooms, or examples of an oriental "other," and permitted the use of masks, blackface, or stereotyped characterizations that appeared as clumsy, foolish, or ineffective. All of this will be offensive to modern audiences, yet I have tried to present it in the context of its own time, in an honest effort to acknowledge the deep roots of difficult issues that are part of our national story.

The images presented here allow us to see visual representations of widely held ideas and meaningful narratives. Time-honored topics presented over many years illustrate people's pride in being Americans and their affection for the country and its history. Although Old Home Days, community anniversary celebrations, and specific historical topics reflect personal affection for New England history and enhance a sense of place, they often romanticize handcraft and an agrarian past. In truth, many of the parades seen on these occasions also express pride in industrial innovation and deliberately illustrate a bustling economy favorable to business. At the same time that parades celebrate tradition and progress, some expose deeply ingrained prejudice and racism, offering hints of anxiety caused by perceived threats to what has been believed to be a stable, reliable world.

To enrich the widespread understanding of the cultural importance of parades, this book illustrates the impact and creativity of floats, banners, civic decoration, and costumes, rather than the uniformity and power of long lines of marching men. Many parade components were heartfelt expressions of very ordinary people, not the products of trained artists or designers. Indeed, the floats can be seen as a form of folk art: original, narrative, ephemeral, and filled with meaning. These are the kind of parade portrayals that an attendee on the Fourth of July in one Vermont town described to me as "touchingly ridiculous but I never want to miss it."

It will be readily observed that this is not a comprehensive study. In addition to being centered on a defined geographic region, it is highly selective, relying on the best possible images and arbitrarily ending at the beginning of World War II. These selected examples cover a period of slightly more than 150 years, illustrating a variety of occasions, ideas, and themes, some of them popular for only a few years, some spanning the entire time frame, and others for which meaning changed over time. Circus processions, religious festivals, sporting victories, commencement processions, military encampments, and boat parades have been excluded in order to concentrate on celebrations of a more general civic nature, thus giving a window into the mindset of very ordinary New Englanders as well as the priorities and accomplishments of its people in both small towns and growing cities.

All of this is briefly seen in an exciting public moment, each idea presented by a float or marching group succeeded by the next, only to disappear until the next year, but leaving lasting memories of reassuring symbols and sparkling innovation. Importantly, we are challenged to understand how ideas have been shaped over time and changed by circumstance, even as perceptions of the past are still evolving and questioned in the present.

The book begins and ends with images of patriotism. Chapter 1 uses Independence Day presentations to introduce most of the topics seen in greater detail throughout the rest of the book; Chapter 8 allows us to revel for a moment in nostalgic patriotism—those celebrations of the red, white, and blue that are still central in any parade, where cherished symbols, shared emotion, and broad community participation give people a chance to express their love of country, its history, and their pride in being Americans. We can hope to see such feeling regain its strength and meaning as we move forward with healing and work together to embrace and celebrate our shared identity as citizens of the United States of America.

NOTE

Some descriptions and images in this publication include outdated language and/or depictions of people and cultures that we now recognize as harmful or offensive. While they reflect the times in which they appeared, both the author and the publisher understand that the creation and perpetuation of these negative stereotypes was hurtful in earlier times and continues to be so. Our hope is that their inclusion in this book will provide important insights about our past and a platform for conversations about today.

1

CELEBRATION

As a member of the Continental Congress in Philadelphia, Pennsylvania, on July 3, 1776, Massachusetts delegate John Adams wrote to his wife, Abigail, at their home in Braintree, describing his feelings about the successful vote for Independence taken late the previous evening:

> ". . . I am apt to believe that it will be celebrated by succeeding generations as the great anniversary Festival. It ought to be commemorated, as the day of deliverance, by solemn acts of devotion to God Almighty. It ought to be solemnized with pomp and parades. With shows, games, sports, guns, bells, bonfires, and illuminations, from one end of this continent to the other, from this time forward, forevermore."
>
> —*Letter from John Adams to Abigail Adams, July 3, 1776* [1]

Debate was closed the next day and it has been the Fourth of July that is celebrated as the birthday of the country ever since.

Independence Day

Adams' predictions of pomp and parade, bonfires and illuminations, games and guns on the Fourth of July have proven prescient, although there has been some change. Pomp and parade, games and guns continue, but bonfires and illumination of buildings by candlelight have largely been moved to other occasions. Fireworks, band concerts, baseball games, boating, and picnics are now the big thing. Independence Day activities have always been lively, noisy, and thrilling. Since at least 1812, they have also been red, white, and blue.

Bristol, Rhode Island, has declared itself the location of the oldest and grandest celebration of the Fourth of July in the entire country. Indeed, the small town on Narragansett Bay appears to have an almost unbroken history of Independence Day observances variously including patriotic exercises and orations, picnics, band concerts, fireworks, and all sorts of land and water sports. The first parade, in 1785, was a procession of citizens escorting dignitaries to the meetinghouse for special exercises. With only a few exceptions, Bristol has held some kind of parade on the Fourth ever since.

As in others all across the country, the form and focus of New England's Fourth of July parades have varied over time. At first, they were dignified civic processions composed of governmental officials, community leaders, and military units marching in orderly divisions to rhythms established by a drummer. In most cases, these men served to escort local luminaries, the Congregational minister, and the men selected as Orator of the Day or the reader of the Declaration of Independence, accompanying them to the spot where formal exercises were to be held. The early orations usually reminded people of the human cost of the Revolution and recounted the blessings of liberty. Fourth of July speakers have also discussed local as well as national political issues and current hot-button topics like temperance, abolition, immigration, or pacifism. At the same time, they seek to stimulate feelings of patriotism and loyalty through comforting repetition of ritual and stirring remembrances of the past.

Independence Day celebrations soon came to resemble military Training Days, with soldiers marching to stirring drumbeats, cannon firing, church bells ringing, sporting contests, excited children darting in and out, booths selling gingerbread and hard cider, punctuated by fireworks and ammunition exploding well into the night.

Soon after 1800, Fourth of July parades began to include floats with young ladies representing the thirteen colonies or the growing number of states of the Union. The 1830s saw the first rowdy and satirical processions of young men called Fantastics, Odds and Ends, or Horribles. By 1841, the date was often chosen by Sunday schools for the presentation of floral processions with bands of children carrying floral crosses, lyres, hearts, and bouquets in addition to a sequence of pretty allegorical or historical floats. Bristol saw its first Fantastics in 1857, a floral procession in 1865, and the Antiques and Horribles first stepped forth there the following year.

Fourth of July traditions continued after the Civil War and they have ebbed and flowed throughout New England ever since. The centennial year of 1876 was a national high point after which many states, as well as towns and cities, pulled out all the stops for their own civic anniversaries. At the turn of the century, enthusiasm for personal fireworks triggered widespread public concern about rising numbers of related injuries and deaths. The resultant pressure by physicians, newspaper editors, public officials, and women's groups for a "Safe and Sane Fourth" suited the Progressive spirit of the era, and legislation prohibiting the use of fireworks was enacted in many places in 1909 and 1910. Civic officials tried to substitute huge bonfires and more elaborate parades as preferred modes of celebration. It worked for a few years, but soon the fireworks were back, bigger and noisier than ever. Celebrations featuring parades waned during times of war and depression and surged again whenever a new group was inspired by idealism, patriotism, prosperity, innovation, or simply by aversion to the boredom of long speeches.

In this first chapter we will encounter some of the typical components of many parades. Every chapter of this book includes examples of the creativity of spirit and the kinds of varied concerns and special interests expressed in these Fourth of July parades. Each reflects its own time and place, but the unifying cord of patriotism is still celebrated. A few examples will set the stage:

Southbridge Light Infantry

Southbridge, Massachusetts, July 4, 1826

Captain Luther Ammidown sought to preserve his memory of the July 4, 1826, celebration marking the nation's Jubilee, the fiftieth anniversary of the signing of the Declaration of Independence, by creating this meticulously detailed ink-and-watercolor sketch (*see next page*). It shows the moment when the parade of soldiers, four abreast, had split and moved apart to stand at parade rest facing an elevated stage where an imposing lady in a plumed hat holds a tall flagstaff. On her left is an empty chair and a man in a tall hat who may be about to step up and deliver an oration or read the Declaration itself.

1826

Behind the soldiers are several lines of men and women, patiently waiting for the speaker of the day. Behind them are a few men on horseback and one couple arriving in a large carriage. Further from the platform, some people are less focused on the speaker, being engaged in conversation, strolling together, or supervising children. Others are simply continuing to go about their daily business on foot or driving vehicles on the surrounding roads.

Hinsdale Town Band

Hinsdale, New Hampshire, July 4, 1855

Even before the Civil War, brass bands were organized by young men in many New England towns. Since members were usually unpaid, they solicited public and private contributions to support purchases of uniforms and instruments—usually eighteen or twenty various horns and one or more drums. These bands marched with parades and performed in concerts on the Fourth of July and, after 1868, on Decoration Day as well as at other civic celebrations, fairs, reunions, or other special events. Sometimes tavern keepers offered free food and drink to band members. In some places, public funds supported specific band concerts or the construction of a community bandstand, but public support for a band itself was indeed rare.

Considerable local pride was invested in the appearance and skill of a town band. Friendly rivalries that developed between communities fostered the acquisition of new instruments and uniforms, development of new skills, and expansion of the musical repertoire. Membership in a band offered men a special elevated status in the community and the fraternal pleasures of participation in a defined group.

THE
CONSTITUTION
AND THE UNION, THEY
MUST BE PRESERVED
OUR COUNTRY.
UNION.
LIBERTY
JUSTICE
JULY 4
1776
LIBERTY.
JUSTICE.
JULY 4
1861
NATIONAL ARCH.

The Constitution and the Union, They Must Be Preserved

Portsmouth, New Hampshire, probably 1861

This elaborate National Arch with its timely patriotic symbolism is the frontispiece in an unpublished manuscript, *The Floral Architect, and Decorator's Companion. Containing Designs and Rules for Projecting Forty Triumphal Arches and Monuments, Fifty Cars and Chariots, for Floral, National, Horticultural, and Firemen's Processions . . .*, written by James Head (ca. 1830–1869), a bookseller, decorator, and author in Portsmouth. Perhaps as early as 1845, Head was actively involved in planning and producing street decorations and floats for civic celebrations and floral processions in his native city. In *The Floral Architect*, he provided watercolor illustrations and detailed handwritten instructions for constructing and decorating forty-three different civic arches and monuments in addition to ninety-three parade floats or "cars" illustrating a variety of allegorical subjects and historical narratives. His naïve and colorful drawings show the floats pulled by smiling oxen or caparisoned horses and embellished with arrangements of flags, flowers, and painted mottoes. Detailed newspaper descriptions comparing floral processions at Portsmouth with those in many other New England cities and towns between 1851 and 1860 indicate that Head's work illustrates the full vocabulary of float design before the age of widespread outdoor photography. His illustrations are an unusual visual record of what mid-nineteenth-century parade floats actually looked like. Some of the designs in *The Floral Architect*, however, are so top-heavy and ambitious that it is probable they were never actually built.

Head may have designed the National Arch to inspire patriotism on July 4, 1861, early in the Civil War, but there is no evidence that it was constructed. Crowned by trophy of flags and a spread-winged eagle, the topmost beam, identified as "Our Country," supports the words "The Constitution and the Union, They Must Be Preserved," an idea that must have been the primary concern of those celebrating the holiday at that fraught moment. Over the pillar on the left stands a figure of Justice looking somewhat disappointed with her scales let down and her sword pointing to the words "Union" and "Justice" above the date "July 4, 1776." On the right a figure of Liberty stands with her symbolic cap on a tall pole while she looks to heaven for support in securing the founding principles of the nation. Beneath her are the key words "Liberty and Justice" and the date "July 4, 1861," a time when these ideals were threatened by the secession of the southern states and the fierce fighting between North and South that had already begun. As Head compiled his ambitious manuscript during the early 1860s while the Civil War was raging, his selection of his design for a National Arch for a frontispiece is telling. The iconography is an excellent summation of the emotions and ideals of the fractured nation.

Honoring Public Servants

Marblehead, Massachusetts, July 4, 1884

Most civic processions include firefighters, either the entire force of the sponsoring community or delegations from neighboring places. Here Marblehead firefighters wearing parade uniforms consisting of red jackets, dark pants, white leather belts, and their protective leather helmets were joined by several men in civilian dress as they stood beneath an arch of evergreen before the Independence Day parade in 1884. The men were proud of their oldest piece of equipment, a refillable water tank and pumper of the type commonly known as a hand tub, decorated for the occasion with flowers and evergreen.

Car of Young Ladies Representing Thirty-Eight States
Thomaston, Maine, July 4, 1887

As the country grew and more states were added to the Union, larger vehicles were needed for this kind of popular parade presentation in which an array of young ladies represented the individual states of the Union. At Thomaston in 1887, this large farm wagon was fitted with benches to carry thirty-eight young women in white dresses with matching caps and diagonal sashes. Their number reflected the admission of Colorado eleven years earlier. The wagon was lightly trimmed with swags of evergreen along the sides and a cluster of bunting at the front. Pennants hung over the sides of the wagon, each bearing the name of a different state. A woman in a gown with bands of stripes at the neck and waist above a starry skirt stood on the driver's seat, holding a tall liberty pole. Her very traditional representation of Liberty was uninfluenced by the design of the Statue of Liberty that had been dedicated in New York Harbor in late October of the previous year.

Stereographs like this appeared as three-dimensional images when the two nearly identical pictures were viewed through two lenses in a hand-held device known as a stereoscope, not unlike the once popular View-Master. Viewing stereographs was a popular kind of parlor entertainment and the cards were produced by the thousands in the last half of the nineteenth century. They were sold singly or as boxed sets, preserving memories of local events and individual travel, illustrating comic memes, and expanding the worldview of many.

Remember the Maine

Greenville, New Hampshire, July 4, 1898

These young boys donned sailor suits to ride on a very timely float during a Fourth of July parade in 1898. Their small motor launch had been fitted with a short central mast before being mounted on a utilitarian wagon draped with bunting. Their effort was in support of the American response to the unexplained explosion of the USS *Maine* and the loss of 260 members of its crew while the ship was at anchor in Havana Harbor on February 15. The *Maine* had been sent to Havana the previous December to protect American interests in the face of tensions caused by Spanish colonialism. "Remember the Maine" became a rallying cry and by April the United States and Spain were at war. In the Philippines, the American fleet under Commodore George Dewey, won a thrilling victory over the Spanish navy in Manila Bay on May 1, and by August the Spanish American War was essentially over.

Part of Parade
South Shaftsbury, Vermont, July 4, 1908

New England's Fourth of July parade tradition has been strong enough to draw forth public participation and support for nearly 225 years. Sometimes there are long lines of marchers, elaborate floats, and multiple bands, but at other times, as seen here, it seems to have been enough to trim the wheels of a bicycle or carriage, hitch up the family horse, dress in costume or one's Sunday best, and join the line as it moved through town.

Horribles Presented by Hall Farm Owners and Employees

North Bennington, Vermont, probably July 4, 1912

The distinctive New England tradition of satirical and fantastical parades known as the Fantastics, the Antiques and Horribles, or simply the Horribles was well established even before the Civil War. Usually held on the Fourth of July, in some places there was a completely separate parade of Horribles that stepped forth in the early morning hours, often at five or six o'clock, well before the official civic procession began. In other places Horribles were confined to a separate division of the official procession. Occasionally a single float like this one at North Bennington was just tucked into the line of march, offering a bit of comic relief. This fern- and flag-decked wagon was organized by the owners and employees of Hall Farm, all of whom were masked.

Since at least 1868, masks had been advertised widely

as essential Fourth of July supplies, often being sold along with fireworks of all kinds. In this case one man on the waagon was dressed in his everyday work clothes and wide-brimmed straw hat, but the others appeared as farm animals. The man in suspenders on the front seat seems to represent a pig, for his mask has a definite snout and two perky ears. How and why such things came to be features in Fourth of July processions remains unknown. It is worth remembering, though, that one of the stated purposes of many parade participants was simply to have a good time.

Centennial Parade
Southbridge, Massachusetts, July 4, 1916

Although many towns have a parade every year on the Fourth of July, the years that mark civic anniversaries—the centennials, sesquicentennials, bicentennials, tercentennials, and, soon, in 2026, the bicenquinquagenary or quarter millennial (250th anniversary) of the United States—are always pretty special. Extra effort and expense result in the arrival of many distinguished visitors and family members who live at a distance, elaborate civic decorations, more musicians, a review of historical events, souvenirs, commemorative publications, and extraordinary parade floats.

In this centennial parade we have a glimpse of an historical feature adjacent to social and policial advocacy. The costumed frontiersman walking alone is followed by white horses pulling the idealistic float of the local women's club. The ladies inside wear white togas with sashes expressing their support of education, conservation, motherhood, and other important concerns of women in a modern community. Not surprisingly, these forward-looking women were also advocates of women's suffrage. Following them in the line are two women bravely riding astride well-groomed horses and a marching troop of white-clad suffragettes.

If We Farmers Miss the Prize, Blame the Weather Man
Canterbury, New Hampshire, July 4, 1916

Within the seclusion of their communal villages, members and wards of New England's Shaker communities enjoyed many of the same traditions celebrated in the outside world. These three girls residing with the Shakers presented this float focused on farming in their community's own Fourth of July parade in 1916. Two of them carry a funeral bier on which is a small model of a farmyard with a sign reading "If We Farmers Miss the Prize, Blame the Weather Man." The bier is covered with a white cloth, the sides of which are painted with a team of horses pulling a hand plow that appears to be driven by the girl in Shaker garb as she holds up her end of the bier. They posed for a photographer beside the Dwelling House, North Shop, and Water Tower of the community. Other floats presented and photographed that day included representations of buttermaking, canning vegtables, cleanliness, and Shaker fancywork. Shaker understanding of innovations in lighting was illustrated with girls dressed as a tallow candle, a kerosene lamp, and an electric light bulb. A float representing "Reading, Ritin, and Rithmetic" emphasized Shaker commitment to the education of the children entrusted to their care.

Alfred Conte's Float

Lenox, Massachusetts, July 4, 1921

In 1921, a self-employed thirty-year-old shoemaker, Alfred Conte, entered this float in the Fourth of July parade at Lenox. The Conte family had emigrated from Italy in 1906 and Alfred now lived in Lenox with his Italian-born wife, Sarah, their three-year-old daughter, Estalia, and his widowed mother, Rosalie. The rather awkward float reflected his dual loyalties, carrying flags of both the United States of America and Italy as well as two crowned young women in costumes representing each country, along with another holding a white umbrella trimmed with flowers and wearing a simple white dress with a red, white, and blue sash.

Which of the three men standing here is Mr. Conte is unknown. Having wrapped a truck in red, white, and blue bunting and trimmed it with flags and floral bouquets in tall vases, one can only assume that he and the two men seen here have helped the three young women to climb on top and are now prepared to drive very carefully through Lenox in the parade, peeking through a tiny clear area on the windshield. It's hard to imagine that either the girls or the tall flower vases made it safely to the end of the ride, unless there were some kind of strong supports hidden behind them.

Ratification of the Constitution

Less than forty-eight hours after Massachusetts became the sixth state to vote in favor of ratification of the new federal Constitution on February 6, 1788, a small committee of Boston artisans and mechanics had organized a celebratory procession. Modeled on the processions of the London Livery Companies that date back to medieval times, Boston's ratification procession may have been like nothing ever seen before in New England. The inclusion of men of many classes and occupations reflecting agriculture, the arts, manufactures, and commerce embodied the democratic ideals of the delegates who had drafted the new Constitution. Their enthusiastic participation in the procession offered tangible evidence of both their commitment and their wide range of skills, boding well for the prosperity of the new nation.

Stepping off at eleven o'clock on the frosty morning of Friday, February 8, 1788, when the ground was covered with snow, more than 1,500 men moved through the Boston streets in occupational groups with identifying banners. Newspapers throughout the country published extensive descriptions, helping to set a high bar for ratification processions elsewhere and a model for other future events. The line of march was led by sixteen foresters with axes and brush scythes symbolically clearing the land. Next, to underscore the idea that agriculture would be the foundation of a successful society, farming was personified by a man with a plough, followed by sowers strewing seed from baskets, reapers with sickles, mowers with scythes, hay makers with rakes, yokes of fat cattle, and husbandmen with hoes, spades, and other farming utensils. There were also two ox-drawn carts with elements of sustenance and raiment: the first was loaded with fresh cuts of beef and followed by eight master butchers walking in clean white frocks. The other carried flax dressers preparing linen fibers for spinning. Following them were twenty-eight groups of tradesmen, each man carrying the tools of his trade decorated with ribbons. Ship builders exhibited a sled, on which was a large work yard with thirteen vessels under construction. On another sled printers operated a press and handed freshly printed messages to people along the route. The symbolic heart of it all was the ship, *Federal Constitution,* also on runners, drawn by thirteen horses, another representation of the thirteen states now united in a common purpose.

In the new United States, the idea of a "Ship of State" quickly became a part of popular culture, an emblem of both the government and the nation itself. Following the Boston example, Baltimore's procession on May 1 and Charleston's in mid-June both included ships named *Federalist.* Later in June when New Hampshire became the ninth state to ratify, the ship *Union* was drawn at Portsmouth by nine horses and accompanied by a tenth representing Virginia, harnessed and ready to join the rest as soon as a vote could be taken. On the Fourth of July, New Haven's grand procession included the ship *Constitution.* Later in the month, on July 23, the great procession in New York included the federal ship *Hamilton.*

According to the diary of the Reverend Ezra Stiles, president of Yale College at New Haven, the procession there was formed by "a committee of all descriptions . . . according to the idea conceived at Boston at their rejoicing last winter." Once again, the line was led by a sower and oxen, followed by reapers, rakers, groups of tradesmen, and then a federal ship, after which came local officials, merchants, clergy, and Yale students, all together forming a procession nearly a mile and three-quarters long.

Model of the Ship Constitution

New Haven, Connecticut, July 4, 1788

Astonishingly, this is the very ship that appeared in the center of New Haven's ratification procession on July 4, 1788. Described then as a "Federal Ship with all sails flying and manned by a Captain and Sailors," this ship model appears to be the oldest surviving object ever used as a parade float in New England. Said to have been found floating in the English Channel in 1768, it was carried in a procession at New Haven, celebrating the end of the Revolutionary War in 1783 as well as in the ratification procession there in 1788. Indeed, it was used in so many subsequent New Haven processions that by the time of New Haven's 250th anniversary in 1888, the ship was called "quite a familiar sight." In 1883 the model was bequeathed by local antiquarian Joseph W. Bennett to the New Haven Colony Historical Association, now known as the New Haven Museum, where it remains.

Abolition Day

Splendid Celebration, of the "BOBALITION" of Slavery, by the African Society (detail)
Boston, Massachusetts, 1823

In response to the abolition of the slave trade in 1808, several hundred free Black members of a mutual aid group known as the Boston African Society processed through the city annually on June 14, continuing through the 1820s. Even though slavery itself continued to be legal in much of the country, the men in Boston celebrated what was known then as Abolition Day.

The early progress toward equality was not widely heralded, however. In 1823, this image appeared as part of a racist broadside satirizing the African Society and their events. The lengthy text uses black dialect in an outrageous parody of the many published reports of the activities, toasts, and sermons of Boston's Black community. Three years earlier, when white spectators hissed and booed the marching men and gangs of whites followed the processions, mimicking and taunting the participants, the editor of the *Boston Recorder* hailed June 14, 1821, as "the one day in the year in which the sons of Africa may know that they are men, and exercise something like national feeling."

Victory

Perhaps the most heart-felt topics for parades are the departures of soldiers and the successful conclusion of war. Although crowds of proud and anxious people turn out for civic processions that salute departing troops, nothing compares with the combined emotions of joy, pride, sadness, loss, and general relief that surface as survivors are welcomed and celebrated, first upon their return and then again on subsequent celebrations of the Fourth of July, Decoration Day, or Armistice Day. Triumphal arches and an abundance of flags salute some returning soldiers and sailors, but there is little evidence of floats as part of the welcoming processions. The following selection of images illustrates some of these tangible expressions of what must have been widespread and powerful feelings of happiness, gratitude, patriotism, and hope for the future.

Victory
Portsmouth, New Hampshire, ca. 1861–1865

Apparently not designed for a specific occasion, *The Car of Victory* is an allegorical design that float designer James Head considered one of his best. Crowned by a figure of Liberty specified as one-third larger than life, the towering float was to be adorned with stars, shields, and laurel wreaths as well as military trophies, eagles, and portraits of both George Washington and the Marquis de Lafayette. Reflecting the influence of circus wagons that toured New England each summer, Head's ambitious *Car of Victory* was to be drawn by four white horses adorned with long plumes and caparisoned in purple and gold. Each horse was to be ridden by a "warrior" in

steel armor that could be rented from a professional costume supplier.

From time immemorial, parade floats have featured women in scanty garments and Head's ideas for female participants were no different. He specified that pretty young ladies of equal height were to ride as "living caryatids" representing goddesses of victory. They were to wear long white dresses with low-cut necklines, short sleeves, and few underskirts as they stood at each corner of the vehicle and pretended to blow cardboard trumpets covered with silver paper. Because Head knew well the importance of providing support for people riding on lurching floats, he specified that each lady have an iron bar to hold tightly as well as a strong leather strap secured around her waist. Safely protected by the warriors riding nearby and representing a classical ideal, Head's Victorian girls were expected to push the limits of propriety in a very public place.

Civil War

All Honor to Our Gallant Army & Navy

Worcester, Massachusetts, July 4, 1865

On the Fourth of July in 1865, many cities celebrated the end of the Civil War and the return of local soldiers with special parades, public exercises, and elaborate civic decorations. During the war, the Fourth had been marked throughout New England with prayer and picnics, but there had been very few parades or displays of fireworks. In the months following Lee's surrender at Appomattox on April 9, people began to talk about much more ambitious festivities. Appointed on May 30, the planning committee at Worcester made arrangements for elaborate civic decorations and not one, but two, processions on the Fourth of July, just five weeks later. One would be a display of the industries and resources of the community and the other an ovation to the soldiers including the Goddess of Liberty as well as thirty-six young ladies, each symbolizing a state of the Union.

This celebratory arch opposite Harrington's Corner at the junction of Pleasant and Main Streets was one of five erected at prominent locations in the center of the city. Each arch had red, white, and blue trimming, and signs naming the major battles in which local soldiers had participated. The arches must have been dazzling at night when open flames of liquefied coal gas burst forth from the straight and circular pipes standing high above. The blazing corona at the apex of the design must have been a sight to see!

ALL HONOR TO OUR GALLANT
ARMY & NAVY.
POPLAR GROVE CHURCH.
WELDON RAIL ROAD.
NEW MARKET.
PIEDMONT.
LYNCHBURG.
CEDAR CREEK.
FORT GRIGG.
HATCHERS RUN
FORT STEADMAN
RICHMOND.

The Car America

Augusta, Maine, July 4, 1865

As dawn broke on The Fourth of July in 1865, people rejoiced in perfect summer weather and prepared to celebrate what the editor of the *Kennebec Journal* called "the nation's recovery from its great disease." Everyone recognized the importance of marking simultaneously the eighty-ninth anniversary of the Declaration of Independence and the reunification of the country following the end of the Civil War in April. The *Journal's* editor noted that "the glorious banner of the Free, the dear old flag," was displayed everywhere, from flagstaffs, treetops, and dwellings. Further, the streets were full of people and "joy illuminated every countenance."

The highlight of the day in Augusta, as in so many other places, was a grand procession of civic officials and veterans, especially the returned officers and soldiers of local Maine regiments. They were followed by features that included, among others, one titled *The Moss Covered Bucket*, which was an open wagon on which white-clad children sat beneath a tall well sweep, singing "The Old Oaken Bucket" and other temperance songs. Additional floats represented a local white family costumed as American Indians riding in a wheeled "Indian Wigwam" they had built themselves, and six young boys in sailor suits riding in a wheeled boat.

The main feature of the Augusta procession was this large and elaborate wheeled float *America*, a tableau representing "Our Country! Its Arts and Its Arms!"—a complex personification of national greatness and power. The car itself was twenty-five feet high, thirteen feet wide, twenty feet long, and richly festooned with flowers and evergreen. At the top was an American eagle, presumably a specimen of taxidermy. At the base were seated young ladies wearing wreaths of flowers on their heads. Dressed in white, they represented the female purity and innocence thought essential to secure the rights of the American citizens. Each of the thirty-six girls wore a diagonal ribbon sash with the name of a single state, including the newest, Nevada, which had been granted statehood during the war, in 1864. Most importantly, the group included all of the states that had left the Union to join the Confederacy in 1861. In recognition of the recent reunification of the country, the girls had linked arms.

Above the circle of girls representing the states was supposed to sit a little child in fairy dress, holding red, white, and blue ribbons that extended to the horses' heads. At the time this photograph was taken, however, she had retreated to safety in the lap of one of the five older girls sitting a little higher where they held emblems representing the army, the navy, agriculture, commerce, and laws. Higher still, surrounded by shields and silken flags, was a young girl representing America. She was dressed as an "Indian princess," supporting a staff on which was placed a Liberty cap, holding a bow and arrow in her left hand, and wearing a gilded quiver of arrows at her back. It must have been really scary for the girls near the top of this huge vehicle as it lurched and swayed over the rough grassy field where it was assembled and then as it was drawn through the unpaved streets of Augusta on a long route that wound around the statehouse and ended at the courthouse. The car was escorted by a military guard of honor and drawn by ten horses decorated with flags and flowers, each led by a "colored groom in Turkish costume," as seen in this extraordinary photograph.

The *America* was designed by John Cochrane, an architect then serving as Maine's Deputy Secretary of State. He was well known in the area for his designs of building decorations and ornamental features used in ballrooms and civic celebrations. The superiority of this design was recognized a month later, on August 3, when Cochrane was presented with a silver water pitcher and tray in appreciation.

Reviewing the iconography of the float *America* reveals the fundamental symbols of American identity from the early national period to the end of the Civil War: America personified as an "Indian princess," the presence and power of the Liberty cap, the unification of the individual states, the supremacy of the eagle. From today's point of view it also reveals the marginalization of Black people with their inclusion as servants in stereotyped "Eastern" costume.

Reception of Company A, 14th Regt. of N. H. Volunteers and other Returned Soldiers

Westmoreland, New Hampshire, August 17, 1865

After the tragic events and devastating losses of the Civil War, there was rejoicing everywhere as the surviving soldiers slowly returned home in the summer of 1865. More than four months after Lee's surrender at Appomattox, at a small hamlet in the Connecticut River Valley town of Westmoreland, "ladies and citizens" assembled on August 17 for a welcome reception in honor of the returned local soldiers. The tiny group was escorted by the Winchendon Cornet Band to the same spot in the South Village where a much larger group had assembled three years earlier to hear speeches and prayers before men marched off to war. The 1865 ceremony featured words of welcome from local dignitaries, after which they all walked across the street to the town hall for dinner.

The modest Congregational Church, a Universalist Church, the Town Hall and the grassy open space at the confluence of several unpaved roads drew people to Westmoreland's South Village throughout the week. The large brick store with its ample supply of stacked firewood not only served the community with a wide variety of merchandise but also accepted local goods and farm products for credit. Houses in a variety of architectural styles sat with their barns within neat fences that protected dooryard gardens from wandering farm animals. Surrounded by both open pastures and dense forest, the Village was typical of those in many New England towns. The lack of ornamental street trees and the worn paint on the church reflect hard times.

Peace

When the welcome news arrived that an armistice ending the war with Germany had been signed in Compiègne, France, at eleven o'clock in the morning on the eleventh day of the eleventh month, November, in 1918, there was great rejoicing. Public celebrations were muted, however, because of the devastating pandemic, then known as the Spanish flu, that had swept the country since February of that year, eventually killing more than 50 million people.

A lull in infections in the fall of 1919 opened the way for planning a nationwide celebration on November 11, 1919. Unfortunately, these mass gatherings led to a resurgence of cases in many places. Even so, ever since then the day has been celebrated annually, first as Armistice Day and much later as Veterans' Day, which now recognizes all who have served in the armed forces of the United States, no matter where or when.

Liberty

Lebanon, New Hampshire, October 13, 1919

Unwilling to wait until November 11 to celebrate the first official Armistice Day because the weather might be cold, the town of Lebanon, New Hampshire, organized an ambitious Welcome Home celebration for returning servicemen on October 12 and 13, 1919. Parade day on the thirteenth turned out to be a perfect autumn day, with bright blue skies, a light breeze, and brilliant foliage. Although October 12 was informally recognized at the time as the appropriate date to honor Christopher Columbus, it was not yet an official federal holiday.

In the same way that Worcester had celebrated the return of its Civil War soldiers in 1865, Lebanon called upon the whole community in 1919 "to welcome the boys

of whom they were so justly proud." Where Worcester had thrilled to the sight of brilliant gas lighting above its triumphal arches (*see page 21*), Lebanon enjoyed hundreds of red, white, and blue electric lights strung around the Common and forming a huge shield over the town hall. The parade that day included bands and schoolchildren, local politicians and soldiers, fraternal organizations, firemen, and decorated automobiles, as well as a few large flags carried horizontally. Fortunately for us, local photographer Alfred Pauze set up his camera in a good spot facing the oncoming line of floats with morning light coming over his shoulder, thus enabling him to capture a series of fine images. This automobile covered with fringed strips of crepe paper, a flag, and a standing figure of Liberty received the first prize of fifteen dollars.

Victory and Peace

Lebanon, New Hampshire, October 13, 1919

The second prize of ten dollars awarded at Lebanon in 1919 was for this ambitious float titled *Victory and Peace*. Presented by the Fireman's Association, it was a wonderful example of the new kind of parade vehicle, having no visible means of locomotion, that truly appeared to float. In this case, the base was a large fire engine totally concealed by masses of evergreen. At the rear was a triumphal arch ornamented with flags and shields, surmounted by an eagle, and proclaiming "VICTORY." Within the arch stood a woman costumed as Columbia, since 1776 the personification of the nation. A large, gilded eagle spread its wings over the front of the vehicle with its proclamation of "PEACE 1919," whereas crossed flags of Great Britain, France, and the United States were mounted above the arch at the rear. Two uniformed firemen stood in or on the concealed cab; the actual driver must have been peeking out from inside the vehicle.

Columbia

Bath, Maine, November 11, 1919

Wrapped in a large flag and wearing her usual crown of stars, Columbia rode high on an automobile, on Armistice Day, 1919. At least two uniformed Boy Scouts preceded her float in one of many joyous parades celebrating the end of The Great War, optimistically hoped to have been "the War to End All Wars."

Disarmament

Montpelier, Vermont, November 11, 1921

A group of "American Citizens of Italian Descent" won the first prize of $100 for entering this compelling float presented on behalf of Montpelier's American Legion Post No. 3 in the city's parade on a snowy Armistice Day in 1921.

Uncle Sam is shown standing precariously on top of the world still bleeding from the wounds of war. He appears to have withdrawn the first of the many swords plunged in all around the equator and to be preparing to present it to one of the young girls dressed as angels of peace. Flags and four uniformed soldiers represent America's four allies of the Great War: France, Great Britain, Italy, and Japan. The body of the horse-drawn cart was covered in red, white, and blue bunting bearing a partially visible message promoting disarmament "We fought for liberty, now let us. . . ." The other two prize-winning floats in Montpelier that day also represented themes of peace, a powerful sentiment in the years following the horrors of World War I.

DISARMAMENT
FOUGHT FOR LIBERTY
NOW

Armistice Day

Lynn, Massachusetts, November 12, 1928

Twelve women wearing white robes with red, white, and blue sashes and starry golden crowns braved a chilly November morning to ride on this flag-bedecked float celebrating the tenth anniversary of the Armistice in 1928. The banners they are holding indicate that they are members of four separate local subgroups: the Oakwood, Evergreen, Arbutus, and Paradise Lodges of the Independent Odd Ladies. Having both a moral and ethical purpose, these women worked together to pursue a variety of benevolent, charitable, and patriotic activities.

2

HONOR

Parades and processions provide a public stage on which people use a variety of texts and symbols to communicate about things that are important to them as individuals and as members of a community. The hierarchical order of the procession immediately establishes rank and significance. Marching units, colorful flags and banners, and symbolic objects help to communicate the identities of individuals and groups within the line. Honor is given to the institutions and organizations that are central to the lived experience and that are perceived as beneficial to all. Community members are honored and feel flattered by the arrival of distinguished visitors, and they reciprocate with a public display of welcome that offers the guest an opportunity to see and be seen. Funerals bestow honor and affection on people of all ranks. Public funeral processions reflect the perceived importance of the deceased, but death affects us all.

Ritual and recognition are awarded to almost every participant. Public monuments extend these honors and are often dedicated after a formal procession. Many of the dedication ceremonies for both public buildings and monuments include the laying of ceremonial cornerstones, often with Masonic ceremonies and processions.

New England Institutions

Not surprisingly, the valued institutions that are believed to be the bedrock of New England communities are honored on celebratory occasions. A toast offered at Worcester, Massachusetts, on the Fourth of July in 1833 hailed "New England—Her condition displays the intelligence of her people and the value of her best institutions—her course is onward." At Marblehead, Massachusetts, in 1884, the toast was to "Free Schools. The Arch on which Free States must rest." Schools were often toasted as "nurseries of science" preparing youth for virtue, usefulness, and immortality. To this day, especially on civic anniversaries, parade floats depict schools, meetinghouses, town meetings, or courts of law. Others honor prominent individuals, first ministers, and beloved teachers. Some pay tribute to those who have provided funding for schools, monuments, hospitals, libraries, musical societies, or other valued institutions. Private charity and poor relief are less likely to be honored on the public stage.

First Meeting House 1727

Concord, New Hampshire, July 4, 1927

This was one of 160 floats in the three-and-one-half-mile-long parade celebrating the bicentennial of the city of Concord, New Hampshire, in 1927. The log building suggested early times and served more as a theatrical stage set than a realistic recreation of the city's first meetinghouse.

The convivial congregation wore old-fashioned clothing of varying dates. Two of the women carried the portable foot stoves that would have offered a modicum of comfort during hours-long sermons and prayers in an unheated building. Two men stood nearby, ostensibly to protect the group from possible attack by natives, one with a gun and the other with a long pole, perhaps intended as a pike. The man in a black suit, ruffled shirt, and white wig impersonated the Reverend Timothy Walker, the first minister of Concord, who served the

congregation for his entire adult life, from his ordination in 1730 to his death in 1782.

In addition to the spiritual refreshment and self-examination prompted by listening to long sermons and intense private prayer, regular Sunday attendance at Congregational meetings offered people an opportunity to observe fashion and behavior, as well as to visit with friends and neighbors.

The First Meeting House on the Rocks, 1660s

Norwich, Connecticut, July 5–6, 1909

Almost as stereotypical as these black-and-white "pilgrim" costumes is the little white church with its tall steeple presented by members of the First Church of Norwich as the only church float in the 250th anniversary parade of the town. Both represent popular, but mistaken, early twentieth-century ideas of colonial life and architecture.

Behind the ox-drawn float is Meeting House Rock, where the first Congregational meetinghouse in Norwich was constructed soon after the town was settled in 1659. In all probability the first meetinghouse was an unpainted square-framed building that lacked a steeple in its earliest years, in no way resembling this iconic, white-painted meetinghouse with its square belfry, a style of building unknown in Connecticut for another hundred years or more. All in all, the design is a reminder that historic memory is often imprecise and meaning can be conveyed by symbolic objects used again and again.

"Meeting House" floats like this celebrate public buildings that served both town government and the established Congregational church in early New England, rather than religious freedom, a subject that first appears in parades after the Civil War with the floats created by Roman Catholic churches, parochial schools, and some ethnic groups.

Justice in 1786

Portland, Maine, July 5, 1886

Tableau Eight in the centennial parade at Portland honored respect for the common law with a float carrying a courtroom with a judge and solemn lawyers in wigs and black gowns trying cases at the bench. In front of the building, various kinds of arcane punishments were demonstrated—by a "criminal" standing uncomfortably with his head locked in a pillory, and another tied to a whipping post while enduring vigorous lashes—suggesting that it "would perhaps still do good if the same penalty were in force today."

Inauguration of Governor George P. McLane
Hartford, Connecticut, January 1901

Severe weather almost never stops a scheduled event in New England. Parades are held year-round to honor distinguished individuals or officially designated public ceremonies and holidays. As a result, people sometimes find themselves confronting a situation such as that seen here in Hartford in January 1901. Despite subfreezing temperatures and driving snow, stalwart New Englanders came out to cheer as the civic and military procession honoring Connecticut's new governor George P. McLane took place on Inauguration Day as planned. Following the street railway tracks, the line of carriages following these military units had no trouble keeping a straight line as they proceeded south on Main Street in front of Hartford's major department stores, Brown Thompson & Co. and G. Fox & Co.

Ready to Move
Center Sandwich, New Hampshire, 1899

Every parade planner has to contend with local traditions concerning the participation of schoolchildren. In many places if one child participated, every child participated, even if they numbered in the thousands, as at Boston in 1851 or Danvers in 1856. The pupils of each district school, class, or grade walked or rode together, usually in ascending order according to their age. Sometimes they were separated by gender within those groups. Many of the children carried identifying banners, while some wore identical costumes, or, rarely, school uniforms. Often the schoolchildren were at the end of the entire procession, in a position where they could drop out, if necessary. Because the routes were long, sometimes covering several miles, and weather was unpredictable, large wagons or public horsecars were sometimes used to carry the children, contain their excitement, and reduce potential mishaps. This large wagon decorated with greenery and striped bunting served the purpose for the Center School as a parade formed in front of the Baptist Meeting House in Center Sandwich in 1899.

Ye Deestrick Skule

Marblehead, Massachusetts, July 4, 1903

Only after 1900 did a few parades begin to include replications of a one-room schoolhouse, with a stern-looking teacher holding a long pointer beside a blackboard and a mischievous lad in a tall, pointed dunce cap sitting on a stool in the corner. Many such buildings in rural areas continued to be in active daily use, so it is no surprise that not until the rise of consolidated school districts in the 1960s almost every Old Home Day parade had a float romanticizing a one-room schoolhouse.

This nostalgic example at Marblehead on July 4, 1903, caused great amusement among the spectators, who recognized the local high school principal seated at the teacher's desk in a tie wig and a tail coat, trying to suggest both the formality of his teaching style and the strict discipline of his old-fashioned classroom. The scene vividly illustrates difficulties encountered by many teachers of adolescents. Whispering girls in gingham aprons who are seated on hard, old, schoolhouse benches pay little attention to the teacher or to their books. One is even eating an apple. The young man seated at the rear holds his open book up high but he cannot conceal from us his amusement at the other boys who are pulling the girls' long braids and throwing paperwads at the master.

Distinguished Guests

The practice of greeting distinguished guests upon their arrival in a town or city and then providing an official escort throughout their visit is a well-established tradition in England, New England, and elsewhere. Upon their arrival, governmental officials and returning soldiers have long been greeted and escorted throughout their visit by civic officials and military detachments. Visiting clergymen, political candidates, firefighters, Masonic and other fraternal brethren are more often greeted and escorted by men of similar affiliation. The more important the visitor, the larger the escort, the longer the route of the initial procession, ensuring that important people could see and be seen by a large segment of the population. Sometimes the routes were planned to pass places of historical significance and the residences of prominent citizens where the line halted for formal salutes.

In both towns and cities these welcome processions were a familiar sight, and their courtesies were expected by arriving dignitaries. For a long time, individuals rode in open carriages; later open convertibles were sometimes substituted. Visiting groups usually walked. In many cases, especially when the welcome procession included large numbers of marching units, the honored guests and welcoming dignitaries were escorted to a stage or platform from which to review the moving procession in its entirety. Afterward, a much smaller group provided escort throughout the remainder of the visit. Upon departure an honored guest was escorted all the way to the boundary of the next town on his itinerary, where he would be greeted by a new escort representing the next community. When railroad travel supplanted horse-drawn carriages, arrival and departure ceremonies were held at train stations, but escorts continued to accompany distinguished guests within localities as they do today.

PRESIDENT GEORGE WASHINGTON VISITS BOSTON, 1789

When word arrived in Boston that George Washington would visit the city in late October of 1789, plans were quickly put in place to welcome and honor the Chief Executive. Having been in office just six months, Washington wanted to meet New England citizens as well as visit those with whom he had served on the battlefield and in government. He also wished to familiarize himself with a part of the country that he had never seen, and to assess the state of the region's economy and resources.

Memories of the city's recent ratification procession were still fresh, and enthusiastic tradesmen were eager to repeat that stirring spectacle. On the fifteenth of the month, an anonymous tradesman suggested in the *Massachusetts Centinel* that there would be no better way to honor the president during his visit than to plan a "SOLEMN GRAND PROCESSION" during which large numbers of people would be able to see the president and pay their respects to him. Apparently counting on widespread volunteerism and private generosity, the tradesman suggested that there would be very little public expense required. He emphasized that since Washington had never seen a procession of this kind, he would no doubt be impressed by the large number of participants as well as the wide variety and usefulness of the various trades, handicrafts, and arts of the city, clearly hoping that these would receive the fostering care and attention of the chief executive.

The tradesman's suggestion was well received, and plans were quickly formulated for a parade to be held less than a week later, on Saturday, October 24. Newspapers and a hastily published broadside announced the date and provided a detailed list of participating officials and marching groups. Headed by military units, civic officials, merchants and traders, ship captains and members of the Marine Society, and the "Scholars of several schools with their masters," the line would feature fifty groups of artisans, tradesmen, and manufacturers, arranged alphabetically from bakers to wheelwrights, some carrying their tools as they had in the ratification procession.

This time each group was to be identified by a white silk flag four feet square with an applied border of rich silk fringe. The flags were painted with emblems of the work such as a picture of one distinctive tool or a product, the name of each specific group, and their sequential number in the procession. The cordwainers and a few other groups illustrated ancient coats of arms that had originated with London livery companies. Two of the groups displayed mottoes articulating hope for America's future economic success: the rope makers expressed their wish for widespread "Success to American manufactures" and the paper stainers (wallpaper manufacturers) expressed their desire for female agency: "May the Fair daughters of Columbia deck themselves and their walls with our own manufactures."

Well aware of symbolism, the president wore a Continental officer's uniform and was riding a white horse. As Washington passed by, the lines turned in upon themselves, with those at the end now first in following him. This countermarching gave every participant an opportunity to see the entire procession.

Colonnade and Arch Built for the Procession Welcoming President George Washington

Boston, Massachusetts, October 24, 1789

On arrival at the Massachusetts State House, seen here on the right, Washington was conducted through this arch designed for the occasion by architect Charles Bulfinch. He then entered the building and walked upstairs to exit through the door of the Representatives' Chamber and step onto the balcony over this impressive colonnade built for the occasion. The space was furnished with armchairs, rich Persian carpets, and a figure of Plenty with her cornucopia. The president found himself facing a cheering crowd estimated at twenty-four thousand people, more than the entire population of the city. After listening to a chorus singing his praises in an especially composed song titled "To Columbia's Favorite Son," he reviewed the entire procession.

Bulfinch's triumphal arch was rich in symbolism, with a tall canopy crowned by an eagle, a frieze ornamented by thirteen stars on a blue ground, and an abundance of inscriptions celebrating Washington's military leadership during the siege of Boston in 1775–1776 and identifying him as "A Man who Unites All Hearts" and, of course, "Columbia's Favorite Son." Intended to honor the president and further dignify the occasion, this arch was one of thousands that would be built in the coming years to enhance New England's festive culture.

1824–1825 LAFAYETTE: THE NATION'S GUEST

General Lafayette's Visit

New England, 1824–1825

The Marquis de Lafayette was an idealistic young French aristocrat who volunteered to serve as a soldier in the American army during the Revolution. While in service, he became a close friend of General George Washington. Fifty years later, invited by President James Monroe to travel again to America and join in the celebration of the nation's Jubilee, Lafayette returned and was hailed as a hero wherever he went.

Lafayette arrived at New York on August 14, 1824, with his son, George Washington Lafayette, and his secretary, Auguste Levasseur. Almost at once they began a nationwide tour that lasted more than a year. The marquis was greeted by enthusiastic crowds and public honors at every stop, with lavish military and civic processions as well as formal escorts in and out of each town before moving on to the next. Extensive newspaper descriptions of these visits were printed and reprinted across the country, focusing public attention on both the travels of the visitor and the ideals soon to be celebrated in the 1826 Jubilee. This widespread response to Lafayette's tour laid a foundation for a common vocabulary of national symbols and patriotic activities that were then socially binding and that resonate even today.

Early in his tour, Lafayette came to Massachusetts

where he visited the sites of the first encounters of the Revolution at Lexington, Concord, and Charlestown. While in Boston he agreed to return the following year in order to be present at ceremonies marking the fiftieth anniversary of the Battle of Bunker Hill on June 17, 1825. That occasion featured another brilliant civil and military procession described, of course, as the "finest pageant that had ever been seen in this country." Seven thousand people marched from Boston to Charlestown to observe the laying of a cornerstone for a 221-foot granite obelisk to be constructed by the Bunker Hill Monument Association in commemoration of the 1775 battle and honoring the soldiers who had participated. The procession included 190 survivors of the battle, most of whom were able to march up the hill as a regimental drummer beat the rhythm of *Yankee Doodle*. Members of the Bunker Hill Monument Association were accompanied by the Massachusetts Society of the Cincinnati and The Grand Lodge of Massachusetts. Honored guests included President John Quincy Adams, the Massachusetts governor and legislature, city officials, presidents of colleges, heads of various societies, including the Massachusetts Historical Society and the Pilgrim Society, judges, diplomats, militia officers, and citizens of Massachusetts. The cornerstone was laid by the Most Worshipful Master of the Grand Lodge of Massachusetts, John Abbott, who then handed the trowel to General Lafayette who wore a Masonic apron as he spread mortar over the stone. People then moved to an amphitheater with seats, an awning, and a stage surmounted with a gilded eagle. On either side were platforms protected by awnings, on which an audience of ladies had long been waiting for the next part of the ceremony to begin. The event was already three hours behind schedule when Daniel Webster began an hour-long oration celebrating the success of the American Revolution in establishing a country based on principles of liberty that should serve as an example to the entire world.

Pro Patria, Kennebec Guards

Portland, Maine, ca. 1825–1830

Don't assume that art always resembles life. By the time the Bunker Hill Monument reached its full height, the man shown standing here in front of it was dead!

This handsome banner of Maine's *Kennebec Guards* (*see next page*) was painted by Charles Codman, an artist who specialized in "Military Standard, Fancy, Masonic, and Sign Painting" in Portland. It featured a faithful image of General Lafayette based on a lithograph of his favorite portrait, many copies of which he brought to present to his hosts in America. The scene behind him, though, is strictly aspirational, for it shows him standing in front of the completed Bunker Hill Monument in Charlestown, Massachusetts. Because construction of the monument was delayed by unsuccessful fundraising, Lafayette never saw it. The completed monument was finally dedicated in 1843, nine full years after Lafayette's death in 1834.

Welcome Lafayette
Boston, Massachusetts, 1824–1825

Many different souvenirs were sold throughout Lafayette's long tour. Probably the most popular were silk ribbons imprinted with the words "Welcome Lafayette" and an image of the Frenchman in the heavy brown wig he wore throughout his visit. Hundreds of people pinned ribbons like this to their clothing before standing in line to shake Lafayette's hand, wave from a second-floor window, or join cheering street-side crowds anywhere along the route of his year-long travels. Other souvenirs bearing Lafayette's image included white gloves, sashes, handkerchiefs, teapots, plates, jugs, and even baby shoes.

Reception of President Fillmore at the Boston and Roxbury Lines by the Municipal Authorities
Boston, Massachusetts, September 17, 1851

Civic traditions persist for hundreds of years, although the details change in response to industrial innovation and changing taste. In 1851, much in the same way that George Washington had been greeted in Boston in 1789, President Millard Fillmore was greeted by municipal officials and huge public crowds when he came to Boston for the Railroad Jubilee in September 1851. After arriving in Roxbury by rail, the president stepped onto a platform trimmed with bunting and carpeted with

evergreen. He then entered an open carriage with three local dignitaries. Drawn by six elegant gray horses, guarded by twelve mounted members of the National Lancers, and followed by sixteen other carriages of various officials and gentlemen, military companies, and marching bands, the presidential party moved toward the center of Boston. Greeted along the way by cheering crowds, they were met at Meeting House Hill in Roxbury by 1,500 children who had decorated their hats and bonnets with flowers and evergreen wreaths. The children stood together in groups with banners identifying each school and competed "in uttering the loudest huzzas." Three hundred citizens of Roxbury joined the line on foot, escorting the presidential entourage to the city line where bells were rung, guns were fired, and tumultuous cheers added to the welcome. President Fillmore and Mayor John P. Bigelow of Boston then toured the city in a single carriage on their way to the Revere House, the hotel where the president was to stay throughout the Jubilee.

GEORGE PEABODY VISITS DANVERS, MASSACHUSETTS, 1856

Arch Near Baptist Church Danvers Port

Danvers, Massachusetts, 1856

Winslow Homer's drawing shows the procession escorting banker and philanthropist George Peabody as they entered his hometown of Danvers, Massachusetts, after his twenty-year residence in England. Peabody rode in an open carriage with the governor of the Commonwealth of Massachusetts near the head of the line, passing first under this eagle-topped arch of evergreen sprigs with its dependent banner proclaiming "Danvers Welcomes the Nations' Guest" as this diverse crowd of men, women, and children filled the streets, some waving hats or handkerchiefs. Three little boys had climbed to the top of a stagecoach on the sidelines in order not to miss a thing.

As the procession honoring Peabody moved further into the city of Danvers, it was joined by a group of women on horseback, identified as the Ladies' Cavalcade. Each carried a large bouquet of flowers which she tossed into Peabody's carriage as it passed by. The ladies' participation in the official procession was praised for adding novelty and variety to the celebration, but the only women shown in any of the fifteen illustrations in the extensive publication that described the event were spectators. Indeed, it was very unusual for women to have an official role in a civic event of this kind in the years before the Civil War. The horsewomen may have been proud of their appearance in their neatly tailored riding habits, and of their genteel welcome to Mr. Peabody, but no doubt their participation was shocking to many at the time.

DANVERS WELCOMES
NATIONS GUEST
A
T. J. MELVIN
C. WEBSTER
HAT STORE
SHOE MANUFAC

THE PRINCE OF WALES VISITS PORTLAND, 1860

Welcome to the Prince of Wales

Portland, Maine, October 20, 1860

After three months spent touring an area that extended from Nova Scotia to Montreal, Detroit, Chicago, Washington, Philadelphia, New York, and Boston, Britain's Albert Edward, Prince of Wales, arrived by train at his last stop, Portland, Maine, on October 20, 1860. Queen Victoria's eldest son had been sent on a goodwill tour, travelling unofficially as Baron Renfrew. The eighteen-year-old had been feted by receptions, parades, and grand balls at every stop. Portland was no exception and crowds turned out to cheer as the prince was driven through the city in an open barouche so all could see him. Ladies tossed bouquets in his direction as the Prince made his departure under an evergreen arch. He was then conveyed by barge to the HMS Hero, which he boarded and sailed for home accompanied by the pounding noise of a twenty-one gun salute.

PRESIDENT ULYSSES S. GRANT IN BANGOR, MAINE, 1871

President U. S. Grant en route to the opening of the European and North American Railway
Bangor, Maine, October 18, 1871

In this scene President Grant can be seen standing in an open carriage in the midst of a huge crowd in front of the Bangor House Hotel where every window was decorated with a flag. Men in military uniforms had formed long lines on every street, prepared to join a procession that would also include civic officials, fifteen fire companies with their engines, and more than 750 lumbermen employed at mills owned by Bangor men. Grant had come to Bangor to meet with Lord Lismore, the governor general of Canada, and to celebrate with him the opening of the new European and North American Railway, which was expected to link Canada and the United States through Maine. Not unlike the 1851 Railroad Jubilee in Boston or, indeed,

the Crystal Palace in London that same year, the Bangor celebration twenty years later symbolized public belief in industrial progress and the potential of international interconnections to enhance the current economy and promote peace. Unfortunately, this proposed railroad line joining Maine and Canada was never completed.

Painted on the arch in front of the hotel were several mottoes: "Our President Peace Welcomes You, The Sword of Appomattox, Let Us Keep the Peace," and "The Treaty of Washington 1871, Peace Through Justice," referring to both the recent end of the Civil War and the ongoing 1871 negotiation of the Treaty of Washington refining boundary lines and establishing fishing rights between the two countries. Although Grant was officially in Maine to celebrate the beginning of the new international railway, extensive publicity like this certainly raised his profile in advance of his campaign for re-election the following year.

Let Us Remember Our Forefathers,
Ceremonial Arch
Bangor, Maine, October 18, 1871

Crowned by a patriotic eagle and flags, this is one of several decorated arches that spanned major streets during Grant's visit to Bangor. These elaborate, but ephemeral civic decorations are, in themselves, a kind of folk art that is rich in symbolism and adds greatly to the sense of public pride generated by such a celebration.

OLDEST CITIZENS

In addition to honoring important visitors, local dignitaries, and aged veterans, some parade organizers singled out local citizens of great age. For example, on the Fourth of July at Newburyport in 1865, the procession stepped off at 8:00 a.m. with various civic officials and the orator of the day, followed by a carriage carrying ninety-four-year-old Captain Richard Lunt, the oldest man in the city, a patriotic gentleman who remembered every war in which the country had ever been engaged. In 1873, the Jaffrey, New Hampshire, centennial parade included Mrs. Dorcas Rice, 104 years old, reputedly the oldest lady in New Hampshire. Many of the centennial processions in 1876 included people designated as "Aged Citizens in Carriages." This kind of honor continues to be observed, although today the oldest citizens ride in a red convertible, the most expensive car in town, or an antique horse-drawn carriage, depending on the taste of the community and the resources of the parade organizers.

Oldest Residents
Manchester, New Hampshire, September 7, 1896

Having been identified as the oldest native residents of Manchester, the four people riding in this open carriage had accepted invitations to be honored in the huge Civic and Military Parade to be held on Monday, September 7, 1886, the first day of a three-day event celebrating the semicentennial of the incorporation of the city. Their carriage appeared near the end of the enormous first division, following carriages containing fifty-two former governors, senators, congressmen, mayors, clergymen, and other many dignitaries from all over the state, along with military units and current city officials.

The four elders wore signs publicizing the year of their birth, thus somewhat obscuring their actual age. Both of the women had been born when the community was known as Derryfield, before it was named Manchester in 1810. It must have been thrilling, uncomfortable, and perhaps a bit frightening for this group of people aged between eighty-five and ninety-five to ride for what must have been a very long time before a crowd of spectators reported to have been more than fifty thousand people.

Funerals

Funerals observe ancient traditions and are rich in symbolism. Special mourning garments, black drapery, lengthy eulogies, and solemn processions honor the dead at the same time they document personal relationships and social hierarchies. Funeral processions include dignitaries and anonymous admirers in addition to grieving family and friends, moving on foot or in lines of carriages or black automobiles. Wartime casualties are escorted by lines of soldiers marching with muffled drums and shrouded banners. Civilians carry floral bouquets and wreaths of evergreen. No matter the circumstances, the goal is to show respect for the dead and to create a lasting memory in the minds of the family and the community.

Funeral Notice for Joshua Bailey Osgood, Esq.

Biddeford, Maine, June 6, 1791

This unusual, although not unique, newspaper notice illustrates the typical tapered hexagonal shape of an eighteenth-century wooden coffin. It also documents both the traditional hierarchical arrangement of participants in a funeral procession as well as the honors conferred by lowering flags to half-staff.

PORTLAND.

Biddeford, June 2, 1791.

Died here, the 30th ult. and yeſterday was intered with military honours, JOSHUA BAILEY OSGOOD, Eſq. of Brownfield, one of the Juſtices of the Peace in the county of York, and Colonel of the 5th regiment of militia, in the 6th diviſion.

THE PROCESSION.

A Company of Militia in uniform, commanded by Major Jordan.

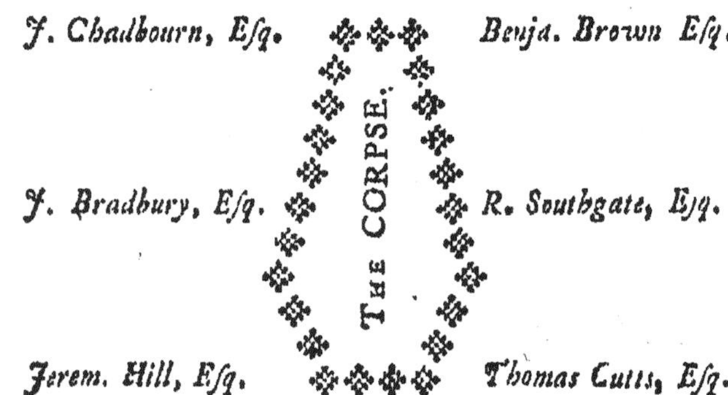

J. Chadbourn, Eſq. | *Benja. Brown Eſq.*

J. Bradbury, Eſq. | THE CORPSE. | *R. Southgate, Eſq.*

Jerem. Hill, Eſq. | *Thomas Cutts, Eſq.*

MOURNERS.

CLERGY.

MAGISTRATES.

MILITIA OFFICERS.

Followed by a very large concourſe of CITIZENS.

All the veſſels in the Port ſuſpended their colours half maſt high. And every thing was conducted with decency, order, and ſolemnity

As he lived beloved, ſo he died lamented.

Funeral of Mrs. Emily Egerton
Royalton, Vermont, 1828

Covered by a black pall ornamented with tassels, the coffin of a local widow was carried at the head of a long pedestrian procession that extended from her front door to the meetinghouse in Royalton, Vermont, in 1828. No doubt her three surviving children wore black mourning garments as they walked at the head of the line. After the funeral service in the meetinghouse, Mrs. Egerton was carried to her grave in the town cemetery nearby, to be interred under the sheltering arms of the weeping willow tree.

Webster's Burial Case
Funeral Procession of the Late Hon. Daniel Webster
Marshfield, Massachusetts, October 1852

Daniel Webster's remains were placed in an enameled metallic burial case with silver handles, described as "an elegant piece of work." Made by Hayden and Putnam of New York, the case was shaped like a human body. Its rippled surface resembled the drapery of a shroud and an oval glass window covered the face. A new and innovative design, burial cases like this were thought to be airtight and thus prevent deterioration of the body within.

According to his wishes, Webster was buried on his estate at Marshfield, Massachusetts, in the family tomb he had recently constructed to house the remains of his first wife, Grace, daughter Julia, granddaughter Mary, and his most honored Pilgrim ancestors, Governor Edward Winslow and Peregrine White.

This was not a simple country funeral, however. Although thousands of people, including the governor of Massachusetts and a delegation from the New York Historical Society had gathered in Marshfield to pay their respects after Webster's death on October 24, the honors of the occasion were focused on the family and the community. The pallbearers walking on either side of the wagon bearing the burial case were described as "sturdy old farmers." They were followed by Webster's son Fletcher with his three children, domestic and farm employees, neighbors, the great orator's personal physician, local clergy, and the selectmen of Marshfield.

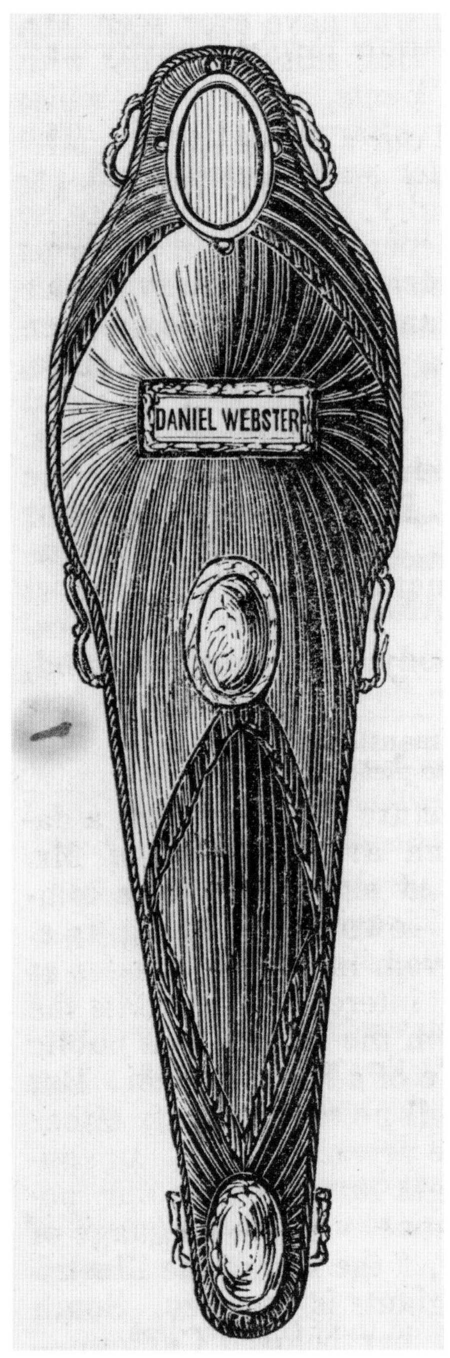

Only then did the usual hierarchy of dignitaries join the line, led by the governor.

A little more than a month later, in Boston on November 30, the public Webster was further honored by a massive memorial procession attended by a large number of spectators, described as "the largest ever seen at this season of the year." Twenty-eight volunteer military units, nine divisions of governmental officials, fraternal organizations, and others, all wearing black mourning badges, marched together through the streets to Faneuil Hall, passing buildings draped in black. Within the hall, surrounded by black drapery and other solemn decorations, they listened to a lengthy eulogy honoring New England's fallen "oak leaf."

Funeral Car for Three Soldiers with Masonic Procession

Taunton, Massachusetts, February 2, 1864

Members of the Masonic brotherhood assembled near the snowless Common in Taunton, on February 2, 1864, to honor three local soldiers whose bodies had been shipped home from Louisiana.

The dead were all members of King David's Lodge in Taunton and nearly 250 men from Masonic Lodges in Taunton and nearby towns turned out to honor them. Wearing their Masonic aprons and other regalia, the brethren assembled near the Common, as we see here. Accompanied by the Taunton Brass Band, they walked together in procession to the church. There the three coffins had been placed on pedestals beneath the pulpit after individual funeral services at the homes of the bereaved parents.

After the service at the church and the closing dirge,

the coffins were placed on the tall eagle-topped funeral car draped in solemn black that is seen in this remarkable photograph. The vehicle was built for the occasion by Philo and Philo T. Washburn, a father and son working together as coffin makers and upholsterers in Taunton. Once the car was loaded, the Masonic procession reformed and escorted the coffins to Mount Pleasant Cemetery where they were "deposited in their receptacles." After final ceremonies and a parting hymn, every Mason present walked past the three coffins and tossed on each a sprig of evergreen symbolizing eternal life.

How their mothers must have wept!

Funeral of Connecticut Governor, Thomas H. Seymour

Hartford, Connecticut, September 7, 1868

The funeral of a major political figure is still usually an elaborate public occasion, showing respect, affection, and veneration. That of Connecticut governor Thomas Seymour in 1868 can be seen as typical. After hundreds of people viewed his body in an open rosewood coffin at Christ Church in Hartford, it was moved to an elaborate horse-drawn hearse with black drapery and stately plumes. Escorted by eight distinguished men designated as pall bearers, the hearse was near the front of a long procession that included public officials, clergy, military units, fraternal groups, family members, and "invited friends from abroad." The line was followed by hundreds of men designated as "citizens on foot," and "citizens in carriages." They all moved through streets crowded with spectators in the center of the city on a wet and chilly day. As seen in this sketch, immediately preceding the catafalque were Hartford's famous Colt's Armory Band and members of the celebrated Putnam Phalanx, wearing their tricorn hats.

Monuments

Monuments serve to honor and commemorate both events and people. In the same way that tombstones and individual cemetery monuments honor individuals, large public monuments honor community leaders and commemorate significant public events, often those associated with wartime victories and battles. The cornerstone laying or dedication of a public monument is usually a formal ceremony, frequently accompanied by a civic procession. These occasions always have a powerful impact on both the participants and the spectators. People from all parts of a community, joined by friends and dignitaries from near and far, are drawn together by the patriotic feeling generated by such a memorable experience.

Two examples commemorating the first encounters between British regulars and patriot minutemen in the spring of 1775 illustrate the complexity and some special circumstances encountered in planning and creating meaningful public monuments.

BUNKER HILL MONUMENT

In 1840, sixteen years after Lafayette laid the cornerstone of the Bunker Hill Monument in Charlestown, Massachusetts, the obelisk was still unfinished. Fund raising efforts were faltering. Still needing twenty thousand dollars, the men of the Bunker Hill Monument Association ultimately agreed to cooperate with a group of women who felt certain that the sum could be raised by holding a benefit fair in Boston. Spurred on by Sarah Josepha Hale, editor of the popular *Godey's Lady's Book,* women throughout the region spent the summer knitting, crocheting, painting, and otherwise working to make useful or fancy goods that would be sold to benefit the completion of the monument. The Ladies' Fair was held at Quincy Hall for seven days in September 1840, opening on Tuesday the eighth when large numbers of people had come to the city for a Whig convention. The Fair attracted sympathetic crowds that must have been in a buying mood. After paying rent and expenses, the Ladies' Fair Committee contributed $29,635.00 to the Bunker Hill Monument Association, ensuring the completion of the project at long last.

Five years later, reflecting on the successful completion of the project, the Bunker Hill Monument Association praised the role of New England women as "an illustration of what they may yet do in aiding to form and complete the lofty idea of a true Republic. . . . May the women of the country—without whom indeed there would be no country—aim to elevate Public Sentiment, which is the ultimate and supreme ruler, and to set up a high standard of virtue, self-denial, and right-living."[2]

Sketched on the spot, by W. Sharp.
Printed by Sharp Michelin & Co.
Remarks—As this print will remain long after all who beheld the brilliant spectacle shall have passed away, it may not be amiss to stamp upon it the interesting fact, that on this same "10th of September" a Fair was held by Ladies in the City of Boston, for the purpose of obtaining funds for the completion of the Monument (which is here presented in its unfinished state) The object was entirely successful— This drawing was taken from Mr. Phipps' house, South East of the Monument, and represents the moment of time when the Cavalcade having countermarched, are about returning to the City; while a portion only of the Delegates on foot have yet reached the hill.
FREEMENS' QUICK STEP.
As performed on the "Glorious 10th of September" Composed and dedicated to the
Delegates
TO THE
BUNKER-HILL WHIG CONVENTION of 1840.
BY
GEORGE HEWS.
BOSTON
25 cts. nett.

Freemen's Quick Step (detail)
Boston, Massachusetts, 1840

During the week of the 1840 Bunker Hill Fair, on Thursday, September 10, Daniel Webster, as president of the Whig convention in Boston, led a huge procession of delegates to the site of the unfinished monument in Charlestown. (*see previous page*) This view shows the rows of assembled militia and more men arriving at the moment when the cavalry was about to return to the city, even though many others were still streaming up the hill and had not yet reached the monument grounds. Clearly, Webster hoped that the sight of the unfinished obelisk would inspire them all to make a visit to the fair in Quincy Hall where both cash contributions and purchases of fancy goods, souvenirs, homemade candies, or other treats would all benefit the construction project.

Ladies Fair Quincy Hall (detail)
Boston, Massachusetts, 1840

The women's fundraising fair during the 1840 Whig convention in Boston was held in the Rotunda, the central assembly room on the second floor of Quincy Market, then known as Quincy Hall. Forty-three subcommittees had each taken responsibility for stocking a separate circular sales table with donated goods and staffing it throughout the eight days of the fair. Four thousand people attended on the opening day, paying a special price of fifty cents, double that of a daily ticket, to have the first opportunity to view the fair and purchase choice items. A daily paper, titled *The Monument*, was printed in the hall on a rotary power press. Having literary contributions from female authors and poets, historical accounts, and information about the fair, it was edited by Mrs. Hale and added more than five hundred dollars to the sum raised.

An inspiring tall model of the monument, the completion of which was to be the beneficiary of this great group effort, was on display near the center of the room. The model attracted special attention from the Whig delegation from Louisiana whose members purchased it and shipped it to New Orleans where it was displayed until it was destroyed in a fire several years later.

"'76" Quick Step

Boston, Massachusetts, 1843

In 1843 the Bunker Hill Monument was finally finished and yet another huge parade was held on June 17, the anniversary of the battle. Like that in 1825, this monumental celebration was considered the finest ever witnessed in New England and Daniel Webster was again the orator. President John Tyler was in the line along with thirty bands of musicians, and the usual groups of militia, officials, Masons, and others. They were joined by survivors of the Revolution from throughout New England, all in carriages this time. On the top of the carriage in which the surviving Lexington minutemen rode, was a miniature model of the Lexington Monument, the first to be erected in honor of those who had fallen on the nineteenth of April in 1775.

Standing out among the many groups assembled at the base of the completed monument, the only legible banners are I. O. O. F. (Independent Order of Odd Fellows), the Bunker Hill Monument Association, and the Massachusetts Charitable Mechanics Association. The Ancient and Honorable Artillery Company in their tricorn hats and continental uniforms can also be discerned, along with the Boston Light Infantry in their distinctive, flat-topped Pulaski-style helmets.

A description in the *Boston Daily Courier* described some of the elaborate street decorations on this occasion, mainly flags, streamers, banners, and arches. In addition, both an antiquarian relic identified as "the old chair of General Washington" and the popular Whig symbol of a log cabin were displayed together with a large white banner inscribed "1776" on an arch across Clark Street.

Webster's oration on this occasion was highly regarded, especially for his definition of the American Revolution as an example to the world in establishing the principles of liberty and bringing to America great progress in knowledge, law, arts, commerce, and liberal ideas.

Captain George Fishley (1760–1850)

Portsmouth, New Hampshire, June 11, 1850

One of the veterans of the American Revolution who attended the dedication of the Bunker Hill Monument in 1843 was George Fishley of Portsmouth, New Hampshire, At age eighteen he had joined the 3rd New Hampshire Regiment, serving at the Battle of Monmouth, New Jersey, in June 1778 and seeing further action in New York and Pennsylvania in the following year. He was honorably discharged in 1781, after which he returned to Portsmouth and became first a privateer and then a coastal trader. In the last decade of his life, he enjoyed considerable attention as a Revolutionary War veteran and, dressed in some semblance of a Revolutionary War uniform, took part in many patriotic celebrations and parades. Still savoring his reputation as a Continental soldier, he posed for this daguerreotype on his ninetieth birthday, June 11, 1850. After his death, just six months later, it was said of him that his "very existence was the spirit of '76—and on all fitting occasions, it was prominently visible. With him, the last of our cocked hats has departed. He was an amiable man, a good citizen, and beloved by all who knew him."[3]

Monuments to the Battles of Lexington and Concord

Dedication of the Monument at Acton
Acton, Massachusetts, October 29, 1851

Commemoration of the April 19, 1775 encounter between British regulars and Masachusetts minutemen began early in both Lexington and Concord. At nearby Acton in 1851, this "stern and substantial column," seventy-five feet high, was erected in the center of the Green as a monument to local minutemen who had walked to Concord early

in the morning of April 19, 1775, responding to news of the approach of British regulars in the first organized American attack on British troops. Acton citizens wished to further honor the contributions of Captain Isaac Davis and Privates Abner Hosmer and James Hayward, the Acton minutemen who fell that day.

Honoring the Heroes

Acton, Massachusetts, October 29, 1851

Acton Green was thronged with visitors from near and far, perhaps because of a unique part of the ceremonies. A few days earlier, the remains of Davis, Hosmer, and Hayward were removed from nearby Woodlawn Cemetery, their graves were filled, and the tombstones left in place "to instruct future generations." The bodies were reported to be in a good state of preservation, with hair on the skulls and the hole made by a musket ball still evident in Hayward's cheek. The remains were put into three separate compartments in a walnut coffin with three engraved silver plates carrying the men's names fastened to the lid. On the morning of the dedication, the horse-drawn hearse seen here in *Gleason's* brought the coffin to Acton Green where it was placed in a special compartment in the base of the new monument.

The Boston Brass Band and two aged veterans of the Concord fight were in attendance for exercises that included an oration, a poem, prayers, and music. At a dinner for 1,200 in Yale's Mammoth Tent on the Green, numerous toasts, and speeches further honored the fallen patriots.

This was not the last monument to be erected in honor of Isaac Davis. On the centennial of the battle, April 19, 1875, along with a presidential visit, a huge parade, and another public dinner, the town of Concord unveiled Daniel Chester French's statue of *The Minuteman*. It features Davis standing with his left hand on the handle of a plow and his right hand holding a musket. French's first public sculpture, it was erected on the far side of Concord Bridge, the place where Davis had met his death one hundred years earlier. Although there were numerous photographs taken that day, apparently, none show the dedication of the monument.

Civil War Veterans

After the Civil War, membership in the Grand Army of the Republic (GAR) was open to all honorably discharged Union soldiers. The nation's first Decoration Day was observed in 1868 after GAR commander-in-chief, John A. Logan, issued his General Order No. 11 instructing GAR chapters across the country to set aside May 30 as "a day for decorating the graves of comrades who died in defense of their country during the late rebellion, and whose bodies now lie in almost every city, village, and hamlet churchyard in the land." Recommended activities included strewing the "choicest flowers of springtime" upon soldiers' graves, "raising above them the dear old flag they saved," and conducting whatever form of ceremonies seemed locally appropriate. In most New England cities and towns Decoration Day activities featured civilians as well as veterans walking in procession as they carried bouquets of flowers, evergreen wreaths, and miniature flags to the cemeteries. May 30 seems to have been the chosen date for these activities at least partly because spring flowers were expected to be in bloom throughout the country at the end of the month. It could be said that General Logan may not have been familiar with the vagaries of springtime in northern New England, where the preferred lilac blossoms and lilies-of-the-valley are sometimes felled by frost, leaving evergreen wreaths as the most reliable substitute for grave decoration.

Decoration Day

Keene, New Hampshire, May 30, 1868

Anticipating a day that would honor their fallen comrades and tug at the "mystic chords of memory," cited in Lincoln's first inaugural address, Civil War veterans who were members of Keene's John Sedgewick GAR Post No. 4

posed in civilian clothing on either side of the handsome floral car that was the focus of their first Decoration Day procession. In addition to the veterans, the line included other soldiers and sailors who were not GAR members, civic officials, and the orator of the day all riding in carriages, a company of engineers, firemen with the fire engines *Neptune, Deluge,* and *Niagara,* a hook-and-ladder company, high school students, and the Keene Brass Band, all followed by a crowd of "citizens on foot."

Donations of flowers and evergreens had been requested by parade organizers during the last week of May and made into the crosses, wreaths, and garlands that ornamented the car before being used to decorate the graves of Keene's Civil War dead in the city's new Woodlawn Cemetery. One of the white horses that pulled the floral car can be seen behind men standing at the right. It may have been either very hot or raining, for at least four people stand under large umbrellas.

Decoration Day

Keene, New Hampshire, 1869

A year later, GAR members created a new floral car to be used in the Decoration Day ceremonies at Keene. Described as a "large and splendid affair," the car was decorated with flowers and evergreen and topped by a floral cross. In the center a uniformed soldier leaning on his rifle and a white-clad sailor standing beside an anchor flanked a white monument topped with an urn and inscribed with the names of Keene soldiers and

sailors buried away from home. The car itself was flanked by two men, one in full uniform, the other wearing a rumpled suit and standing on a peg leg.

This procession was larger than that of the previous year: members of Masonic Lodges, Knights Templars, Odd Fellows, Fenians, and the entire fire department joined the marching men. Twenty-nine graves were decorated at Woodlawn Cemetery as well as an unrecorded number at the old cemetery and others on the outskirts of the village.

After intense discussion and several votes in Chester's Town Meeting, no final decision had been made about a suitable monument. Some wanted a statue, others wanted a memorial hall with brass plaques inside the new town hall. On November 3, 1884, Chester resident Hugh Henry, commander of the local GAR Post, apparently took matters into his own hands and signed a contract for a bronze statue of a soldier to be acquired from the Ames Manufacturing Company of Chicopee, Massachusetts. Henry paid the $1,200 bill himself, although he was later reimbursed by the town, which also paid for the granite base and the bronze plaques.

Dedication of Monument to Civil War Soldiers
Chester, Vermont, 1885

In the years following the close of the Civil War, many towns saw a growing interest in erecting permanent monuments to honor local veterans, but success was sometimes elusive. Planning discussions were emotional. Decisions about appropriate locations, format, and design, were seldom easy. There was debate about the use of public funds. Private fund raising took time. When the goal was accomplished, veterans and townspeople assembled for dedication ceremonies sometimes recorded by a photographer, like this one at Chester, Vermont, in 1885.

The Ames Company is well known as having been a manufacturer of swords, hundreds of thousands of which were made for the Union Army. After the war, they made hundreds, if not thousands, of statues of generic uniformed soldiers, standing at parade rest, with their hands holding the barrel of a musket standing in front of them. Because the uniformed soldier's cape concealed any insignia that would have identified him as being a member of either the Union or the Confederate forces, Ames and other northern foundries were able to sell statues like this to be used as soldiers memorials in cities and towns in both the North and the South.

Decoration Day

Peterborough, New Hampshire, 1893

In 1893, members of the GAR Post in Peterborough, observed Decoration Day on Sunday, May 30. Because the Monadnock area was experiencing an unusually late spring, the Post had appealed to the public for contributions of whatever flowers were available to ornament small evergreen wreaths for decorating soldiers' graves. Those making the wreaths were asked to be sure they did not exceed eight inches in diameter, a size considered appropriate for display on even modest tombstones. Since the number of veterans' graves now exceeded the number of veterans expected to participate in the ceremonies, the GAR Post invited schoolchildren to join them for the event, marching together in the procession and bringing their own bouquets.

Led by a flag bearer and officers carrying swords upright, the veterans are seen here on Main Street wearing white gloves and regulation GAR hats while carrying the small wreaths of evergreen and flowers. They are followed by two drummers, a host of schoolchildren escorted by their female teachers, and the usual "Citizens on foot or in carriages" as they all walk down the hill on their way to both the Pine Hill and the Village cemeteries and then on to the Soldiers Monument in Putnam Park. Coming down the sidewalk from the brick town hall, on both sides of the street, a number of people are walking along toward the cemeteries on what appears to have been a chilly spring day. On the left, they are passing under a great elm tree that may have been defoliated by gypsy moths, the invasive insects that had begun their relentless attacks in New England only a few years earlier.

Dedication of the Memorial to Robert Gould Shaw and the 54th Massachusetts Regiment

Boston, Massachusetts, May 31, 1897

Decoration Day in Boston, on May 31, 1897, has been long remembered for this moment, when sixty-five surviving members of the Massachusetts 54th Regiment marched up Beacon Street, some carrying swords, others with floral bouquets. To the music of "John Brown's Body," the men stood by for the unveiling of Augustus Saint Gaudens' bronze relief honoring them and their white leader, Colonel Robert Gould Shaw, who had been killed alongside nearly half of his men in their siege of Fort Wagner. (*see next page*) Those present all recognized that the site was the very same from which the men had departed for duty in South Carolina on May 28, 1863, one of the first Northern corps of Black soldiers to enter the fray.

Standing at the corner of Boston Common, opposite the Massachusetts State House, this was the first civic monument to Black soldiers. It remains a testament to their bravery and sacrifice as well as to the imagination and talent of the sculptor. Saint Gaudens modeled Colonel Shaw astride his horse, riding in the midst of a large number of marching soldiers. Casting aside racist stereotypes and in contrast to the generic statues of white soldiers then being erected by the hundred in towns throughout the North and South, these figures were modeled on Black men whom Saint Gaudens invited into his studio in New York in order to capture their individual appearance. Immediately after the dedication, the monument was praised for its artistic success and realistic qualities. The *Springfield Republican* exulted on June 1 that "there has been nothing nobler done. It is the work of profound and serious thought." Indeed, it was.

Tenting on the Old Camp Ground

Hadley, Massachusetts, 1909

As years went by, the appearance of veterans in parades became less mournful and more a celebration of the survivors. For example, at Hadley, Massachusetts, in 1909, GAR members of Company F of the 37th Massachusetts Volunteers mounted this vignette of camp life on a float for the parade that was part of the celebration of the 250th anniversary of the town. Inspired by Uncle Sam carrying a sign urging them "To The War," the small group of elderly men in civilian clothing and regulation GAR hats stood before folding chairs and firmly gripped the chairbacks ahead of them to help maintain their balance on the horse-drawn float. Behind them can be seen a tent, a pyramid of stacked arms, and a representation of outdoor cooking with brass kettles and a tea pot suspended over a rather haphazard pile of firewood. A sign above the tent lists the places where the Hadley men saw action during the war.

US Grant Relief Corps

Biddeford, Maine, September 16, 1916

As part of the Tercentenary Parade on September 16, 1916, in Biddeford, Maine, members of the local US Grant Relief Corps received an Honorable Mention for this patriotic float. Established in 1888 to promote patriotic work and care for the graves of Civil War veterans, the group was the women's auxiliary of the local chapter of Grand Army of the Republic (GAR).

Trimmed with American flags and bunting that must have been red, white, and blue, the float carried four veterans seated around a white-robed woman wrapped in a flag and wearing a crown to represent Columbia. Four "married women" also wearing white robes stood at the corners, each grasping a pole on which was mounted an American flag. A valued piece of fire equipment, Biddeford's old horse-drawn steam pumper, *Saco* No. 2, crowned by flowers and another flag, is just visible in the background at the right, waiting for the line to move.

G•A•R Yankee Boys of '61 to '65

Bangor, Maine, ca. 1910

Trudging bravely along the streetcar tracks next to parked automobiles in Bangor, Maine, aging veterans of the Civil War continued to honor their fallen comrades in street parades as long as they were able. (*facing page*)

G·A·R
YANKEE BOYS
OF
'61 to '65

GAR Veterans

Lexington, Massachusetts, April 19, 1930

Four elderly Civil War veterans wearing their medals and the GAR emblem on their official hats were honored by a ride in this flower- and flag-decorated automobile in the Lexington parade on Patriots Day in 1930. Each year there were more graves to decorate in May and fewer veterans to undertake the task. Well before this date a new group, the Sons of Veterans, had been organized to assist.

3

IDENTITY

At its very heart, any parade defines two things for its participants: personal identity and position in civic society. No matter whether one's place is conferred by birthright, occupation, or association, almost no one in a parade is anonymous. Even in carnival processions and parades of Horribles where masking and disguise are employed to break down societal norms, participation adds nuance to individual identity and status.

Parades have always included long lines of people moving together in a vivid display of governmental and social hierarchy, national origin, fraternal association, occupational identity, and/or ideological harmony. Groups are identified collectively and individually by banners, badges, distinctive uniforms, and specialized equipment.

Without question, underlying factors such as gender, race, class, and national origin affect participation, but marching with military units, firefighting companies, political parties, advocates of reform, or any kind of ethnic or fraternal organization illustrates a person's chosen place in the larger community. Some people have more than one choice and may appear with different groups on different occasions, depending on the message they wish to convey.

Parade planners work carefully to develop the sequence of participant groups. Because the assigned places instantly convey information about both the identity and significance of each individual group and float, it is a delicate task to create a line of march that reflects both long-established traditions and ongoing change while offending as few people as possible. Further, the planners must identify individuals who will feel honored by an invitation to be a marshal and then be willing to serve on parade day in an unpaid disciplinary role, helping participants find their places in line, keeping the moving units on time and in step, maintaining order in the crowded streets, and responding to unanticipated events that might range from a bolting horse to a flat tire or a terrified child.

Trades Pre-1845

Beginning in medieval times, parade displays by groups of artisans throughout Europe focused on traditional hand skills rather than products. Not surprisingly, these traditions appeared almost at once in the parades of the new nation.

> *Each Tradesman turn out, with his tools in his hand,*
> *To cherish the arts and keep peace thro' the land;*
> *Each apprentice and journeyman join in my song,*
> *And let your full chorus come bouncing along.*
> *Happy, and free, happy and free, all are united,*
> *happy and free.*[4]

This cheerful song, believed to have been written by Benjamin Franklin while watching the ratification procession in Philadelphia on July 4, 1788, may suggest the spirit of many subsequent parades in which tradesmen and mechanics participated during the years before the Industrial Revolution changed everything.

On July 3, 1786, marking the successful completion of the Charles River Bridge between Boston and Charlestown, Massachusetts, 120 workmen identified as "artificers"—those who had been employed in construction of the bridge—carried their different tools as they walked across the new bridge as part of a civic procession. As we have seen, two years later, similar processions in many cities celebrated the ratification of the new federal Constitution.

On other occasions, the groups of tradesmen used painted banners (also called standards) in addition to their tools to represent their special identity and skills. This format appeared in a parade organized on a snowy George Washington's Birthday in Boston in 1815. Members of the Washington Benevolent Society were celebrating not only the country's first president, but also the news of peace at the conclusion of the War of 1812. Eliza Susan Quincy, daughter of Josiah Quincy, president of the WBS, left this description in her journal: ". . . all the representatives of the Trades, [were] drawn on sleds with appropriate standards and carrying their tools. The bricklayers were building a house, they broke their bricks and worked busily. The carpenters were erecting a Temple of Peace. The printers worked a small press, struck off handbills, announcing peace, and threw them among the crowd."[5]

Cordwainers Banner
Boston, Massachusetts, 1789

Boston's cordwainers carried this banner when they marched in twelfth place as part of a line of forty-six groups of artisans, tradesmen, and mechanics welcoming George Washington to Boston on October 19, 1789. The image is derived from the ancient coat of arms of the Worshipful Company of Cordwainers of London, organized there in 1271. The three goat heads represent the use of kidskin for the kinds of high-quality shoes made by skilled cordwainers for centuries. Clearly the men were proud of the ancient origins and longstanding traditions of their craft as well as their reputation for fine-quality workmanship and their mastery of unique hand skills.

Only a few of these silk flags carried by tradesmen in the Boston procession honoring Washington have survived. No records have been found that identify the people who did the work. It seems likely that many of these flags were created by professional painters of military standards and shop signs, but with so little time to prepare fifty different flags, some of the groups may have turned to Boston's few portrait or landscape painters, or even to coach or chair painters, most of whom had little or no experience in designing or painting emblems and legible alphabets.

The appearance of groups of workmen in civic processions continued even as factory production expanded in the nineteenth century, and their inspiring banners were part of an attempt to raise the public profile of middle-class workingmen. This is well documented by the remarkable survival of seventeen painted banners of the Maine Charitable Mechanics Association, an organization formed in Portland in 1815 to provide relief to injured or distressed members and their families, to promote innovation and improvement in their skills and trades, as well as to advocate for various good causes, especially temperance. The banners were painted by local sign painters for a procession of MCMA members in 1841, fifteen of them by ornamental painter William Capen alone. They were used in processions over the years and kept safe in the Association's headquarters until sold at a thrilling auction to a consortium of sixteen Maine museums in 2010.

Banners of the Maine Charitable Mechanics Association
Portland, Maine, 1841

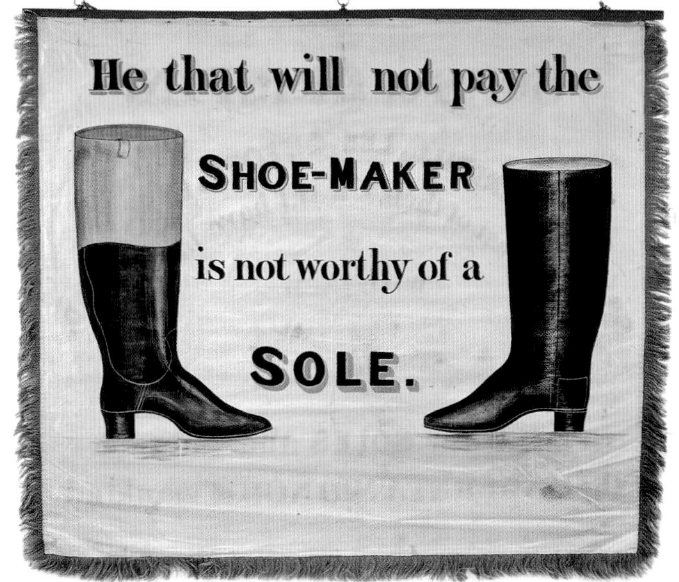

New England Militia Prior to 1860

To provide for the common defense and ensure public order, the United States Militia Act of 1792 required every able-bodied white man between the ages of eighteen and forty-five to be enrolled in his state's militia, equipped at his own expense with a musket or rifle, bayonet, knapsack, powder horn, cartridge box, and flints. In most New England states, militia members were also required to appear equipped for inspection and ready to participate in two annual Training Days or be subjected to a monetary fine. Most men enrolled in local infantry companies, but some resented or outright resisted this obligation and its attendant costs.

Those who could afford the additional expense of expensive uniforms, high-quality weapons, and specialized equipment could choose to serve in the strictly disciplined and elite volunteer companies of infantry, cavalry, or artillery units with impressive names such as Fusiliers, Dragoons, Rangers, Guards, or Light Infantry. There they elected their own officers and enjoyed social activities as well as the higher status and political clout of those groups. Volunteer units became a familiar sight as they marched frequently with their silken banners and bands of musicians escorting dignitaries and participating in civic parades and ceremonies. Some later served with distinction in the Civil War and for many ensuing years.

Salem Common on Training Day 1808

Salem, Massachusetts, 1808

Spring and fall Training Days, called Muster Days in some places, were popular community festivals. Here, in Salem, (*see next page*) excited women and children have left home to watch the military spectacle and some Black families have come out to join the fun. Everyone enjoyed visiting with friends and neighbors, viewing peddlers' wares, listening to itinerant fiddlers, feasting on the gingerbread, rum, cider, and other treats sold at temporary booths set up along the fence, and listening to the stirring music. The military high points of the day were the inspection of uniforms and equipment, demonstrations of marching and drilling, and the vigorous sham fight at the end. For many, the level of enthusiasm afforded by Training Day approached that of the Fourth of July.

Maine Militia Standard, 1822 (fragment)

Probably Boston, Massachusetts, 1822

After Maine became an independent state, separating from Massachusetts in 1820, various symbols were used on the official seal and flag, notably tall pine trees, the North Star, and sometimes a large moose with an impressive rack of horns. For militia banners, these images were used selectively in combination with the state motto, "Dirigo" (meaning "I lead" or "I direct"), and text identifying individual units. This fragment represents one of the first designs for a Maine militia standard. Believed to have been painted in Boston in 1822, it was part of a flag long treasured in the family of Alvin Doe of Parsonsfield, an active member of the local militia and later a member of the legislature. In all probability, torn and tattered edges of the original were cut away at some point in time, but clearly, the owners could not bear to part with these beloved symbols of the State of Maine.

The Ancient and Honorable Artillery Company on Tremont Street in front of the newly erected Tremont House Hotel
Boston, Massachusetts, ca. 1830

Boston's Ancient and Honorable Artillery Company, founded in 1638, is the oldest chartered volunteer military unit in the western hemisphere. For many years it trained officers for other volunteer companies in the Massachusetts militia. Since the 1920s, members of the company have worked to support patriotic and historic traditions in the city of Boston. Centered in the city's elite families, membership has often continued through successive generations. With their distinctive uniforms, disciplined marching, and individual prestige, the Ancients, as they are often known, always attract attention.

Traditionally, the Ancient and Honorable Artillery Company elects new officers on the first Monday of June. Following their own tradition, the men parade through the city to the Boston Common for a commissioning ceremony where the old officers resign and the insignia are passed to the newly elected leaders, after which the festive entertainment concludes with sentimental, political, and philanthropic toasts. The company appears again on other historic occasions such as Bunker Hill Day and the Fourth of July when they parade the short distance from their headquarters at Faneuil Hall to the Old State House, where a member has read aloud the Declaration of Independence almost annually since 1776.

During the 1830s, a growing demand for sheet music suitable for parlor piano performance paralleled the establishment of new volunteer militia companies and the rise of lithography as a new process for making handsome and inexpensive pictures in large quantities. One result was that Boston's entrepreneurial lithographers and publishers produced a series of song sheets with illustrated covers featuring historical landmarks in the city. Many of the pieces were for the sprightly marching tunes called "quick steps," which moved along in double time, usually 120 steps per minute. Not surprisingly, the sheets were often dedicated to the officers and members of elite volunteer companies who were sure to be ready customers.

Winthrop's Quick Step (detail)
Boston, Massachusetts, 1835

Like other elite companies, the Boston Independent Fusiliers were highly praised for being tastefully dressed and well equipped, their disciplined marching and execution of military tactics, and their civil and gentlemanly behavior. This was widely evident during their month-long trip to Washington, DC, in June 1835. The men returned by train to Roxbury on Friday, June 26, and marched into the city in the early evening, in plenty of time to head home for a rest before joining in celebration of the Fourth of July the next week.

As depicted on this cover, one wonders if they had arrived ahead of schedule, otherwise it is hard to understand why there are no cheering crowds as they march on State Street toward the old Massachusetts State House, for this elite company, and their commander, Captain G. T. Winthrop, usually attracted crowds of people anywhere they went. Alternatively, it may have been purely artistic license, an effort to focus on the primary subject rather than illustrate a detailed and accurate street scene.

Capt." E. G. Austin's Quick Step (detail)
Boston, Massachusetts, 1837

The Boston Light Infantry was a well-disciplined elite volunteer militia company. Their eye-catching Polish-style headgear emulated a distinctive European military fashion with a close fitting leather helmet surmounted by a square mortarboard raised high by a tall, cloth-covered cardboard cylinder.

The troops are shown climbing to the Charlestown Navy Yard from the Charles River shoreline where, anchored midstream, is an American frigate, believed to be the USS *Constitution*, which has been known as *Old Ironsides* ever since her decisive victory over HMS *Guerriere* early in the War of 1812. On the far shore is the Boston skyline with the steeples of many houses of worship and the dome of the Massachusetts State House seen directly ahead, a gentle reminder that at this point in time such architectural features and the masts of tall ships were the tallest things most people had ever seen!

"Our Country is Safe" The Berry Street Rangers Quick Step (detail)
Boston, Massachusetts, October 4, 1837

Passing two of Boston's bow-front brick houses on Berry Street, with the Reverend Dr. William Ellery Channing's Federal Street Church on the corner beyond, are the Berry Street Rangers marching on October 4, 1837. Only a few years earlier, they had been a nearly defunct volunteer militia company when a new captain sought to revitalize the unit and elevate its public reputation by upgrading their equipment, improving their marching and drilling, and parading more frequently. To enlarge the group, men of all social classes were invited to participate. To keep costs down, the men eschewed expensive uniforms and drilled in ordinary dark-colored

coats and hats, carrying their own various firearms, usually either a musket or a rifle. Despite the captain's efforts, the 1838 parade of the Berry Street Rangers was neither well attended by its members nor well disciplined. It was reported in the *Hingham Patriot* that "every man appeared to be his own officer." The disorder was such that several commentators feared that the new troop would serve more to promote insubordination than to elevate the militia as a whole.

"North-End Forever" Hull Street Guards Quick Step (detail)

Boston, Massachusetts, 1838

The Hull Street Guards were another new volunteer militia company, raised in the North End of Boston in 1837. Here we catch a glimpse of the Guards parading through their own neighborhood as part of their effort to attract attention and support. That goal seems unfulfilled in this image where there are no real spectators and the children playing in the street pay no attention to the marching soldiers in front of Christ Church (Old North). This is the steeple in which two signal lanterns, hung on April 18, 1775, triggered the battles at Lexington and Concord the next day, the first of the American Revolution. After the 1861 publication of Henry Wadsworth Longfellow's poem "The Midnight Ride of Paul Revere," the church became a hallowed symbol for all Americans.

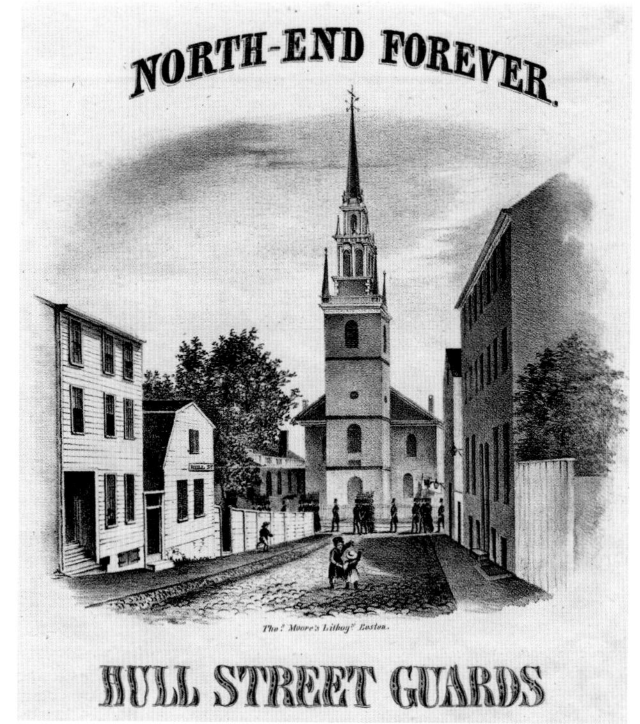

Presentation of an Elegant Standard by the Ladies of Manchester (detail)
Manchester, New Hampshire, September 22, 1842

Undoubtedly, this kind of scene was repeated many times in the years before the Civil War, as militia companies lined up at attention to receive a painted banner, or standard, as these flags were often known at the time. Standards were often paid for and presented by groups of ladies, frequently the wives and sweethearts of members of the company. In most cases the silk was painted by a professional artist, often a fancy painter who specialized in coach and standard painting. Usually, the women had raised money by making foods and fancy goods which they sold at a benefit fair; less frequently the funds had come from personal savings or solicitation of friends, family, and community members.

On this occasion five hundred people assembled on a damp and cloudy day to observe the presentation of

what was called "one of the handsomest standards in the state" to the Stark Guards as they stood at attention in front of Colonel Chase's house on Amherst Street in Manchester, New Hampshire. The standard was presented to the Guards' Captain Morrison by Miss Eliza Wheeler on behalf of the Manchester Sewing Circle. After the two exchanged appropriate remarks, the ladies of the Sewing Circle left the sheltering front porch and were escorted by the Guards as they all walked to the town hall to listen to a formal address.

The Stark Guards standard was designed and painted by Thomas P. Pierce, a New Hampshire artist little known today. According to a newspaper account, the standard featured the coat of arms of the State of New Hampshire surrounded with rich scrollwork on one side and on the other the inspiring words "We are always ready . . . For Our Country and our Country's good" along with a portrait of the Guards' namesake, General John Stark, the hero of the August 16, 1777, Battle of Bennington.

Participation in elite volunteer military companies like these brought prestige and pleasure to their members, but few men could afford the expense of fine uniforms and equipment or the time required for extensive drilling and military exercises. To fulfill their obligation under the Militia Act, most men joined local infantry companies, but in the years after the conclusion of the War of 1812, enthusiasm waned. By the 1820s attendance at Muster Days and military discipline had deteriorated badly, especially in rural areas. The enrolled companies lacked status and were typified by their spotty attendance, casual appearance, disreputable garments, makeshift weapons, and undisciplined behavior. Their Training Days attracted crowds of enthusiastic spectators, but often featured widespread drunkenness as well as rowdy and outrageous behavior.

Muster Day

Saco, Maine, 1843

Although Charles Granger's picture of a Muster Day at Saco in 1843 (*see next page*) provides a glimpse of militia drilling in the distance, he focuses our attention on the ineffective, but impassioned speaker at the podium. No one in the crowd appears to be listening to his message, which may well be advocating temperance. In the booth next to the speaker, a garrulous man, assisted by a woman, is pouring tumblers of rum from green glass bottles, and a drunken soldier has fallen to the ground in front of them. In all probability the rum seller would have been even busier once the troops were dismissed.

In the face of widespread disorder, as well as changing attitudes and circumstances, compulsory military training was abandoned in the 1840s. Soon, the energy and spare time of many middle-class young men were transferred to the fraternity and work of volunteer fire departments. The elite volunteer military companies continued drilling and appeared on ceremonial occasions in large cities, but, needless to say, everything changed when shots were fired at Fort Sumter in 1861.

The Militia Muster

Boston, Massachusetts, 1828

David Claypoole Johnston's image of a training day satirizes the degeneration of the militia system. The tall man at the right with his bayonet attached to a corn stalk seems fairly serious as the swaggering commander in his pretentious uniform attempts to call the group to attention. Further down the line, things are more out of control as the men step on each other's feet, laugh out loud, and mimic the officer. One man has snagged another's hat on his bayonet while his neighbor takes a long pull from a bottle of whiskey or rum. It's more than they can do to stand still.

Col. Pluck (detail)

Boston, Massachusetts, ca. 1824

Colonel Pluck was an illiterate stable hand elected colonel in the 84th Regiment of the Pennsylvania militia in May of 1824, when respect for military hierarchy there was already in serious decline. After being court-martialed for outrageous behavior in 1826, Pluck traveled often to New York and New England in the 1830s and 1840s, appearing as an honored guest at political and Masonic meetings and marching in military parades. He was also imitated by local men wearing huge and extravagantly feathered chapeaux de bras and carrying yard-long swords. The character "Colonel Pluck" appeared in many satirical antimilitia cartoons and often was a prominent officer in parades of Horribles and Fantastics, appearing at civic events in New England for more than one hundred years. To this day, "pluck" is a word sometimes used to identify either bravery or people with bombastic personalities.

Standing Company

Boston, June 1832

Comic almanacs published in the 1830s also seized on the deterioration of good order and the general disrespect for its traditional standards in the militia. This image was one of twelve amusing, but mostly outrageous woodcuts in an 1832 Boston publication titled *Broad Grins*, or *Fun For the New Year.* Ranging from the pompous commander with his tall feathered hat and might upright sword, the scene gradually deteriorates as it moves from the energetic drummer and determined rifleman at the right to three dissolute characters sharing only one weapon among them, a tall broomstick. Their unsteady posture indicates that they have also been sharing the open bottle of rum. They may mean well, however, for the man at the end of the line is wearing the slumped woolen Phrygian cap that has symbolized LIBERTY since ancient times.

Many New England town histories contain descriptive text that makes clear the way service in enrolled militia companies changed throughout the region in the years between 1825 and 1840. Not having been called to active duty since 1815, there was less and less agreement that the expense of equipment or the discipline of training days accomplished anything useful. Widespread mocking of the requirements of equipment and active drilling replaced good order, and training days were usually lubricated by abundant alcohol. Consider this description from New Bedford, Massachusetts, as a typical example:

> There was a time when the military system was in eminent repute—when to become Captain of a company of militia was the summit of common ambition, and when to be elevated to the post of Lieutenant or Ensign was esteemed 'glory enough for one day'. . . . But this time has passed away. The last May training that we remember, under the old regime, was worthy of being the last. Such a display was never before witnessed—so unique, so picturesque—it was eminently worthy of forming the finale of the whole system. Falstaff's army would have shewn like a troop of regulars in contrast. The Captain was an old man, hard upon eighty, who by some misfortune had been deprived of the free use of his pedal appendages, and mainly depended for support upon two crutches, which were handled with great dexterity and one of which supplied the office of a sword. The subaltern officers were chosen with similar discrimination, but the rank and file embodied all that fancy could suggest of the ludicrous and grotesque. Guns without locks and stocks without barrels, staves, pitchforks and broom sticks constituted the arms of the corps—codfish supplied the place of knapsacks, and of caps there was a variety not to be equaled in number by the names of the most distinguished of the Castilian race—the whole, marching to the inspiring music of tin pans played with exquisite taste by ragged urchins assisted by a band of performers on willow whistles and penny trumpets. The appearance was indeed picturesque, but the drill and evolutions—the manual and the march—the inspection and the parade—we will not describe them—and the sham fight in the afternoon and the real fight at night—all these we remember, but they are not to be portrayed on paper, and least of all with the pen. It was the last of the May trainings. The law existed afterwards, but the troops could never be assembled again, and thus the whole system passed away.
>
> *The New-Bedford Register,* June 7, 1843 [6]

Firefighters

A vital part of New England's long and thrifty tradition of relying on dedicated volunteers as essential parts of a successful community has been the availability of people who turn out to battle fires and serve in other public emergencies. Participation in an organized and uniformed fire company brings honor to both individuals and the group. Firefighters were usually recognized for being brave, sober, and strong, highly disciplined, and people of high moral tone. Until recently, they were also exclusively male and overwhelmingly white; few fire companies enrolled women or Black men. Even as many of the generous volunteers have been replaced by paid staff, firefighters are still honored as heroes.

New England's brave firefighters have always loved to display their expensive equipment, smart uniforms, special skills, and strong horses or powerful trucks. It seems that almost no parade has ever marched without at least one contingent of proud firefighters savoring both fellowship and public accolades. Nowadays they come from miles around, often bringing their children in the cab, throwing candy to the crowds along the way, and keeping their sirens screaming. No matter whether volunteers or paid employees, firefighters appear in parades as citizens dedicated to public service and safety. For nearly two hundred years, they have also organized day-long "musters" to which they invite other companies to compete in tests of strength, speed, and skill. Not surprisingly, these events often begin or end with loud and colorful parades.

While most fire companies polish up their newest equipment for display at musters and on parade days, it has long been a tradition for them also to roll out their oldest apparatus. The contrast between old and new equipment and documentation of the increasingly effective means of firefighting became more and more dramatic as steam pumpers replaced manpower, public water hydrants replaced bucket brigades, and motorized trucks replaced massive horses. Interest in preserving the old equipment and keeping it in working order prompted establishment of the New England League of Veteran Firemen in 1890. From the time of their first muster, at Lowell, Massachusetts, on September 25, 1891, the group and its successors have sponsored popular competitions that test the strength and stamina of both men and machines.

Sometimes wives and children were called to assist in the task of decorating firefighting equipment for parades with flags, garlands of evergreen, or baskets of flowers. In 1846 it was reported in the *Hampshire Gazette* on July 5, that at Springfield, Massachusetts, on July 4, the *Niagara* Company's machine was "particularly resplendent in the gifts of Flora. Indeed, all the machines looked as if they had fallen under the touch of fairy fingers." Of course, problems could develop, for firefighters are always on call. Three years later at Northampton, the *Ocean* Fire Company from Springfield brought a machine that was beautifully decorated "but they were obliged to remove the work of their taste and skill to attend a fire."

These accounts remind us that fire companies were often named for their use of water: not only *Niagara* and *Ocean*, but also *Torrent, Fountain, Deluge, Cataract*, and *Neptune* were popular names for fire companies. Others are identified with their style of work as *Invincibles, Tigers, Eagles*, or *Volunteers*, or by the height of the water thrown from their hoses: usually *Excelsior* (meaning very high).

At first firefighters had no uniforms, wearing their own everyday work clothing when called to action. Usually, they chose garments that were loose, comfortable, and probably old, things that could easily be discarded if they were badly torn, singed, or otherwise damaged. Wool was preferred because of its resistance to flames. Soon after 1825, special uniforms and helmets began to be adopted for parade use only. Described variously as "appropriate," "neat," or "new" and "showy," parade uniforms usually consisted of black or white pants with distinctive red woolen shirts and sometimes patent leather or white leggings and matching belts. Styles change over time, of course, and in Providence, Rhode Island, after a parade on July 4, 1875, older citizens remarked with a feeling akin to sadness the absence of the "joyful firemen with their red shirts, as of old."

Like the military, fire companies marched in groups, sometimes identified by distinctive badges or painted banners. The banner of the *Deluge* Company of Northampton, Massachusetts, painted on white silk by a Mr. Elwell in nearby Springfield, showed on one side "a sea of swelling waters overhung with dark clouds—representing the Deluge . . ." and on the opposite side a view of the First Church in Northampton, with "firemen throwing a stream of water to the top of the steeple and the words Excelsior . . . Ever Ready to Do Our Duty." Sadly, that banner, like so many, has been lost to the ravages of time.

Men took special care of the oldest equipment, but danger lurked. A sad example occurred in 1938 at Hampton, New Hampshire, when a high-spirited horse bolted and ran away with a hundred-year-old piece of apparatus, smashing it into a front porch and destroying both the fire engine and the porch.

Participating in parades helped to build support for firefighting companies at the same time that demonstrating the expensive equipment stimulated confidence in their effectiveness. Training together enhanced physical and communication skills. Frequent meetings and shared exposure to danger strengthened ties between the individuals. These bonds of fraternity offered personal rewards and inspired selfless service in times of need. Further, marching as part of a well-respected, easily identifiable, uniformed group raised the self-confidence of individual members and gave them a certain level of status in the community.

Preparing for a Muster on Middle Street

Portland, Maine, September 30, 1846

This rare window into public life in pre-Civil War Portland was opened when daguerreotype artists George S. Hough and Charles J. Anthony set up their new camera on Middle Street. The Portland *Advertiser* on the twenty-ninth announced the men's intention to capture a view of the planned parade and drill of Portland's fire departments the next day, and urged everyone on the scene to "remain as stationary as possible" during the exposure in order to assure success. At four in the afternoon at least three exposures were made, showing fire companies assembled in parade dress on Middle Street, the city's principal thoroughfare. Afterward the fire apparatus was described as being "in good order" and the men "most promising."

In this view, we are able to see five groups of uniformed men with their engines. At least three different uniform styles are discernable—farthest away are five rows of men in shiny, or white, flat-brimmed hats and gray wool pants, lined up on either side of their hand tubs. Another group standing closer to the camera flanks an engine with one of its long pumping brakes raised. They wear white pants and braces with a different style of hat, with the kind of flap at the back intended to protect their necks, more like a modern fire helmet in shape. Closest to us are members of *Casco* Engine Company No. 1, wearing white pants, dark jackets, and leather helmets with shiny faceplates. Their banner, mounted on a pole nearby is blurred by the breeze, but it appears to show a landscape surrounded by a wreath.

The busy scene includes crowds of spectators in the street, on sidewalks, on exterior staircases, and in windows. There are horse-drawn vehicles on both sides of the street, and, at the lower right, a newly arrived stagecoach loaded with trunks and other luggage.

During the next few years, many of the eighteenth-century houses and Federal-era stores seen here were swept away as returning prosperity brought change to the city center before the beginning of the Civil War. Sadly, the handsome domed granite building, the Portland Merchant's Exchange, burned to the ground in 1854. Even worse, the steepled Second Parish Church and all the new buildings visible here were destroyed on July 4, 1866, when a disastrous fire sparked by celebratory fireworks destroyed 1,500 buildings, fully one-third of the city, and left ten thousand people homeless. Firemen from as far away as Boston traveled by train to assist in fighting the conflagration, proving the skill and readiness they so proudly displayed at public musters and parades.

FEATHERS

Lexington Battle Monument. S. Danvers with Residence of Hon. R. S. Daniels
Danvers, Massachusetts, 1856

This company of firefighters in parade-uniform coats and caps is seen hauling equipment in the 1856 procession welcoming philanthropist George Peabody to Danvers, Massachusetts, the city of his birth. The engine with its large water tank and long pumping brakes on each side, may have been that known locally as the *General Foster.* Behind it a few men are pulling a hose reel. Overhead are the flags of the United States and Great Britain along with a banner proclaiming "Honor to Him Who Loves to Honor His Country," referencing both Peabody's current residence in England and his philanthropic contributions to his native Danvers.

The tall obelisk they are passing commemorates the

Battle of Lexington. One of the first public monuments honoring events of the American Revolution, it had been erected in 1835 on the seventy-fifth anniversary of the early morning encounter on April 19, 1775, at Lexington Green, as British troops marched toward Concord in their quest to destroy Patriot military stores. George Peabody's contribution of one-third of the cost of the monument is an early example of his local philanthropy (*see pages 47 and 206*).

Before the Parade

Northampton, Massachusetts, 1879

This company of Northampton, Massachusetts, firefighters lacks parade uniforms, wearing instead white shirts, straw hats, and pants of various colors. Having decorated their horse-drawn ladder truck with long garlands of flowers, they paused under the elms in front of the First National Bank for a photograph in 1879.

Ready for the Muster

Village Fire Company, Chester, Vermont, ca. 1905–1910

Men of the *School Street* Fire Company, Aid No. 1 stand in parade uniforms before departing to participate in a regional firemen's muster or a parade. They may have mounted their old horse-drawn hose reel on the bunting covered flatbed truck behind them in order to display it or to enter it in a competition at the muster.

Fraternal Organizations

Throughout American history people have come together to participate in organizations for various purposes such as self-improvement, social activity, community service, and political action. For a long time, many of these groups were openly called secret societies because they observed restrictive membership based on ethnicity, religion, race, gender, occupation, personal interests, and/or financial resources. Within each group, people enjoyed friendships, the sense of importance conferred by admission to the select membership, a high moral tone, and participation in activities with demonstrated public benefit. These bonds were cemented by complex private rituals, coded symbols, distinctive uniforms, and emblematic badges. Access to private libraries, lodge rooms, and other spaces, knowledge of organizational secrets, and pledging loyalty to the values of a well-defined group elevated members' sense of self-worth and belonging. While uniforms and traditions honored the past, especially the group's history of service to the larger community, the activities, social activism, and benevolence of most fraternal and social groups usually focused on the present. In some places, members prized the availability of alcoholic beverages on Sundays or during Prohibition, when otherwise prohibited by blue laws.

Many fraternal organizations are national in scope, with separate subsidiary subgroups in various states. Membership was long restricted to men, although some groups had separate, often subordinate, organizations for women and children. In recent years, the gender barrier has largely disappeared.

The number of fraternal organizations expanded in the years after the Civil War. Veterans joined the Grand Army of the Republic (GAR) and successor organizations like the American Legion. Businessmen joined the Rotary, Elks, Loyal Order of Moose, or similar groups. Physicians, lawyers, professors, and other professional men established special affinity groups. Immigrants formed associations based on ethnicity. Farmers and their families joined the Grange. Laborers joined benevolent associations and unions. Even the Ku Klux Klan recruited members by offering family-based picnics and athletic competitions in addition to their threatening and violent nativist activities.

As women began to step onto the public stage in the years after the Civil War, they also established gender-specific organizations to facilitate their good works and to support each other. Few New England towns lacked a female charitable society, a women's book club, or a sewing circle. In 1890, the General Federation of Women's Clubs brought together sixty-three clubs from across the country, and the number of individual clubs and their membership then grew rapidly.

After 1890, some women joined the National Society of the Colonial Dames of America or the Daughters of the American Revolution (DAR), and men became members of the Sons of the American Revolution (SAR) or the Society of Colonial Wars. Members of these and other lineage societies honored their proven ancestors by preserving historic sites and engaging in a variety of patriotic projects while enjoying the social activities and elite social status conferred by their eligibility.

Fraternal groups, like so many others, participated in parades. They often marched proudly together, wearing badges or carrying banners to proclaim their identity. By the 1870s, some fraternal groups created wonderful parade floats, and these became more and more common as time passed.

The Procession Passing the Boston Museum, Tremont Street
Boston, Massachusetts, October 25, 1848

A group of Masonic officers wearing their symbolic aprons, as well as the rich and dazzling jewels that served as emblems of their individual offices within the brotherhood, led other fraternal groups in the great parade celebrating major improvements to the city's public water supply. This was a major feature in Boston's Water Celebration on October 25, 1848 (discussed further as an example of Progress in Chapter 5).

The line seen here is passing through the monumental Water Arch erected between the Boston Museum and the Tremont Hotel on Tremont Street. Designed in the Moorish style by Boston architect Hammatt Billings and made with its wooden frame covered with cloth, the arch stood fifty feet high. It was bordered with crimson and gold trefoils and further embellished with quotations from Shakespeare. Looking south in this image, both King's Chapel and the steeple of the Park Street Church are visible in the distance. Just coming into view is the great feature of the Marine Division, a full-rigged sloop-of-war manned by twenty-five sailors, drawn by eight fine horses, with streamers flying and cannon protruding from her portholes.

In addition to scores of Freemasons, there were Washingtonians, Sons of Temperance, members of the Father Matthew Temperance Society, the Boston Temperance Society, Rechabites, and other temperance organizations from all over New England enthusiastically joined in celebrating the newly available abundance of pure water in the city. Civic officials, military units, firemen with decorated engines and hose reels, truckmen with their massive draft horses, members of Salem's East India Marine Society carrying their Indian palanquin, Irish and Scots charitable societies, and a host of businesses and tradesmen walked in the procession, which was nearly five miles long.

Palanquin

Calcutta, India, before 1803

Among the fraternal organizations that entered features in the Boston Water Celebration procession were members of Salem's East India Marine Society, local men who had served as supercargoes or masters

of ships that had ventured near or beyond Cape Horn or the Cape of Good Hope. Established in 1799, the group collected tangible souvenirs of their extensive travels, things that were termed "artificial and natural curiosities," which they displayed in their headquarters museum. Among them was this palanquin from Kolkata (formerly Calcutta), given by five members in 1803. Featuring an enclosed chamber with louvered sides in which a person could recline in privacy while being carried on the shoulders of two or more strong men, the gift was intended to "gratify the curious" and offer Westerners an opportunity to view this unusual form of transportation from a mysterious foreign land.

In the early years of the East India Marine Society, members paraded with the palanquin through the streets of Salem after their annual business meeting, some of them wearing exotic clothing or carrying objects that had been donated to the collection. Over the next fifty years occasional events like this proved entertaining, but they also began to attract criticism. In the Water Celebration parade, the Society's entry included two large ship models along with the palanquin in which was a "fair young boy reclining in oriental style" while being carried by "six stout negro bearers dressed in white oriental costumes, with white turbans." By 1848, members of the Society themselves declined to participate in this vignette.

As we will see, this kind of exotic display was by no means unique in nineteenth century New England. Turbaned Blacks served as grooms or drivers of many horse-drawn parade floats. Combining tangible elements of African, Turkish, Indian, Chinese, and Japanese cultures, overt racism, and stunning insensitivity to individual identities, the rosy glow of romantic orientalism appealed to some as both admirable and fascinating at the same time that it struck others as grotesque and offensive, much as it does today.

Inauguration of the Statue of Franklin

Boston, Massachusetts, September 17, 1856

After a long procession organized by the city of Boston, this huge crowd gathered in front of City Hall on School Street to observe the dedication of a statue honoring Benjamin Franklin, the printer and patriot who had been born just around the corner 150 years earlier, on January 15, 1706. On this occasion, Franklin was honored as both a civic leader and a self-made man who championed wide dispersal of science and useful knowledge.

On guard at the rear of the crowd were the volunteer militia in its accustomed splendor and mounted members of the National Lancers. Among the participants were many fraternal organizations, easily identified by their badges and the Roman-style banners suspended from cross bars. Among them were about two thousand members of various Masonic orders, along with delegations from the Massachusetts Charitable Mechanics Association, Scots Charitable Association, Kossuth Lodge, East India Marine Society,

MUSEUM

German Society of the Sons of Liberty, Germania Gymnastic, Kossuth, United Shamrock Society, Medical Association, Harvard College Faculty, Hebrew Mutual Relief Society, Humane Society, Merchant Seamen, Massachusetts Society for Promoting Agriculture, Massachusetts Horticultural Society, New England Historic Genealogical Society, Mechanics and Apprentices Library, and YMCA, along with numerous additional Masonic Lodges, Odd Fellows, and the Bunker Hill Monument Association, as well as a wide variety of historical, scientific, literary and musical societies, and representatives of forty-seven different trades, all reflecting varied interests and affiliations of men in the city.

These groups, along with the name of every participating business and school, were carefully described in the *Franklin Statue Memorial,* a 412-page account of the event. Although the organizers had expressed a desire to arrange a holiday inclusive of all classes of Boston citizens, the published list of participants illustrates the limited definition of citizen at the time, for it does not include any Black or women's groups, not even the Prince Hall Lodge of Masons, Boston's Black Lodge.

Franklin Statue Dedication Badges

Boston, Massachusetts, 1856

Banner of the New England Historic Genealogical Society

Boston, Massachusetts, 1856

In addition to the painted banners identifying each group in one of these large municipal processions, many of the individual participants also wore membership badges or distinctive ribbons identifying their affiliation. Among surviving examples are ribbons in white, red, and yellow with various texts and images of Benjamin Franklin, either as a full-length standing figure or a portrait bust. Marshals, members of the Committee of Arrangements, and others appointed by the city of Boston wore badges with depictions of both Franklin and the city's seal on white silk ribbons crowned by rosettes with sequined stars in the center. The New England Historic Genealogical Society paid printer George C. Jenks of Boston two dollars to print an unknown number of these distinctive red ribbons for its members to wear as they marched with this silken banner at the 1856 Franklin Festival.

CITY OF BOSTON.
COMMITTEE
OF
ARRANGEMENTS.
Sept. 17, 1856.
BOSTONIA
CONDITA A.D.
1630.

BENJ. FRANKLIN.
Born in Boston, Jan. 17, 1706.
Died in Philadelphia, April 17, 1790
Inauguration of
The Franklin Statue

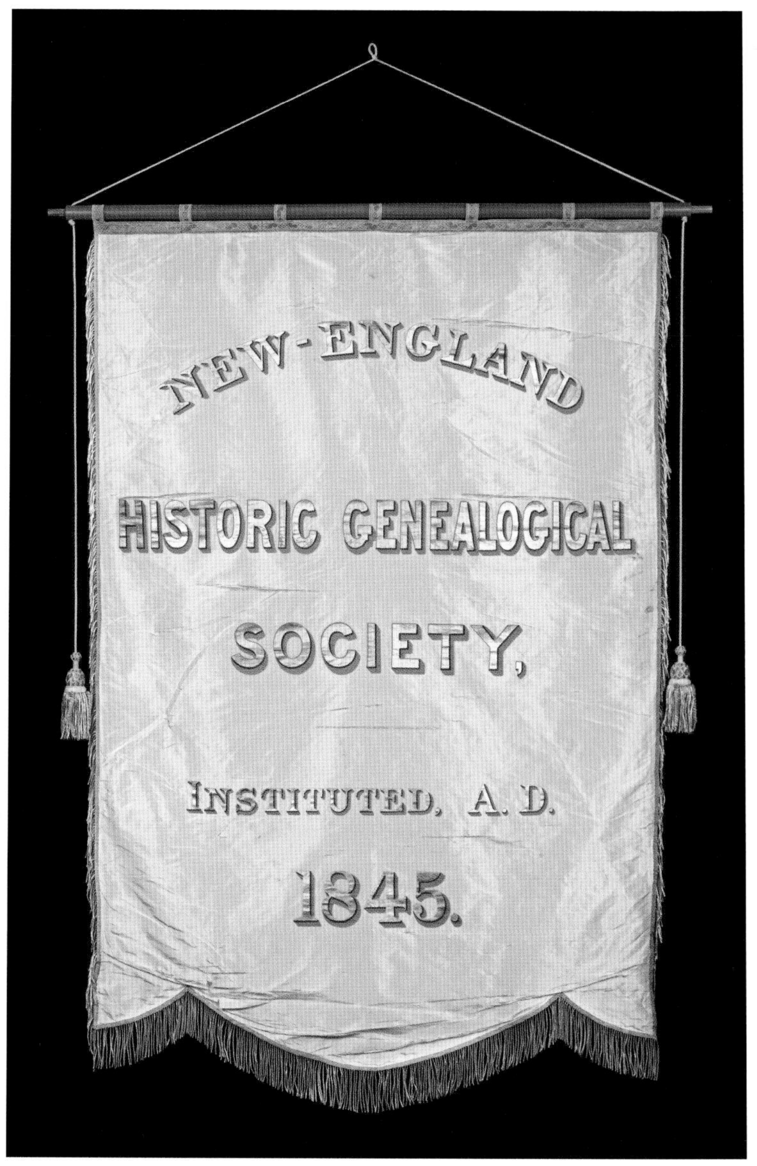
NEW-ENGLAND
HISTORIC GENEALOGICAL
SOCIETY,
INSTITUTED, A. D.
1845.

Members of the Putnam Phalanx
Hartford, Connecticut, 1860

Commemorative military groups like the Putnam Phalanx were established in the 1850s by doctors and lawyers, judges, merchants, and other community leaders who may have lacked the prominent ancestors required for membership in the Society of the Cincinnati or Boston's Ancient and Honorable Artillery Company. Similar quasi-military organizations included the Amoskeag Veterans in Manchester, New Hampshire, and the Continentals in Worcester, Massachusetts.

Unlike the spontaneous and satirical military units who turned out for the parades of Fantastics or the Antiques and Horribles on the Fourth of July in the 1840s and 1850s, these commemorative military groups were fraternal organizations of men who loved military splendor and recalling the stirring events of colonial days. Founded for social and historic as well as mostly ceremonial military purposes, these men were especially proud of their distinctive replicas of historic uniforms and disciplined marching. They escorted dignitaries, attended funerals of prominent men, and conducted annual parades in which they displayed their martial skills and patriotic spirit.

Like members of many fraternal organizations, the men of the showy Putnam Phalanx reinforced their bonds with uniforms, banners, a strictly observed internal hierarchy, and a pleasant collegiality in their spacious headquarters known as the Armory. The men frequently honored their namesake when offering a toast "The True Soldier—Like Israel Putnam—ever ready to do—to dare—to die." Phalanx members participated in official excursions, traveling together by railroad to other cities where they enjoyed elaborate entertainments after marching in procession to visit monuments and historic sites such as Bunker Hill, Mount Vernon, or the Bennington Battlefield. When traveling, they enjoyed the reciprocal hospitality of similar organizations, attended multiple receptions and dinners, and received loud cannon salutes and hearty applause as they marched near the front of the line in public parades. Unlike temperance advocates, the "jolly and substantial" members of the Putnam Phalanx were described as "stout trenchermen" who enjoyed good food and drink. Undaunted by the gruesome reality of the Civil War, these prominent men and boys continued to practice regular drilling in their showy uniforms. Although the Putnam Phalanx is no longer active, some of these organizations continue to this very day.

Pioneers—Grange Division of the Procession

Gorham, Maine, 1886

In small-town parades, like those in major cities, floats presented by members of the National Grange Order of the Patrons of Husbandry illustrated time-honored agricultural activities as well as tributes to the Roman goddesses of agriculture, flowers, and fruit: Ceres, Flora, and Pomona. At Gorham, Maine, in 1886, the Grange section of the 250th anniversary procession included signs proclaiming: "Our farms illustrate the fruit of industry, frugality, and intelligence." To illustrate these ideas, the Grange floats offered tributes to both past and present in addition to the usual allegorical compositions. First came this log cabin with signs reading "Be it ever so humble, there's no place like home" and "1736, They Endured, 1786, We Enjoy." Inside was a domestic scene repeated in many similar parades: a family dressed in clothing of the olden time, with the mother spinning flax and children playing nearby. The next entry, covered in spruce boughs, was deemed a "vivid picture of rustic simplicity," but the costumed people riding inside must have understood the never-ending toil of farm life; their sign declared "Labor conquers all things." It is clear that even as they honored the perseverance and hand skills of the past, the Gorham farmers were well aware of changes resulting from mechanization. Their

confidence that ongoing improvements in equipment and scientific farming practices would open the way for future agricultural triumphs was obvious as they proudly compared a plow of 1776 with one used in 1886 and added a display of their new machinery at the end of the Grange division in the procession.

The men and women of the Grange believed that farming was at once the most useful and honorable profession, but even in prosperous suburbs where farming was no longer the primary occupation, many middle-class white people became Grange members. At a time of rapid cultural and economic change, people found comfort in the rituals and collegiality of an organization that honored traditional agrarian values.

Ten Rod Road Float

Rochester, New Hampshire, 1893

Although lacking formal organization with its attendant rituals and uniforms, informal groups of neighbors have always enjoyed bonds of fraternity. For at least ten years, this group of farm neighbors on Ten Rod Road in Farmington worked together each year to create a new design for the float they entered in the parade at the nearby Rochester Fair. On fair day they looked forward to a

happy time and anxiously hoped that their float would win a prize ribbon. Their effort was encouraged by the Grange and led by one of the best farmers in the area, Joseph Demerritt. He is seen here in 1893 with his readily identifiable white beard, standing near the front of his biggest wagon at the moment it was decorated and ready to go. The finest specimens of the neighborhood harvest had been artfully arranged against a background trimmed with sprigs of evergreen and fresh flowers. The flags, the steer horns, the identifying signs, and the bunting used to wrap the wagon were stored over the winter in Demerritt's barn and used year after year.

Seal of the Franklin County Agricultural Society

Greenfield, Massachusetts, 1897

Established in 1850, the Franklin County Agricultural Society added something new to their annual Agricultural Fair at Greenfield in 1897 when they sponsored a magnificent coaching parade featuring handsome equipage and thoroughbred horses along with a number of elaborate floats. Emphasizing the agricultural roots of the community, the society's float relied on four teams of sturdy oxen, each accompanied by a man in a farmer's white smock and a straw hat. The display featured a plow and a sheaf of wheat

surrounded by fruits and vegetables centered by a living emblem of its seal with a woman in white representing Pomona, the Roman goddess of fruitful abundance.

Some Pumpkins

Greenfield, Massachusetts, 1897

New England farmers have always relished the openly friendly competition that honors the earliest production or the biggest and best products, no matter whether the assessment is in the barnyard or on the fairgrounds. Hard work, special feeding, and plenty of secret tricks to protect selected animals and cold-sensitive crops are employed to produce prize specimens and bragging rights. Even today, champion steers, huge hogs, sparkling jellies, perfect potatoes, lush flowers, and symmetrical arrangements of big, beautiful fruits and vegetables attract lots of attention and win prize ribbons at agricultural fairs.

The "Klondike pumpkin," said to have been the largest product of the vegetable kingdom ever raised in the county, was displayed at the 1897 Franklin County Fair. It was described as a "wondrous specimen . . . which would have made a whole winter-full of the old-fashioned pumpkin pies our grandmothers used to set before us." Mounted on a farm wagon trimmed with cornstalks, the pumpkin was carried in triumph in the coaching parade at the fair, along with exquisitely decorated private carriages, farm wagons, and delicate floats. The "Greenfield giant" was certainly huge, but it pales in comparison to the 2,114-pound specimen that was a recent prize-winner at the Topsfield Fair. These competitions continue, and New England's prize pumpkins still get bigger every year.

Longshoreman's Benevolent Society
Portland, Maine, July 4, 1894

As Irish immigrants began to replace Portland's Black dockworkers in the 1870s, they sought mutual support. Their Longshoreman's Benevolent Society was established in 1880 to protect their jobs and provide assistance to injured members and their families as well as their widows and orphans. To protect their racial exclusivity, membership was restricted by an unfortunate bylaw requiring that "no colored man shall be a member of this society."

Members who chose to participate in this 1894 parade wore suits instead of work clothes. Some rode behind a team of white horses in the wheeled boat while others walked behind, going west on Cumberland Street. The huge banner above the boat proclaims, "United We Stand, Divided We Fall," a motto embedded in the preamble to their 1881 bylaws.

Go Thou and Do Likewise
Biddeford, Maine, September 14, 1905

In 1905, the Laconia Lodge of the International Order of Odd Fellows won first prize in the Biddeford semicentennial parade for this float highlighting the charitable efforts of the group, especially their cumulative contribution of $50,000 in support of various relief and educational efforts in the city.

The tableau in the center of the float presents a bedridden sick man attended by three women, with a watcher and two visiting lodge brothers nearby. All together they illustrate the deep bonds of fellowship and mutual support enjoyed by members of the Odd Fellows.

Old-Time Household Industry

Lexington, Massachusetts, April 19, 1910

The streetcar trolley passengers riding on Massachusetts Avenue in Lexington on Patriots Day, April 19, 1910, must have been astonished when they found themselves passing between the new Lexington High School and this tableau of *Old-Time Household Industry* with costumed women spinning thread and churning butter. The slow-moving, ox-drawn float was the entry of the Lexington Grange in the great local parade commemorating the 135th anniversary of the first military encounter of the American Revolution, that of April 19, 1775, on Lexington Green.

The *Lexington Minuteman* report on April 23 that "the costumes were those of Priscilla and John Alden," might seem irrelevant considering that the Pilgrim couple, celebrated in the well-known poem, "The Courtship of Miles Standish," by New England poet Henry Wadsworth Longfellow, lived in faraway Plymouth, Massachusetts, more than 150 years before the local battle that was commemorated that day in Lexington. By then, Priscilla Alden was seen as a paragon of domestic duty and the couple were revered both as founders of New England and enduring symbols of its virtues and values.

Indian Tribe
Bedford, Massachusetts, 1912

Members of the Shawsheen Tribe, No. 45, of the Improved Order of Red Men won the second prize for floats with this entry in the Old Home Week parade at Bedford, Massachusetts, in 1912. Their fraternal organization, founded in 1834, was a lodge of white male citizens who saw themselves preserving an important part of the American past. They promoted ideals of freedom, friendship, and charity, which they identified with the Native American culture and mistakenly believed to be fading away.

At this period, most New Englanders believed that the American Indians who inhabited the region before the arrival of English colonists looked like contemporary Plains people with their tall, feathered headdresses and tipis. Entrepreneurial merchants selling supplies for various fraternal organizations offered these items as well as tomahawks, drums, buffalo robes, and weapons, along with flags, badges, and other accessories in mail-order catalogues. Acquisition of the full range of goods was promoted as a way to provide a sense of authenticity for the activities of the group as they met in their "Wigwam" lodges or appeared in parades honoring the myth of the "Noble Savage."

Indian Village

Concord, New Hampshire, 1927

It should not be surprising that women of the Hiawatha Council, No. 35, of the Daughters of Pocahontas created this imaginary *Indian Village* on a flatbed truck to set the stage for a series of historical floats in the 1927 parade celebrating the two hundredth anniversary of the settlement of Concord, New Hampshire. Their dramatic pre-contact scene featured the costumes and tipis used in their own lodge activities as well as those of their brother organization, the Improved Order of Red Men. No doubt their patriotic and historical intentions were good, but in reality, their float ignores the impact of settlement on indigenous communities and illustrates a misunderstanding of the clothing and dwellings of New Hampshire's native tribes in 1727, when the city was founded.

Ethnicity

The number of features illustrating ethnicity in New England's traditional parades has expanded over time, reflecting not only ongoing immigration and the increasing diversity of national origins, but also a more inclusive society. Many churches and ethnic fraternal organizations entered floats in larger community events while a few organized their own parades, usually for specific holidays like the Irish St. Patrick's Day or Swedish *Midsommar.* The duality of immigrants' desire to nurture and express the traditions of their own cultural identity and to participate with enthusiasm in American celebrations continues to this day.

Usually the floats created by ethnic groups featured an abundance of flags together with allegorical representations of the homeland, folk costume, and other distinctive features based in history, literature, music, and the arts. In many cases these were combined with American flags and figures of Columbia or Liberty in order to express the patriotic spirit of new citizens. The small selection that follows illustrates some of the more popular formats.

NEW AMERICANS

The Original States of the Union

Haverhill, Massachusetts, July 3, 1890

Anticipating the parade planned as part of Haverhill's three-day celebration of its 250th anniversary in July 1890, members of the city's Irish Catholic parish, St. James, developed elaborate plans to participate in a way "that would be at the same time novel in its idea and also strictly American and patriotic" instead of their usual display of shamrocks, Celtic harps, and the regalia of the Ancient Order of Hibernians. The result was a lengthy series of historical floats that began with Columbus at the court of Ferdinand and Isabella and extended to the Civil War, along with a series of tableaux honoring discoverers, early settlers, soldiers, sailors, statesmen, orators, and poets. As the culmination of their presentation, the *Original States of the Union,* this float was both innovative and impressive. A young man in the costume of a Continental soldier at the time of the American Revolution stood guard near the driver of a horse-drawn wagon carrying a wide platform draped with bunting. A large wooden structure towered over the float with its large American flag and portrait of George Washington, "The Father of Our Country," surrounded by flags of the "different European nations who sent their representatives to America." In an unusual effort to honor the increasing diversity of the growing industrial city, the float carried a group of young ladies dressed in what were called "costumes peculiar to the nations that settled here" instead of the usual white gowns and ribbon sashes.

FRENCH CANADIAN

La Grande Hermine

Lewiston, Maine, June 24, 1897

This replica of the ship *Grande Hermine* was a prominent feature at the head of the line in the parade at the annual Grande Fête de St.-Jean Baptiste in Lewiston–Auburn on June 24, 1897. Maine's French Canadians, many of whom had come to find work in textile or paper manufacturing towns, honored the ship that had brought Jacques Cartier and others to the mouth of the St. Lawrence River in June of 1535. For these communities, the *Grande Hermine* was as significant as the *Santa Maria* or the *Mayflower.*

French Canadian groups sometimes selected float topics honoring the supportive role of the French during the American Revolution, notably the voluntary leadership of the Marquis de Lafayette or the surrender of Cornwallis in the presence of the French fleet at Yorktown. Other French Canadian floats were much like those seen elsewhere but with a French twist. At Haverhill, Massachusetts, in 1890 one of the French Canadian floats titled *Antiquity* carried "an old time Canadian family with the women engaged in domestic work and men cobbling." Yet another offered eight young ladies in white representing states founded by the French. Unfortunately, there are no pictures.

GERMAN

United German Societies

Northampton, Massachusetts, June 7, 1904

Like many groups sponsoring parade floats in cities after 1875 or so, the three United German Societies of Northampton—the German American Citizen's Association, the Order of Harugars, and the Schuetzenverein—sought professional help with their entry for an especially important occasion. For the Meadow City's 250th anniversary parade on June 7, 1904, they hired Richard B. Eisnold of nearby Springfield who prepared a design for this "very artistic" float decked with American and German flags. The tall woman at the center represents Germania traveling through foreign countries accompanied by female personifications of art and music. The float was escorted by costumed heralds and a mounted marshal dressed as Lohengrin, the legendary German Knight of the Holy Grail. Somewhat incongruously, the driver wore a version of American colonial costume, complete with tricorn hat.

IRISH

The Army and Navy Forever

Norwich, Connecticut, July 6, 1909

The figurehead on this nautical float was a crowned figure of the Virgin Mary flanked by three girls dressed in pure white to represent religion and purity. The ensemble was created by the local Sisters of Mercy for the parade celebrating the 250th anniversary of the city of Norwich, in 1909. With young men dressed as cadets and younger boys in sailor suits, aboard what was termed a modern battleship, the float was hailed as a "credit to St. Patrick's parochial school" and described in a patronizing fashion by the city fathers as something "appreciated by the people of Norwich." At this date Catholics were often considered outsiders by the establishment, yet this presentation suggests that, even so, they already considered themselves part of the Norwich community.

Irish Girls

Pittsfield, Massachusetts, July 4, 1911

This real photo postcard was mailed without a signature on July 18, 1911. The sender asked "Do you recognize Columbia? This was our A. O. H. S. float in the parade July 4th." The card depicts the shamrock-trimmed float presented by the local chapter of the Ancient Order of Hibernians in the "Pageant of

Historical Floats" in the parade celebrating the 150th anniversary of Pittsfield, Massachusetts. The sender implies that she participated as Columbia, standing tall near American and Irish flags, surrounded by seated young women in white holding small American flags while wearing matching crowns and sashes that almost certainly were green. Facing the rear of the float, another young woman is strumming a large Irish harp.

The Ancient Order of Hibernians was founded in New York in 1836 and today it is the oldest ethnic organization still active in the United States. In Boston, the Charitable Irish Society, established there in 1737, stepped forth in its first St. Patrick's Day parade in 1862. These groups and other Irish charitable and temperance societies grew rapidly in the years before the Civil War in response to the prejudice fostered by the anti-Catholic Know Nothing movement. The parades of Irish groups have changed over time but have always featured distinctive badges, shamrocks, and plenty of green.

SWEDISH

Viking Ship

Worcester, Massachusetts, July 4, 1892

Not surprisingly, the number of floats honoring Columbus increased markedly in 1892 as towns and cities across the country responded with enthusiasm to President Benjamin Harrison's urging of Americans to prepare to honor the 400th anniversary of what was then termed Columbus's "discovery" of America. As a result, on both July 4 and October 12, the streets were

filled with "the red, white, and blue of the nation and the red and yellow of old Spain."

Although the first members of the Swedish community in Worcester, Massachusetts, had only arrived a few years previously, they recognized the powerful symbolism of the planned commemorations of Columbus's voyage. They seized the opportunity to get ahead of the crowd and make their own powerful statement about immigration. Svea Gille constructed this replica of Leif Ericson's longship and mounted it on a canvas covered float painted with swirling waves. Propelled by horses hidden underneath the float, the boat rocked on large springs that made it look as if it was being tossed on a stormy sea. Crowded with oarsmen dressed as Viking warriors, the ship joined the city's patriotic parade on the Fourth of July in 1892. On the stern, Gille had painted "Anno 999" in reference to the year of Ericson's voyage, almost five hundred years before Columbus' "discovery." Essentially proclaiming "*We Were Here First!*", these descendants of the Vikings asserted their strong claim to a preeminent role in the civic life of Worcester as they passed between the cheering crowds.

Midsommar Maypole

Worcester, Massachusetts, ca. 1917

A Swedish Folk Festival parade in Worcester about 1917 included this verdant horse-drawn float representing the annual June celebration of *Midsommar* with its garlanded maypole and people in traditional folk costume. Despite the vigorous Americanization efforts of local industrialist George Jepson, who was himself an immigrant from Sweden, members of Worcester's large Swedish community continued to observe traditions of the homeland.

ARMENIAN

Buy Liberty Bonds

Haverhill, Massachusetts, 1918

Among the immigrant groups seeking economic opportunity in the massive shoe factories at Haverhill were Armenians who welcomed survivors of Turkish violence and the Armenian genocide of 1915. Many joined local organizations associated with the Armenian National Union, a short-lived umbrella organization that included the group sponsoring this parade float in 1918. Twelve young girls in white are visible on this simply decorated motor truck. It is tempting to think they may represent the thirteen colonies; perhaps one is hiding. Certainly, they represent religious liberty, a cherished benefit of their new life in America. They are escorted by five men with false beards who appear to be wearing the costumes of ancient Armenian warriors. These garments were probably those used in their local church's annual production of a play depicting soldiers led by Vartan Mamikonian who suffered a military defeat by Persian soldiers at the Battle of Avarayr in AD 451. Afterward Vartan became a saint and his followers, the Vartanantz, became martyrs to their quest for religious freedom. The message of this float urging spectators to "Buy Liberty Bonds," as part of their patriotic duty to support the American war effort must have had special resonance among people who had left their homeland under devastating circumstances.

ITALIAN

Sons of Italy

Wakefield, Massachusetts, July 4, 1922

These gentlemen can represent the hundreds of thousands of men who marched in countless parades as proud members of fraternal and ethnic societies over the years. In this case, on the Fourth of July in 1922, the Sons of Italy in Wakefield, Massachusetts, wore their best suits and ties. Although it may have been a very hot day, more than half are also wearing woolen hats, although a few have chosen to wear summer straw. Their officers are distinguished by the medals hanging from striped ribbons around their necks. Unfortunately for us, their signs and banners are almost invisible, with the exception of the prancing lion at the head of the line.

Columbia

New London, Connecticut, 1935

Since at least 1815, Columbia has been a major symbol of the United States, a figure representing the dignity and continuity of the nation and its values. With a sword in her right hand, this Columbia hangs on tightly to a flagpole as this float in the Connecticut tercentennial parade passes through a large crowd at New London in 1935. As usual, her costume is a white classical robe and a blue cap with stars. She is standing under a Doric canopy near two seated women wearing Italian folk costume. On one corner another Doric column is visible, this one capped by an eagle with outstretched wings, a device that may also have been on other corners of the platform. Several red-, green-, and white-striped Italian flags add to the overall effect and strengthen the identity of both the sponsors and the participants.

Columbus Discovering America

Hartford, Connecticut, October 12, 1935

Although his voyage of discovery was funded by King Ferdinand and Queen Isabella of Spain, many Italians honored Christopher Columbus for his Italian birthplace. This version of Columbus's ship, with its masts shortened to fit underneath electric wires and only two sails flying, was entered by members of the Italian-American Societies at Deep River, Centerbrook, and Chester, Connecticut, as one of the twenty floats created by national groups in the tercentennial procession on Columbus Day in 1935 at Hartford. The men aboard eschewed the gaudy Renaissance-style costumes often seen on floats of the *Santa Maria*, appearing instead in their best suits.

PORTUGUESE

Floral Display of the History of Bristol, 1680–1930

Bristol, Rhode Island, September 1930

Members of the Joint Conference of Portuguese Organizations in Rhode Island created this lavish floral float for the parade that was part of the celebration of the 250th anniversary of the town of Bristol. Like many others created by ethnic organizations, it honors both their homeland and the history of their new community. Multiple banners proclaim that "Bristol is the Garden of the State," while one within a large star at the front of the truck names John Walley,

Nathaniel Oliver, Nathaniel Byfield, and Stephen Burton as the "Founders of the Town." On the visible side, the hand-painted motifs include a Portuguese coat-of-arms flanked by alternating Portuguese and American flags. Two women at the front of the float wear robes emblazoned with stars and stripes, while standing high at the back of the float a woman in white represents the Portuguese Lady Liberty. Portuguese emigrants from the Azores moved to Bristol between 1890 and 1921, most seeking employment in the city's textile mills, often taking jobs previously held by French Canadians who had gradually become upwardly mobile.

THE MELTING POT

Sisterhood of Peace

Concord, Massachusetts, April 19, 1925

For the sesquicentennial celebration of the April 19, 1775 battles at Lexington and Concord, this group of eleven women appeared on a simple parade float under the watchful eye of a minuteman. Headed by one woman representing Columbia with an American flag and another as Columbus with an Italian flag, nine others represent countries ranging across the globe as far as Japan and Russia, reminding us once again of the power at that time of the concept of America as a "melting pot."

Civic Identity

Parades often include complex allegorical figures created at great effort and expense. Some of these personify big ideas like liberty, truth, faith, or industry, while others embody the idealized characteristics of a city, state, or nation. Different levels of education among viewers surely led to different degrees of understanding of these symbols and concepts, but everyone could admire the beauty of the overall composition and the costumes as well as the status of the featured individuals. At some of New England's largest parades, especially those celebrating major civic anniversaries, floats carrying imposing allegorical figures are still a culminating feature.

At a time when female modesty was highly prized, it was unusual, and indeed somewhat daring, for women to appear publicly in highly visible places or revealing clothing. Yet, the women chosen to appear as allegorical figures on parade floats usually wore classical robes or diaphanous gowns. Their safety was guaranteed by an escort of marching soldiers or civic officials. Most often they were chosen because of the prominence of their husbands or fathers. Clearly it was considered an honor to represent a great idea.

Tableau XVI, Boston 250th Anniversary

Boston, Massachusetts, September 17, 1880

The great torchlight procession celebrating the 250th anniversary of the city of Boston in 1880 included 325 vehicles and 14,000 men in multiple divisions. For many the highlight was a series of sixteen allegorical tableaux that were praised for their artistic groupings and the beauty of the costumes. Mounted on platform cars from the Metropolitan Horse Railroad, they moved along iron rails in the streets, a feature that was praised for providing smooth, even motion that made it easier for the riders to maintain their poses. While the parade route was illuminated by marching members of fraternal societies carrying lighted torches, the tableau cars were brightly lit by additional torches, locomotive headlights, and calcium lights.

The horsecars carried a series of historical scenes beginning with the landing of the Pilgrims in 1620

and concluding with George Washington's arrival in Boston after the evacuation of the British troops in 1775. Those were followed by an allegory of Commerce, followed by others representing Europe, Asia, Africa, and America. At the end of the line came this culminating figure, Boston herself, resting her elbow on the city seal. Six young women below her represented Peace, Prosperity, Justice, Education, Charity, and Industry. At their feet, a large cornucopia spilled forth Plenty. The women were guarded by uniformed members of the Ancient and Honorable Artillery Company and the Independent Corps of Cadets, the city's two oldest military groups.

Grand Allegorical Car Representing Portland

Portland, Maine, July 6, 1886

This huge triumphal car was considered the grandest feature of the historical display in Portland's 1886 centennial parade and "also the finest allegorical tableau ever seen in Portland." Well-known Portland artist Harrison Bird Brown modeled it after a circus wagon and adorned it with a horn of plenty, a gilded eagle, and the city seal. A crowned young woman representing both Portland and Prosperity sat high under a satin pavilion at the back. In front of her was a smaller pavilion occupied by eight young women representing History, Science, Painting, Commerce, Architecture, Sculpture, Poetry, and Manufactures.

Undoubtedly, these huge, colorful, and detailed floats were thrilling to the crowds of spectators looking on from sidewalks, open windows, and rooftops along the parade route. Understanding their full meaning, though, required a considerable degree of cultural literacy. Even though the horse-drawn cars moved fairly slowly, it is quite possible that not everyone was able to comprehend the significance of every rich detail.

4

PROGRESS

In nineteenth-century America, progress was both celebrated and feared. Increasing mechanization and the growth of factories changed every aspect of everyday life, new transportation systems and public utilities made things faster, warmer, cleaner, brighter, and more comfortable for many at the same time that it disrupted long-established social norms and gender relations.

The completion of new roads and bridges, canals, railroad lines, water reservoirs, and other significant public works was often celebrated with parades. These events usually honored the governmental officials who had allocated funding and supervised construction as well as the artisans and laborers who had actually done the work. Once the benefits of telephone systems and electric power became widespread, their impact on both communities and individual families was also exhibited and celebrated. Detailed newspaper descriptions called attention to the overall prosperity and economic resources of the sponsoring communities. Long columns of text named every participating business and carefully described both machinery and products displayed on elaborate floats.

PUBLIC WATER SUPPLY

View of the Water Celebration, on Boston Common October 25th 1848. Respectfully dedicated to His Honor Josiah Quincy Jr., Mayor, the City Council and Water Commissioners
Boston, Massachusetts, 1848

On October 25, 1848, Bostonians joyfully celebrated the successful completion of an enhanced public water supply system. After two and a half years of construction, a new aqueduct carried water through iron pipes twenty miles from Lake Cochituate in Framingham through several suburbs to a reservoir in Brookline, and thence by way of gravity-fed pipes throughout the city of Boston.

As noted earlier, a highlight of the day was a great procession that offered a vivid illustration of the city's prosperous economy and civic pride. The number of spectators, estimated at 300,000 people, was, as usual, considered the largest ever, apparently exceeding both recent partisan political processions and the usual festivities on the Fourth of July.

Here we see the exciting moment when the procession had halted upon its arrival at Boston Common and the aqueduct was ceremoniously opened. The City Guards, the Independent Cadets, and other military companies stood at attention. Ladies and schoolchildren waited in specially designated areas on each side of the Frog Pond. Civilian and fraternal groups held their banners high, many of them illustrating fountains, water pipes, and even Niagara Falls. Tradesmen and their vehicles loaded with displays of manufactured goods encircled the crowd. Printers on the car of the Franklin Typographical Society paused their work striking off songs and broadsides to distribute to the crowd. The young ladies tossing artificial flowers from their employer *Mr. Partridge's Floral Car* turned their attention to the master of ceremonies. Two people portraying Adam and Eve on the car of the Journeyman Tailor's Society turned their backs on the serpent twining around the trunk of a tall tree in the Garden of Eden. As the fountain in the Frog Pond reached a height of seventy-five feet, people cheered, church bells rang, and cannons fired.

RAILROADS

Just three years later, in 1851, Boston devoted three whole days in September to an even more elaborate celebration of progress and prosperity: the Railroad Jubilee. The events hailed a promising new rail connection to Montreal that made possible short and easy passenger and freight service between Boston and Canada. Importantly, additional new connecting railroad lines between western Canada and Montreal were now linked to Boston's ice-free port and the newly established Cunard steamship service to Liverpool, England.

Massachusetts Whigs had hoped they could count on

the new railroads to enhance the nationwide reputation of New England as a place with wealth deriving from superior intelligence, personal industry, and free labor, a center of commerce linked by new and modern transportation systems. Further, they hoped that the better acquaintance and increased communication made possible by canals, railroads, improved roads, and the newly invented telegraph would lessen sectionalism, reduce misunderstanding, and foster mutual support as well as economic development both in the region and across the nation.

No wonder there was rejoicing that New England skill and enterprise had managed to surmount obstacles and open new opportunities for both travel and trade. Plans for a memorable celebration were proposed in mid-July. Invitations were sent to President Fillmore and committees were appointed to plan invitations, receptions, escorts, and a public dinner for 3,500 people in Yale's Mammoth Tent on Boston Common, as well as decorations on public streets and prominent buildings, harbor excursions, illuminations, fireworks, and the special activities designed to include public schoolchildren.

A committee of merchants met on September 9 to plan the procession that was already scheduled to be held just ten days later. Their goal was to feature the products and processes of manufacturers and craftsmen in the city and its surrounding communities, giving an idea of the character and resources of greater Boston. Enthusiasm was so high that on Friday, September 19, when the procession was scheduled to begin at nine o'clock in the morning, it took two more hours to organize the unanticipated large number of businessmen and artisans with the many different horse-drawn floats on which they displayed their skills and products.

The Railroad Jubilee

Boston, Massachusetts, September 19, 1851

Parades of this kind were nothing new, but it is only thanks to the artists of *Gleason's Pictorial Drawing Room Companion*, who created this two-page illustration published in the issue dated October 11, 1851, that we can actually see the highlights of such a massive civic procession in its full scope. The view extends from the line of policemen carrying a long stick to clear the streets at the beginning of the line, the military escort, and the carriages of dignitaries all the way to the indistinct representation of crowds of schoolchildren, "Boston's brightest jewels," and the even larger crowds of people who walked at the rear. What it does not show are the groups of tradesmen, some with as many as 350 people, marching between the floats in the fifty different occupational divisions. The full line extended three and a half miles, taking more than two hours to pass any given point. (*For more about the elaborate floats representing the arts and trades of Boston see Chapter 7.*)

MUSEUM
ETNA LABORATORY

Dover Street as Decorated for the Jubilee

Boston, Massachusetts, September 19, 1851

Gleason's additional coverage of the Railroad Jubilee in successive issues provides unmatched views of civic decoration and pageantry. These decorations of Dover Street were considered the most beautiful and extensive of those on any street in the city, with streamers, flowers, and evergreen adorning buildings on both sides of the street. In this image, the carriage bearing Canada's Lord Elgin and his suite, flanked by a military escort, proceeds forward on Dover Street where newly planted street trees are protected by wooden cages.

The decorations that stretched overhead included both British and American flags, views of Montreal and Boston, and mottos celebrating international trade by proclaiming "United We Prosper." Others honored the

Cunard Steamship line that was inaugurating its first direct service between Boston and Liverpool. Many identified the themes of the celebration: Mechanic Arts, Industry, and Commerce. A banner with the three links of the Independent Order of Odd Fellows honored the virtues of Friendship, Love, and Truth. Lastly, a flag with an image of two men shaking hands symbolized international friendship.

RURAL COMMUNICATION

Levant Telephone Company

Levant, Maine, ca. 1910

Like many rural communities in New England in the early twentieth century, Levant, Maine, with a population of about seven hundred people, had its own

telephone company to provide local and long-distance service to its subscribers. In all probability, Levant's central switchboard was located in a private house, where women took turns answering and rerouting calls all day and all night.

Very simply decorated with red, white, and blue crepe paper, this float representing the Levant Telephone Company featured simulated utility poles, a crank telephone box, and a switchboard. Perhaps the child wearing the operator's headset was imitating something he saw every day if his mother filled the role of "Central" in their home. The float is followed by Father Time, suggesting the importance of speedy communication in the modernization of rural areas.

PUBLIC TRANSPORTATION

Little Daisy
Concord, New Hampshire, August 20, 1903

Prototype of Modern Electric Streetcar
Concord, New Hampshire, August 20, 1903

The huge workshops of the Boston & Maine Railroad at Concord, New Hampshire, created a number of floats for the city's semicentennial parade in 1903. Among them were these two models of vehicles operated by the Concord Street Railway Company and its successors.

The *Little Daisy*, drawn by four horses, represented the first open car used in the city. Measuring thirteen feet long and only five feet wide, the car could seat just twenty people. During the parade it carried seventeen veteran employees of the B & M shop, including the man who drove the original on its first run in 1878.

People may have felt nostalgic at the sight of *Daisy*, for small, open horsecars like this were soon to be replaced in Concord by much larger electric streetcars, forty-one feet long, that could seat as many as forty-four passengers. This unfinished prototype being built by the Boston & Maine followed *Daisy* in the parade, offering a comparison between the old and new in street transportation.

STREETLIGHTS

Modern Electric Street Lights, York Power & Light Company

Biddeford, Maine, 1916

The partial double exposure of this picture emphasizes the small models of the new electric street lights placed on the corners of this float for the York Power & Light Company in the Biddeford, Maine, tercentennial parade on September 16, 1916. Four women in white hats and summer dresses symbolize the cleanliness of the new regional power source. Several signs urge consumers to embrace new utilities: "Use Electricity for Light and Power" and "Do You Own a Gas Range?"

MODERN HIGHWAYS

The Modern Highway, Broad with Easy Grades, Opening Up New Territory and Developing the Entire State

Portland, Maine, July 5, 1920

In the early twentieth century, as more and more people gave up reliance on horse-drawn vehicles, new standards were developed for the construction and care of public

roads. Recognizing that modern highways were essential to the expansion of automobile sales and tourism, the Automobile Dealers and Allied Trades of Portland, supported this entry in the Maine centennial parade at Portland in 1920. One of twenty floats designed and constructed for the occasion by the New York firm of Messmore and Damon, this depiction of an automobile climbing a hill on a modern highway caught the spirit of the times. Although the original design called for the float to be mounted on an invisible motorized truck, its Portland sponsors apparently saw no irony in using a pair of horses to pull it past the Morse-Libby House (now Victoria Mansion) as part of the parade.

AUTOMOBILES

Almost as soon as horseless carriages were first manufactured, their proud owners polished them brightly and entered them in parades. Accounts of parades as early as 1900 list the names of both the owners and manufacturers of the automobiles in the line. Within a year or two, some automobiles were decorated with flowers or crepe paper and prizes were offered for the best decorated automobile. As early as 1903, the Dennison Manufacturing Company of South Framingham, Massachusetts, published helpful booklets with designs and directions for decorating automobiles with their inexpensive and colorful crepe and tissue papers.

Instructional booklet published by the Dennison Manufacturing Company
Framingham, Massachusetts, 1905

A combination of horse-drawn carriages and automobiles was seen in the extensive quarter-millennial celebration in Northampton, Massachusetts. The dignitaries at the head of the procession rode in twenty-three decorated carriages followed by sixteen private carriages decorated with flowers (*see page 237*). After an impressive array of marching groups, bands of musicians, fire engines, and historical floats, the concluding feature was the sixth division with its "hints of the horseless age": twenty-one decorated automobiles. None carried a sign or represented a theme. Most were driven by their owners, many with their wives and families as passengers. A

few seem to have invited neighbors or professional colleagues to join them. The Springfield Automobile Company presented the only commercial entries—"a twenty-four horsepower car, of the Locomobile touring type, . . . trimmed with yellow chrysanthemums," a Stevens-Duryea machine, and a locomobile surrey, both also decorated with flowers.

Soon, some automobiles were valued for their age. As early as 1911 a car designated as an "antique" was driven in a coach parade at Bethlehem, New Hampshire. Like the old horse-drawn carriages, automobiles were cherished for their distinctive features, noted manufacturers, and increasing age as well as for their associations with historic events or their distinguished former owners. Driving an antique automobile in a parade is still considered an honor, and a testimonial to the patience, mechanical ability, and financial resources of the owner, as well as the quality and durability of the vehicle itself.

Patriotic Display

Lebanon, New Hampshire, October 13, 1919

Trimming an automobile with bunting, crepe paper, and/or flowers and evergreens is a much simpler and less expensive task than constructing a narrative float. Still, dramatic effects can be achieved. Here, in celebration of America's victory in World War I, the red, white, and blue flags and bunting leave no question about the patriotic enthusiasm of the participants.

5

MEMORY

Celebrations of the nation's Jubilee in 1825 and the public ceremonies surrounding Lafayette's visit in 1824 and 1825 stirred memories of wartime bravery and reaffirmations of the virtues and values of the Country's founders. Those who joined Lafayette and Daniel Webster at the cornerstone laying for the Bunker Hill Monument in 1825 were very aware of the changed appearance of aging community leaders and the veterans of the Revolutionary War.

At the same time, New England experienced a growing concern about threats to traditional settled ways of life as opportunity called and population dwindled in response to industrialization, urbanization, and westward migration. Not surprisingly both pride and concern began to be reflected in parades. Many floats offered iconic images of tradition or celebrations of progress. Others dramatized the difference between the hardships of early times and the impact of industrialization, with vivid comparisons of *then* and *now,* focused especially on domestic scenes and demonstrations of traditional women's work.

These simplified presentations were often exaggerated, presenting myth as attractive reality. Some of the ideas were aspirational, illustrating a serene view of New England life, not as it actually was, but as they wished it had been. Many portrayals of the olden times also reinforced gender stereotypes and social convention within visually captivating vignettes that made powerful impressions on enthusiastic spectators at curbside.

In the years leading up to the Centennial celebrations in 1876, memory played an even greater role in the definition of American culture. Public celebrations and parades focused on history as a means of enhancing civic life. Vivid illustrations of American and regional stories were used to expand popular understanding of both identity and place to

celebrate both the natural world and industrial progress. History was invoked to bind together an increasingly diverse population, encouraging new immigrants to observe American traditions and holidays as well as adopt what were defined for them as American values.

Well before 1900, the "Olden Days" were perceived as a vague time before the mills, before urban tenements, before the immigration of people from southern and eastern Europe. Frequent repetition of iconic scenes believed to define both past and present conveyed lessons in American history and values, cementing ideas about national identity and character. Similar ideas are still presented in parades today. Fortunately, there has been ongoing expansion of the story. As many parades have become more inclusive, new ideas and new identities are celebrated and a growing roster of new events calls attention to contemporary issues while still celebrating the nation.

The Ties That Bind

The population of many of New England's agrarian communities peaked in 1820 and then began a steady decline as entire families migrated to the wide open spaces and fertile fields of the Northwest Territory, and young women left to work in textile factories at Lowell, Lawrence, Nashua, or elsewhere. Men seeking to make their fortune in the fields of business and the law moved to large cities, ranging from Boston and New York to Galveston and San Francisco. Well before the Gold Rush, many people sought opportunity far beyond the borders of their ancestral villages.

By mid-century, some of those who had left were both well-settled and prosperous. Those left behind sought to rekindle close ties between friends and family members, hoping to draw the emigrants back to their native towns where they would be honored for their success. One goal was to awaken an interest in local history as both a source of pride and a binding social force. There was also some hope that the returning people might be inspired to share their wealth, not only with family members who remained behind but with local charitable and cultural institutions, once they saw with their own eyes the modest circumstances and occasional disrepair of the places they had once called home.

The Day of Jubilee Has Come
Sons of Portsmouth, Welcome Home

Portsmouth, New Hampshire, July 4, 1853

Published as "a pleasing memento of a glorious gathering," this handsome lithograph records "The Return of the Sons," an innovative and impressive celebration held in Portsmouth on a lovely summer day in 1853. An invitation had gone out to hundreds of businessmen who had left their hometown in order to pursue successful

THE DAY OF JUBILEE HAS COME
SONS OF PORTSMOUTH WELCOME HOME
W.H. FOSTER
THERE IS NO PLACE LIKE HOME
"NO SPOT UPON EARTH IS SO DEAR TO OUR EYES, AS THE SOIL WE FIRST STIRRED IN TERRESTRIAL PIES."
SONS OF PORTSMOUTH RISIDENTS OF BOSTON

careers in distant cities. They were urged to return to Portsmouth to join together with their families and old friends in celebrating the Fourth of July.

Motivated partly by a growing nostalgia for the olden times, the larger goals were to strengthen the attachment of successful people to their native place, awaken a warmer love of country, and foster a resolve to live lives of lofty virtue. Several thousand accepted the call and traveled to Portsmouth where they were welcomed and entertained in grand style. Homes and businesses throughout the city were decorated with flags, bunting, banners, greenery, and flowers. Many families held open houses where friends and family members were welcomed and there were joyous reunions of men who shared memories of schooldays and childhood adventures.

The official celebration began with a huge civic and industrial procession led by the returned men, who walked in groups with banners that identified their current places of residence and expressed deeply felt sentiments such as "There is No Place Like Home," or as silly as "No Spot Upon Earth, Is So Dear to Our Eyes, As the Soil We First Stirred, In Terrestrial Pies." One has to assume this recalled the boyhood pleasure of making mud pies.

The procession began in Market Square under a series of gothic arches made of evergreen, each bearing the name of one of the original thirteen colonies. In addition to the usual marching groups, there was a long line of floats depicting the scope and success of the city's business community. There were sailors firing cannons from a ship model, blacksmiths hammering, printers printing, ropemakers twisting, joiners working wood, tin men with a fire, and painters, masons, and cabinetmakers busy at their crafts, along with many more merchants and minor manufacturers displaying their goods. The whole thing sought to impress upon the visitors that the people of Portsmouth were both prosperous and happy participants in the modern world. The successful event led to the desired result as many of the visitors expressed their pride at being sons of Portsmouth and promised to share their enthusiasm for the city in far-away places. The Portsmouth planners predicted a resultant extension of "the pleasant fruits of social harmony, kind reminiscences, and brotherly love." Subsequent "Return" celebrations that included daughters as well as sons were held after the Civil War, in 1873, 1883, and 1910, the latter attended by over two thousand former residents.

In addition to regional distribution of the lithograph seen here, the first Return of the Sons in Portsmouth received extensive coverage in newspapers throughout the country and it inspired similar efforts elsewhere in succeeding years. At Newburyport in 1854, the invitation to a Return event included distant daughters as well as sons. In succeeding decades, the movement expanded across New England. Even in the town of Limington, Maine, where the population was only about one thousand people, a Return was celebrated in 1883. By 1900, the ongoing popularity of these events was often folded into the new Old Home Day celebrations.

Banners used on the Jacob Wendell House
Portsmouth, New Hampshire, 1873 and 1893

These rare banners are typical of the hundreds of homemade banners that decorated New England houses on festive occasions. Hand-painted on old cotton sheets, these two were kept by Miss Caroline Wendell in a trunk in the barn behind her home at 222 Pleasant Street. They were brought forth to be hung above the front door as part of Portsmouth's successive decennial celebrations of the Return of the Sons. The date 1815 refers to the year when Caroline's father Jacob Wendell purchased the house that would serve as the family home until 1977; 1843 was the date Caroline's brother Jacob II left Portsmouth make his fortune in New York City. He came back for each of the Return celebrations, and it was his financial support that enabled his sister to continue to live in the family home until her death.

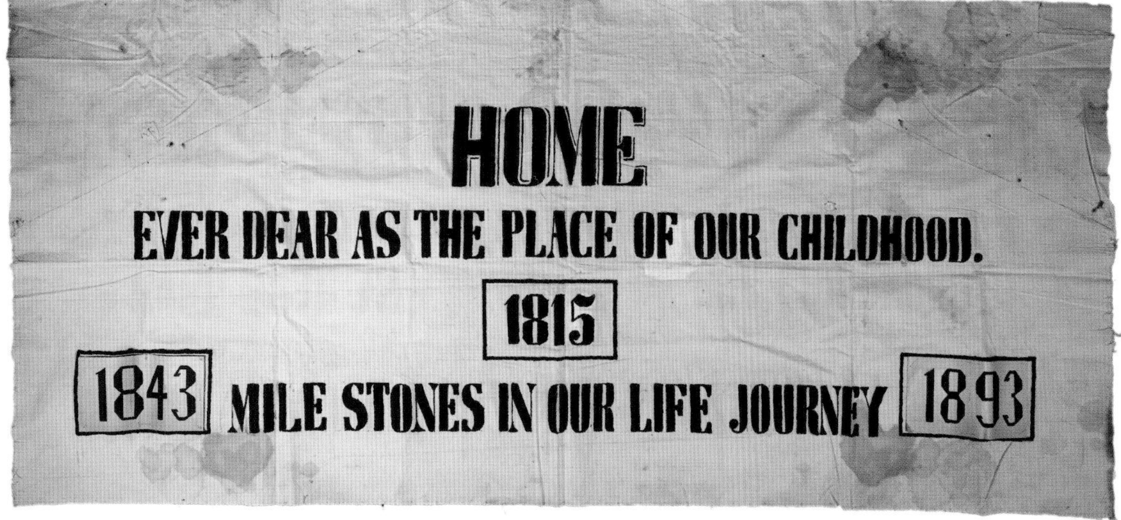

The Procession Forming Under the Arch at the Head of Main Street

Gorham, Maine, May 26, 1886

The sesquicentennial anniversaries observed by many towns in northern New England in the 1880s and 90s reflected both current prosperity as well as memories of the challenges met by the first white settlers in the area. The 250th celebration at Gorham in 1886 is an astonishing example. Townspeople welcomed visits from returning family members and hundreds of day-trippers, many from nearby Portland, who arrived by train.

The highlight of the morning was the grand procession with its array of civil, military, and fraternal marching units, seen here approaching a welcome arch spanning Main Street. The life-sized wooden statue of a war-like American Indian armed with both a gun and a tomahawk standing in the foreground had recently been erected on a pedestal bearing the dates 1736–1886 and the original name of the town "Narraganset No. 7." As would be expected, the anniversary procession included allegorical and historical floats, but the Gorham lineup had an unusual conclusion—a group of white men made up and dressed so that they "looked as though they were in truth aborigines" walking together. The formal

exercises in the afternoon centered on an antiquarian address by the Reverend Elijah Kellogg, the well-known Maine author whose novel about Gorham is titled *Good Old Times.* Late in the afternoon, the emphasis on conflict continued when a "band of Indians led by Chief Presumpeaukett" ran into the center of Gorham. Waving tomahawks and shrieking war whoops, they engaged in a vigorous sham fight representing the "Indian attack during the Seven Years War on the Garrison at Fort Hill." Unsurprisingly, the costumed white settlers of Gorham prevailed, quickly "killing" or routing the entire band before the afternoon events were over. Gorham's simultaneous efforts to dramatize and honor conflict with indigenous peoples of the area in these ways seem unusual. Few other examples of similar statues or sham fights at this date have been found.

Old Home Day

At the turn of the century, the appeal and the activities of these popular reunions were greatly expanded by statewide events first envisioned by New Hampshire's governor Frank H. Rollins in 1897. Recognizing the continuing population decline in rural areas and the number of abandoned farms in the state, he sought to convince wealthy city dwellers to turn those farmhouses into summer homes for their families. Further, he encouraged people who had moved far from home to return on a specified summer day to celebrate both the power of place and the pleasures of healthy food, clear water, and the agrarian way of life. Rollins assured them that their weary lives would be refreshed and strengthened by the sound of the church bell, the inspiration of the local schoolhouse, and the voices of family and childhood friends. If they chose to return for several months every summer, it would be so much the better for them and for the community.

New Hampshire's first Old Home Day was held on August 31, 1899, with happy reunions and a wide range of activities in a number of cities and towns. Old Home Days were held in Maine and Vermont in 1901, followed by others in Massachusetts and Connecticut in 1906. The idea soon spread to Ohio, Indiana, and other states of the old Northwest Territory as well as to Maritime Canada. An Old Home Day Association was soon established in New Hampshire to facilitate coordination of events and sharing of ideas across the state. By 1915 more than fifty towns in New Hampshire alone were celebrating Old Home Day; some expanded the event and celebrate Old Home Week to this day.

Old Home Days are usually held in late summer, a time when the days are long and weather in New England is usually mild, so evening events and outdoor activities can be scheduled reliably. From the very beginning, Old Home Days have been a great success, bringing people to family reunions and town-wide activities featuring orations, parades, community meals, tours of historic homes, churches, and cemeteries, hymn singing, band concerts, dances, baseball games, and both land and water sports. In many places there are loan exhibitions of cherished antiques and local relics. Sometimes these events have led to formation of local historical societies and preservation of historic buildings.

Old Home Day parades often feature an array of old vehicles and floats representing romanticized settings and depictions of formative experiences in the olden times—especially those that originated in the "One-Room Schoolhouse," the "Town Meeting," and by the "Domestic Fireside." Others celebrate unique events in local history and honor men who have made a national reputation in politics, business, or literature. Occasionally they feature well-known local characters. Almost always there are floats sponsored by local businessmen, displaying their products and suggesting both the prosperity and the up-to-date nature of each place.

Although these events were both well-meaning and enjoyable for many, without question there were some people who did not fit the narrative—impoverished families decimated by injury, alcoholism, fire, death of the breadwinner, or lack of motivation. On the edges of many a crowd on parade day there were dirty, thin, hungry, and barefoot children as excited as anyone and hoping for a treat from a stranger. For them, the path to success or even basic sustenance was a daunting challenge that lasted long after the music died.

Some towns still observe Old Home Day every year. In other places the observance fades away for a while, but it is soon resurrected by an enthusiastic committee and a host of volunteers, still fulfilling Governor Rollins' goals for community development and civic engagement.

Old Home Day

Norwich, Connecticut, ca. 1900

Even in some large cities, Old Home Day was celebrated by enthusiastic crowds. Parade floats advertised local businesses and the icons of the preindustrial world at the same time that they honored the founding of a community and featured the fraternal organizations of an increasingly diverse population.

Old Home Day

Pittsfield, New Hampshire, 1908

The pleasures of Old Home Day are on display in this 1908 view of a parade on a tree-lined street in Pittsfield where a line of decorated horse-drawn carriages and wagons carries representatives of various businesses and civic organizations. At the house across the street, flags are flying from the front porch and lined up along each side of the front sidewalk, a kind of Old Home Day decoration that is still popular today. At that front door and at various places on both sides of the street, people have stopped to watch the spectacle or to visit with each other. It must have been a comfortable temperature, for most of the men are wearing suits and with few exceptions the ladies wear white summer dresses. A few teen-aged girls wear large hair bows at the back of their heads; everyone else is wearing a hat or cap of some kind, many of them made of straw. The tall pole with the rectangular box for a transformer at the extreme left indicates that electricity had come to Pittsfield by this date, powering some homes as well as the street light.

Historical Tableaux

In the years after 1840, people in all ranks of society enjoyed dressing in old clothing or military uniforms to take part in scenes called tableaux that were performed in private parlors, public buildings, and on parade floats. Participation involved standing silent and still in a costumed group, posing with props and scenery to recreate a famous painting or illustrate a scene from history, literature, or the Bible. The scenes usually were part of a narrative series, each lasting just a few minutes. On parade floats, the narrative was spread over a series of vehicles, but the participants' task was harder, for they had to hold poses on a moving stage throughout the whole event, sometimes more than an hour.

Ideas for successful tableaux mostly passed informally from house to house as friends and family members sought to replicate and improve on examples they had seen or in which they had participated. Professional advice was offered in 1860, when Portsmouth, New Hampshire's James Head's illustrated book, *Home Pastimes; or, Tableaux Vivants*, was published in Boston by J. E. Tilton and Company. With its detailed instructions for creating the costumes and settings of one hundred topics deemed suitable for presentation to an audience of friends and family, copies were snapped up and the book was reissued five times in just seven years. Publishers of stereograph cards also fed the popular interest by producing cards with staged images of costumed people posing in fashionable parlors. Sets of such cards illustrating different topics or the successive scenes in narrative tableaux increased sales.

Parlor tableaux often included a chronological series depicting important national and local moments in America's story. The topics focused on heroic deeds of founders and patriots, sentimental depictions of home life, and dramatic scenes of discovery, battle, political action, or domestic activity. Some exaggerated human frailty in ways intended to be hilarious. Without question, parlor tableaux had a major role in ensuring widespread knowledge of certain historical events, and a rich, but stereotyped, visual culture. They also fostered strong emotions of patriotism as well as veneration of the first settlers and the Founding Fathers, the Declaration of Independence, Betsy Ross, the "Snug Fireside," and the "Spinning Wheel."

The topics and images presented in parade tableaux formed a foundation for American cultural memory that antedates the historic pageant movement by more than fifty years. The later pageants involved hundreds of costumed people posing in tableaux before massive audiences in a large outdoor amphitheater, on a beach, or on a new-mown hayfield. Their sequence of stationary scenes dramatized many of the same American stories in the way that parades had always done, often with added interludes of dance and other performance art, as well as allegorical references to the future.

In parades, the historical sequences were highly selective, usually beginning with a depiction of American Indian life, followed by "The Landing of the Pilgrims," and then a chronological review of acknowledged landmarks in the American story, sometimes interspersed with pivotal incidents in local history. As early as 1852, a scene depicting Columbus "discovering" America was placed between scenes of indigenous life and the Pilgrims' landing in a parade on the Fourth of July at Portsmouth, New Hampshire, but this was most unusual. Columbus was rarely included in these presentations before the four hundredth anniversary of his voyage in 1892.

When added to the sense of history gained from illustrations in textbooks and in illustrated periodicals like *Gleason's Pictorial Drawing Room Companion, Leslie's Illustrated,* or *Harper's Illustrated*, as well as the inexpensive prints by Currier & Ives or other artists that were framed and displayed in middle-class homes, the sight of historic tableaux repeated year after year helped to embed both ideas and images in the popular mind. They also created a well-understood baseline for American history, fostered white supremacy, and built stereotypes of heroic men and dutiful women, as well as myths of unified experience and unchanging tradition.

Although most chapters of this book present floats organized chronologically according to the date of the parade in which they appeared, the historic tableaux in this chapter are presented according to the sequence of the original events, thus replicating the traditional arrangement and impact of these topics as seen in most parades and in any history book.

Two Centuries Ago

Portsmouth, New Hampshire, ca. 1861–1865

James Head's depiction of Indigenous American life before European settlement (*see next page*) shows the "feathered red men" in a quasi-domestic scene with non-threatening people like these, standing by while a woman tends a large kettle over a cooking fire. Some mid-nineteenth century "Indian" floats depict women caring for children and men carrying weapons as they appear to arrive with freshly killed deer or other game. Others featured heroic figures, embodiments of the "Noble Savage," those icons believed by many in Head's time to have disappeared long ago, despite the continuing presence of indigenous peoples throughout many New England communities.

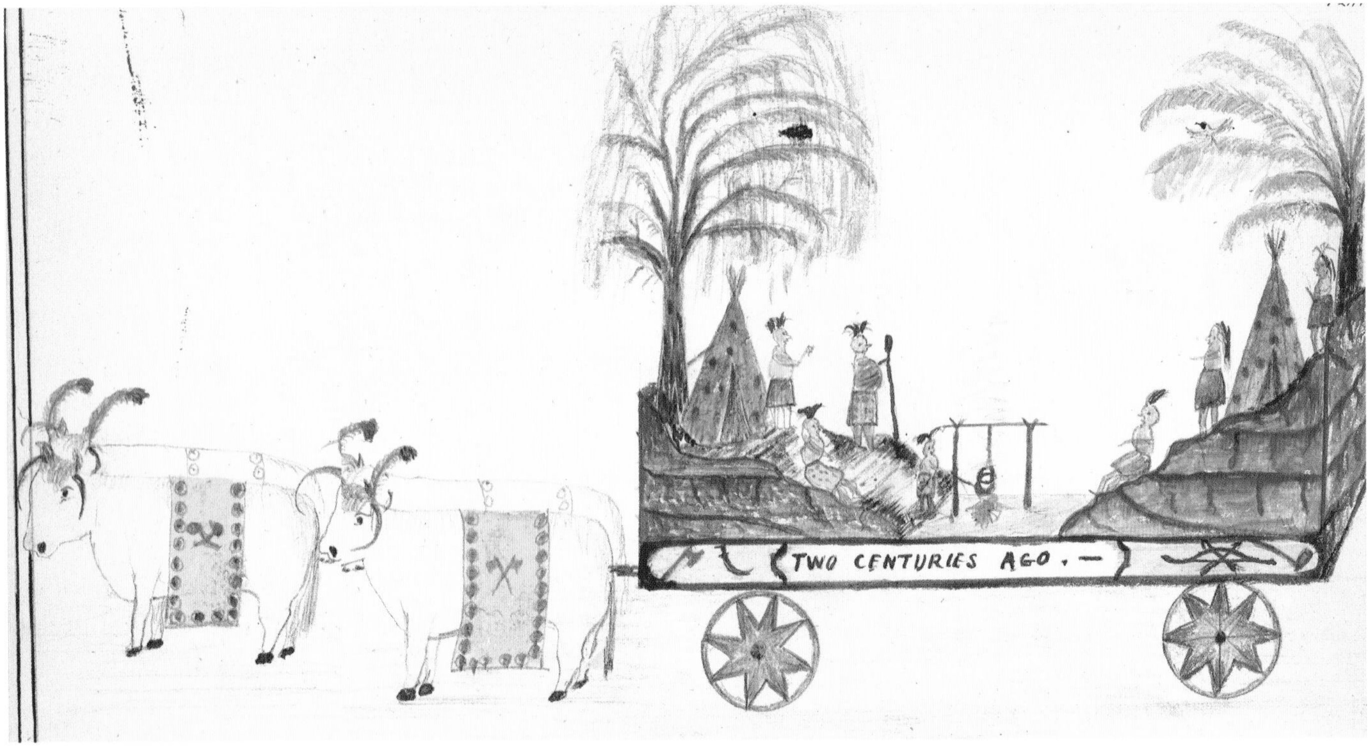

TWO CENTURIES AGO. —

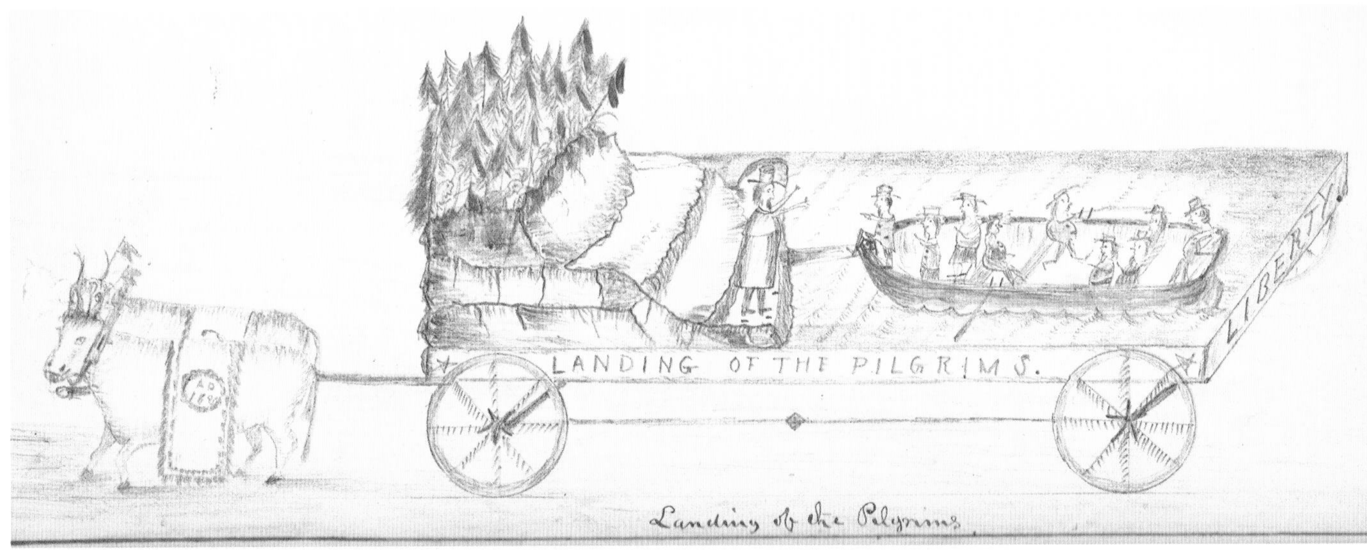

No Craft Ever Bore So Precious a Cargo. Landing of the Pilgrims.
Portsmouth, New Hampshire, ca. 1852–1865

In *The Floral Architect,* James Head explained this idea for a Pilgrim float as an illustration of the snowy forest and the sandy beach near Truro on Cape Cod on November 21, 1620. A small boat, dispatched from the nearby *Mayflower,* brings the first twelve Englishmen ashore for some tentative exploration, a month before their final decision to make their permanent settlement at Plymouth on the opposite side of Cape Cod Bay. Indigenous peoples are shown lurking in pine trees near the seashore with weapons aimed at the approaching boatload of Pilgrims. Head portrays the English leader as having just stepped on the beach and raised his hands in a prayer of thanksgiving, while the others "gaze with thoughtful brows into the frozen forest and listen with attention to the solemn words of their leader." Head specified that the clothing to be worn by the leader should be a loose black coat and breeches, a white shirt with a wide collar, buckled shoes, and a tall black hat with a buckle, an early example of the stereotypical Pilgrim costumes seen in parades, plays, and pictures of New England's "First Settlers" to this very day!

Landing of the Pilgrims, 1620
North Bennington, Vermont, 1907

In the year of the celebration of the three hundredth anniversary of the founding of Jamestown, Virginia, members of the Congregational Church in North Bennington decided to create a parade float focused on New England's comparable event, the landing of the Pilgrims, thirteen years later, at Plymouth in December 1620. Perhaps because it is always difficult to maintain one's balance while standing on a moving float, the Pilgrim woman in North Bennington chose to sit safely on Plymouth Rock rather than pretending to step daintily onto its round surface.

First Thanksgiving, 1621
Plymouth, Massachusetts, August 1, 1921

In Brockton, Massachusetts, a women's group associated with the Independent Order of Odd Fellows, the Independent Rebekah Lodge No. 163, relied on the popular concept of log cabins as homes of the first settlers when they prepared their float depicting a mythical First Thanksgiving for the tercentennial parade held at Plymouth in August 1921. Two additional log cabins were shown in this parade, one representing the home of a first settler in the nearby town of Halifax and the other "Ye Olde Trading Post."

Americans have long seen the log cabin as a symbol of humble beginnings and highly valued character traits such as rugged individualism and self-reliance. As a result, log cabins have often served as an important starting point in representations of the American experience. Despite the fact that there was no British tradition of log building and it is therefore unlikely that the first English settlers would have known how to build such a building, almost every New England parade that includes a series of historical floats has at least one log cabin following a float that depicts the founding of the community.

Although ideas about the appearance of the first Thanksgiving had been crystallized by widespread reproduction of several popular paintings well before 1920, the Brockton women's depiction of the event is somewhat compromised by the limited space available next to the log cabin. Their costumed Pilgrims are gathered around a small table. If any friendly native people were included in the scene, they were out of camera range.

Speak for Yourself, John

North Bennington, Vermont, July 4, 1914

This hearthside scene in the Fourth of July parade at North Bennington in 1914 represents the dramatic high point of Henry Wadsworth Longfellow's popular 1858 poem, "The Courtship of Miles Standish." Set at Plymouth, just a few years after the arrival of the Pilgrims, John Alden was deputized by Captain Miles Standish, the recently widowed Pilgrim leader, to approach the Pilgrim maiden

Priscilla Mullins, on Standish's behalf and seek her hand in marriage. In Longfellow's words, her spunky reply was, "Why don't you speak for yourself, John? Although both men were surprised by her response, it was Alden she married.

In this scene, Priscilla sits beside a large spinning wheel, suggesting her huswifery skills and devotion to duty. One wonders if the North Bennington ladies who designed the float knew how to spin, for they have shown Priscilla beside a "great wheel," the type sometimes referred to as a "walking wheel." Normally, the spinner stands to turn a great wheel while drawing the thread from its long, sharp spindle, but this spindle has been placed well beyond Priscilla's reach. Great wheels were usually used for spinning wool, but since no sheep arrived in Massachusetts on the *Mayflower,* Priscilla probably concentrated on household tasks other than spinning in the first years of her marriage.

Since 1769, Pilgrim descendants have celebrated their ancestors with an annual procession and dinner on Forefather's Day, December 21, the date of the first landing at Plymouth. In recent reviews of American history that have been both meticulous and emotional, the Pilgrim story has become the subject of archaeological investigation, exacting research, and carefully crafted living history as well as a cultural flashpoint triggered by concerns about colonialism, American Indian genocide, forced Christianization, and white supremacy.

Hanging of Witches, Boston Common, 1630

Boston, Massachusetts, 1930

Boston parade planners turned to Messmore and Damon, a successful and well-known firm of parade float producers in New York, to create the major floats for their tercentennial procession in 1930. Among them was a series of historical scenes that, as usual, cemented myth and reinforced stereotypes. Among the most dramatic was this design illustrating the hanging of Boston women accused of witchcraft by Puritan leaders who found their non-conformist and extreme behavior threatening. Despite the fact that Boston's hangings were conducted from the Great Elm on Boston Common, the New York artists conjured up a timber-framed gallows with nooses suspended over the heads of two accused women. A Puritan minister reading from a Bible stood before them, with the hangman pulling on a control rope behind. A nearby man holding a halberd represented the power of the law. Adding to the scene, taut figures of black cats, known today as witches' familiars, were placed by the designers at the corners of the float. The pierced-tin lanterns may have been intended to underscore the antiquity of the scene, but the pumpkin and the books on which the cats are standing suggest something that is less threatening, and much closer to Halloween than to history.

The firm of Messmore and Damon was well known for building props for fun house and "laff-in-the dark"

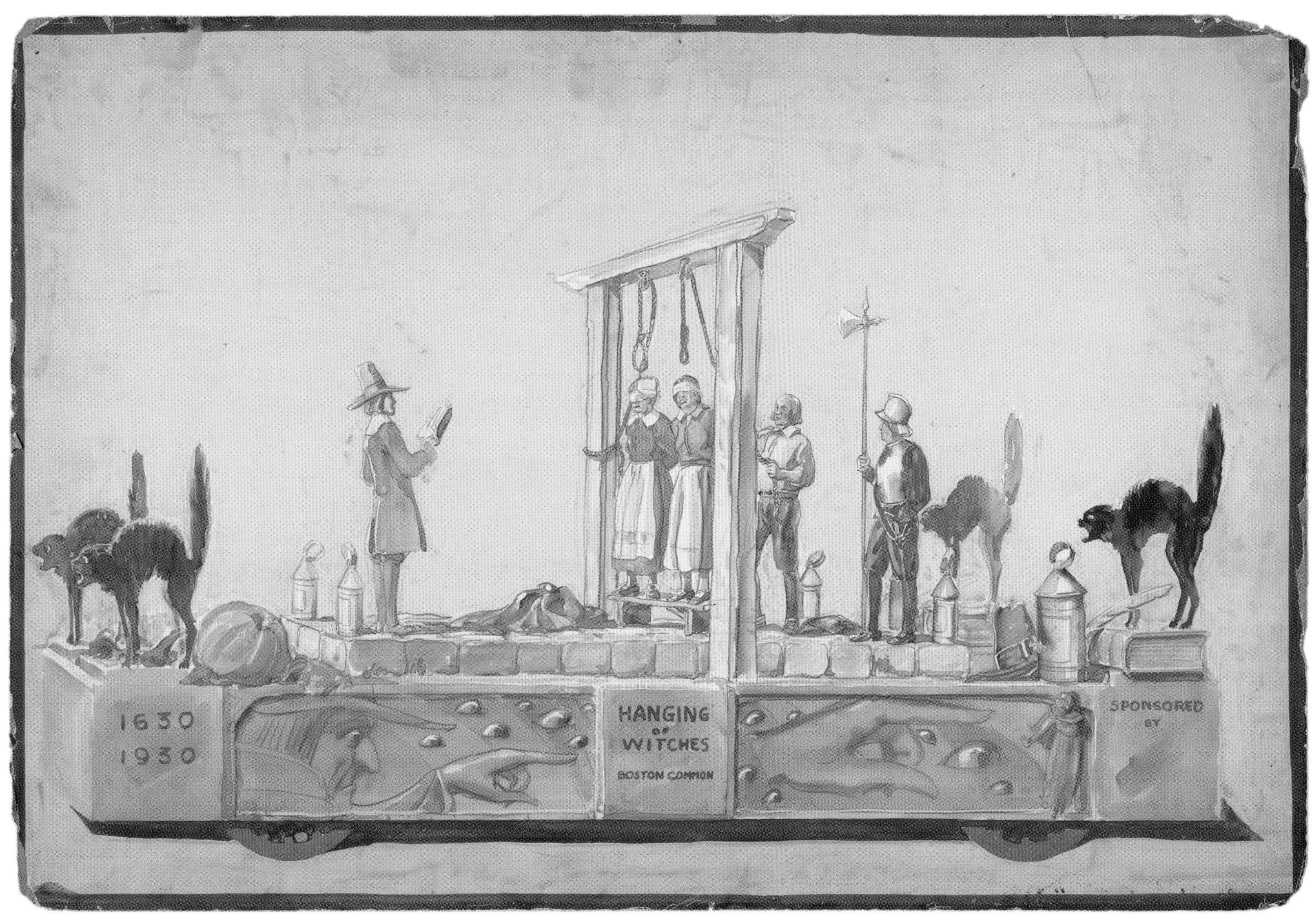
1630
1930
HANGING
OF
WITCHES
BOSTON COMMON
SPONSORED
BY

experiences in amusement parks, as well as parade floats and major features at international exhibitions and World's Fairs. Their earlier work in New England included historical tableaux shown at urban department stores, and twenty-one floats at the Maine centennial celebration at Portland in 1920, which were highly praised. Of those built for Boston in 1930, the *Boston Post* enthused, "Seldom had Boston seen such floats, so ornate and well finished, decked with such groups of beautiful maidens." 'Twas ever thus! (*For more work by Messmore and Damon, see pages 138 and 321.*)

Cleeves & Tucker Building Ye First Log House, 1633

Centennial Procession, Portland, Maine, July 5, 1886

This fanciful tableau of a dwelling house under construction was designed by one of Portland's most well-known architects, John Calvin Stevens. The scene purports to show men of the Cleeves and Tucker families, Portland's first settlers, "deep in the primeval forest and hard at work building their first home." Here again the log cabin served as a symbol of strong, resourceful men working with the materials at hand to create a good foundation for family life in the new world.

Governor John Winthrop brings the Massachusetts Bay Colony Charter and is met by John Endicott, 1630
Newburyport, Massachusetts, 1930

The float, with its painted canvas skirt representing ocean waves, was designed for the Newburyport tercentennial parade by a well-known antiquarian, the Reverend Glenn Tilley Morse, president of the Historical Society of Old Newbury. Morse also appeared in costume as the star of the show: John Winthrop, leader of the first large group of Massachusetts Bay colonists. We see them on their arrival at Salem in June 1630, approaching the shore with Winthrop standing in the bow of a small boat. He holds a large, carved oak "Bible Box," presumably containing the charter of the Massachusetts Bay Colony. The newly appointed governor John Endicott holds out his hands to receive it.

As Float Number Six, this scene was preceded by fanciful tableaux illustrating *The Forest Primeval Before Man Came to the Merrimack*, *The First Americans: The Red Man in the Wilderness*, *Columbus the Discoverer*, and *Captain John Smith*. No surprise there!

The Founding of Concord, 1635

Concord, Massachusetts, April 19, 1925

On Patriots Day in 1925, members of the Concord Grange turned to the first chapter of Lemuel Shattuck's 1835 *History of Concord*, to inform this tableau float portraying the origin of the town. To cast the scene, the Grange members apparently invited a number of Native American people to join them. They all wore stereotypical garb: the Grange members appeared in Pilgrim costume and the Native Americans were wrapped in patterned blankets and wore leggings, dark wigs with dangling braids, and a few articles of traditional dress. Signs on the float refer to the story of the transfer between local Natives and English settlers of six square miles of agricultural land at Musketaquid, which preceded the 1635 incorporation of the town. A powerful example of myth and memory, the people shivering on the truck endured sleet and snow as they sought to bring to life a pivotal moment in the history of Concord. Shattuck published official depositions taken in the 1670s that describe the earlier exchange of wampum, knives, hatchets, hoes, cloth, and other goods "after which the Indians declared themselves satisfied and told the English they were welcome," thus associating the idea of a "purchase" with the relative peace and concord of the first decades. A sign bearing the imagined, but memorable phrase: "Having purchased this land from the Indians, I declare it shall be called 'Concord'" enhanced their presentation of the town's founding story.

Elizabeth Pole Making Her Purchase, 1635

Taunton, Massachusetts, June 5, 1889

Considered "perhaps the most artistic" float in the Taunton 250th anniversary procession in 1889, this scene could also be considered the most far-fetched. Today it may be the most offensive. Although it was described as showing "the fabulous story of Elizabeth Pole handing over her peck of beans to the Indian chiefs," today we can marvel at the depiction of New England indigenous people standing in "war bonnets" as they pass long "peace pipes" and appear to negotiate with Miss Pole, who sits like a princess on a huge log in her pretty white dress and fetching cap.

Elizabeth Pole was a well-born native of Devonshire, who sailed for Massachusetts on the *Speedwell,* in 1635 with two friends, fourteen servants, and supplies for both huswifery and the preservation of commercial quantities of fish. Although she is still recognized as having been a founder of the town of Taunton and she did have large landholdings there, no deed has ever been found for her alleged land purchase. When the tale was first recorded in the mid-nineteenth century by a member of the Old Colony Historical Society, the raconteur asserted that Miss Pole had purchased the land from Native Americans for the famous peck of beans and a few trinkets, including a jackknife. Even now, the story resonates as a rare instance of female agency in a restrictive society. Taunton's motto, a line from the *Aeneid,* "Dux Femina Facti," meaning "this was the deed of a woman," keeps the legend alive to this day.

Going to Southampton to Settle, 1723

Northampton, Massachusetts, 1904

As New England towns grew, there sometimes was insufficient land to divide individual holdings among members of successive generations. While eldest sons might inherit family farms and daughters move to land owned by their husbands, many younger brothers moved away in order to acquire sufficient acreage to establish farms and provide for their own families. In the first few generations, these moves were not far, but as time passed, the new homesteads were farther and farther away, reaching into Ohio and the Northwest Territory in the early years of the new nation, and then progressing ever westward. By the time of the 1904 celebration of Northampton's 250th anniversary, descendants of the community's first settlers returned from homes all across the country.

For the great parade at Northampton in 1904 this group of men illustrated an early example of expanding settlement with their ox cart loaded with furniture, tools, and a spinning wheel. Two walked barefoot beside the cart, while another man wearing a dress sat primly in a chair amidst the household goods. Their sign indicated that they were moving in 1723 to settle in nearby Southampton, a mere nine miles away.

Jonathan Hinsdale and Family, 1750

Lenox, Massachusetts, ca. 1921–1924

It should be no surprise that Jonathan Hinsdale, long thought to have been the first settler at Lenox in western Massachusetts in 1750, would be depicted with a log cabin on a motor truck in a local parade during the early 1920s. However, the effort to illustrate his strength and independent thinking in a primitive situation is somewhat diluted by his wearing the fashionable colonial costume and white wig that assert his identity as a gentleman rather than a hands-on farmer.

THE BOSTON TEA PARTY

1773 Boston Tea Party and Highlanders

Marblehead, Massachusetts, July 4, 1884

A powerful example of citizen protest, the Boston Tea Party was a dram-atic response to British imposition of both a restrictive monopoly and a tax on imported tea. On December 16, 1773, some Boston citizens, many dressed as Indian warriors, boarded three British merchant vessels, the *Beaver,* the *Dartmouth,* and the *Eleanor.* The men threw 360 chests of East India Company tea into Boston Harbor that evening, provoking punitive restrictions quickly imposed by the British government on the colony.

This dramatic event was a perfect subject for historic parade floats and many Boston Tea Parties have appeared in New England over the years. Although the costume details usually lean toward tall, feathered headdresses and the fringed frontiersmen's shorts that enhance masculinity more than they represent historical authenticity, people took pride in celebrating the imagination and daring of the original tea party participants in the early stages of New England's rebellion against British authority.

At Marblehead in 1884, this Tea Party float was followed by a group of young men representing a completely different idea. Inspired by the Waverley novels of Sir Walter Scott, they were costumed as Scottish Highlanders, who also resisted English rule in the eighteenth century.

THE WAR FOR INDEPENDENCE

Isaac Davis and the Acton Minutemen

Concord, Massachusetts, April 19, 1925

At the snowy Patriots Day parade in Concord, Massachusetts, in April 1925, this float from nearby Acton framed a scene celebrating the first military encounter of the American Revolution, the famous moment on April 19, 1775, when patriot troops were confronted by British regulars at Concord Bridge. Upon learning of British troop movements early that morning, Acton's minutemen had marched the seven miles to Concord where they joined the arriving troops from several towns. When Concord's Colonel James Barrett asked for someone to lead the Patriot response if military action were needed, Acton's Captain Isaac Davis replied with the stirring words "I haven't a man that's afraid to go." Shortly thereafter, British regulars fired, killing both Davis and Acton's Private Abner Hosmer. The brave Patriot response to the British troops was made memorable for generations by Concordian Ralph Waldo Emerson's "Concord Hymn." Written for the dedication of the first monument at Concord Bridge on July 4, 1837, and sung that day to the tune of "Old Hundredth," the poem begins with this poignant verse:

By the rude bridge that arched the flood,
Their flag to April's breeze unfurled.
Here once the embattled farmers stood
And fired the shot heard round the world.

(*See pages 63 and 64 for images of the Acton monument to these men.*)

"We Will Be Free and Independent States" —Signing the Declaration of Independence

Marblehead, Massachusetts, July 4, 1884

The builders of this float in Marblehead, Massachusetts, made no effort to replicate the architecture of the Assembly Room in Independence Hall in Philadelphia which was the setting for the discussions of the Continental Congress and the signing of the Declaration of Independence. Twelve young boys in white wigs, dark coats, buckled knee breeches, ruffled stocks, and buckled shoes of colonial style were joined by one whose mother didn't quite get the message when she sent him in a linen coat with matching breeches and a tall straw hat to ride on this float on the Fourth of July in 1884. Before this photograph was taken, the six boys swinging their legs on one side were joined by five standing behind them who probably had been seated on the opposite side of the vehicle as it moved through the streets. In the center another boy is seated in a Windsor chair at a table on which a pen and inkwell are prominently displayed; he may represent Marblehead's delegate to the Continental Congress, Elbridge Gerry, or perhaps John Hancock, Massachusetts' most well-known signer.

Dark Days of the American Revolution
Portsmouth, New Hampshire, ca. 1861–1865

The dreary winter of Washington's army encampment at Valley Forge in 1777–1778 was a scene of cold, sickness, suffering, and death. James Head's float design for this topic proposed a circle of snow-covered log huts with steam rising from iron pots suspended over small cooking fires (actually burning in iron pans) in front of the individual huts. Some of the soldiers were to wear old and patched Continental uniforms; others ragged clothing, with their feet tied in rags and blankets thrown over their shoulders. The bearded men were to have lines painted in India ink on their faces to make them look haggard. A stack of muskets lies half buried in the snow near a flagpole, while Washington himself, in full uniform, stands alone. The oxen pulling the float were to have red, white, and blue ribbons tied to their horns and large saddlecloths with the words "Liberty or Death" and "Our Country and Our Liberty."

Betsy Ross and the First American Flag

Newport, Rhode Island, July 4, 1916

The popular imagination has long been stirred by fanciful illustrations and stories of Philadelphia upholsterer and flag maker Betsy Ross's storied 1777 meeting with George Washington and other members of the Continental Congress. There, her clever folding of a piece of paper and a single snip of the scissors that created a five-pointed star are said to have brought Betsy Ross the flag-making agreement that elevated a working-class woman to an equal position with the founding fathers.

On the Fourth of July in 1916 in Newport, Rhode Island, four members of the William Ellery Channing Chapter of the Daughters of the American Revolution (DAR) dressed in eighteenth-century silk gowns to bring to life the legend of Betsy Ross and three assistants stitching the first American flag in her Philadelphia parlor in 1777. Despite the incongruity of a mid-nineteenth-century architectural setting and the presence of a large spinning wheel that had no part in the creation of a flag, the judges of the patriotic procession in Newport awarded this float the third prize of fifty dollars.

The Newport DAR's choice of Betsy Ross as the subject of their 1916 float was hardly unique. Her growing popularity as an historical icon was furthered in children's literature and she appeared on parade floats throughout New England from at least 1880 up until World War II. She even appeared with George Washington in a parade of Antiques and Horribles at Andover, Massachusetts, in 1912!

Betsy Ross and the First American Flag

Hartford, Connecticut, October 12, 1935

The appearance of Betsy Ross in the tercentennial parade at Hartford on Columbus Day in 1935 was not a product of a local designer and a volunteer decorating committee. Instead, a thirty-two-page illustrated catalog published by the Chicago Artificial Flower Company offered prefabricated components and costumes for this float as one of "twenty-four attractive patriotic floats." Covering the supporting vehicle and providing a base for the design required forty-eight yards of the company's Chrys-cello white floral sheeting composed of "fluffy, curled flower petals mounted on cotton cloth," costing seventy-five cents a yard and guaranteed not to scratch the finish of any vehicle. The catalog also offered a special Betsy Ross flag and a wide selection of artificial flowers and vines to complete the design. Betsy's dress could be rented for an additional five dollars.

The float catalog specified that a flax wheel be placed at Betsy's feet, probably to underscore her femininity and domestic talents, although spinning linen is not a task that has anything at all to do with snipping stars or stitching together red and white stripes. The Hartford parade planners appear to have understood that and were content to let Betsy stick to her sewing.

Design for the Betsy Ross Flag

Chicago Artificial Flower Company catalog, 1935

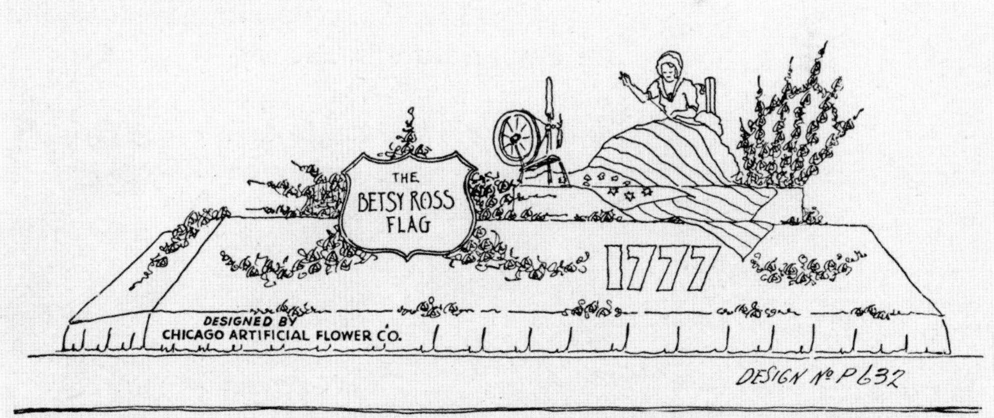

DECORATION No. P-632. "The Betsy Ross Flag" float designed to meet the requirements for attractive patriotic floats — one of a series of twenty-four patriotic float suggestions. Use chassis or flat bed truck. Chrys-celo floral sheeting in red, white or blue. Use any flower vines for decorating. Rental of Costume, $5.00.

EARLY DAYS OF A NEW NATION

Shays Plots Rebellion 1786

Amherst, Massachusetts, 1930

Once the war was over and a new government established under the Articles of Confederation, not everyone was happy. Poor farmers in western Massachusetts banded together in 1796–1797 to oppose new taxes and seek governmental change. Led by Daniel Shays, who had fought the British at Bunker Hill and Saratoga, they participated in a number of violent episodes, soon known as Shays' Rebellion.

People in Berkshire County and adjacent Connecticut River Valley towns one hundred miles west of Boston were proud of Shays' efforts, which ultimately contributed to the overthrow of the Articles of Confederation and the establishment of a new form of government under the federal Constitution. Their pride was commemorated in Amherst's tercentennial procession, where this float showed a room in Clapp's Tavern with its hospitable tavern keeper standing behind his bar ready to pour some mugs of hard cider or tumblers of rum to lubricate the wheels of change.

Log Cabin, ca. 1790
Eliot, Maine, August 1910

Second prize in the centennial parade at Eliot in 1910, was awarded to this float drawn by four yokes of oxen. Representing a home in the Massachusetts District of Maine, it featured a well sweep outside the door of a log cabin, near a tall evergreen tree that suggests the vast forests in what became known as the Pine Tree State. Considered an authentic replica, the cabin was eight feet square and furnished with "handmade" furniture. A fire burning in the stone fireplace emitted smoke from the chimney. Raccoon pelts and strings of dried apples were hung on the outer wall. Four men busied themselves sawing, splitting, carrying wood, or engaging in other strenuous activities. There was no sign of women at work at the log cabin; their indoor activities were shown in a separate kitchen float in the same parade (*see page 178*).

Early Connecticut Homestead
Hartford, Connecticut, October 12, 1935

A substantial log cabin stands behind a costumed couple lifting a bucket of water from a well with a long sweep on the float presented by the New Canaan Grange on Columbus Day in 1935. It was thirty-eighth in the line of 125 floats illustrating "Three Hundred Years of Connecticut Life and Progress" in the tercentennial parade at Hartford. The float exhibited a distinctive new format, one that completely concealed both the supporting platform and the means of locomotion so that it truly did appear to float over the road. To achieve this effect, the New Canaan float made use of a fully encompassing wrap of artificial grass that was intended to represent "amber waves of grain."

Then and Now: Women's Work

With the increasing mechanization of textile manufacturing, the establishment of numerous textile mills, and the resultant ready availability of inexpensive cotton cloth in the years after 1825, the daily work of many New England women changed markedly. With abundant sheeting, shirting, and a multitude of colorful printed goods, many families abandoned the time consuming utilitarian home production of linen and instead purchased inexpensive, easily laundered cotton fabrics. Some of these goods sold for as little as ten or twelve cents a yard. Woolen production suffered a similar change. No one needed to continue to spend multiple days preparing fibers, spinning thread, dressing a loom, or weaving yards of cloth or blankets. To fill their time and contribute to the family income, some women turned to activities like stitching shoe uppers or braiding straw hats and bonnets, which they used for credit at local stores where a wider variety of goods was now available. Some continued to spin wool into knitting yarn, but others turned their newly available time to making more or more elaborate clothing for their families, piano playing, ornamental embroidery, flower arranging, extensive correspondence, reading novels, or doing good works. Within a generation, fears were expressed that the old, useful hand skills would be lost forever when the spinning wheel was exiled to the attic. Many worried that idle hands could easily be led astray, tempted by personal reading, card playing, gossiping, gambling, attending tea parties, or drinking wine.

As a result of these changes and concerns, women's work became an extremely popular topic for parade floats. An early example was a Fourth of July parade in the factory town of Nashua, New Hampshire, in 1853, that was described in the *Nashua Telegraph* as having "A very interesting . . . car upon which some of the mechanical business of the old time was going on. Flax was taken in the raw state, broken, hatcheled, swingled, carded, and spun—the tow upon the big wheel, and the nice flax upon a little wheel. These operations were all carried out by old persons, dressed appropriately for their business, who knew just how the thing used to be done, and could do it now."[7]

Clothing the experienced elderly spinners in historic garments gave apparent authenticity to the display. The reality was that factory production of textiles in places like Nashua had already brought far-reaching change to the New England economy, disrupting daily domestic activity and changing the very fabric of family clothing, bedding, floor coverings, and table linen, as well as spurring the development of new cities, offering cash-paying employment opportunities for women as well as men, and setting the stage for widespread cultural change. Although the Nashua float, and others like it, appears to have been steeped in nostalgia for the good old days, no one really wanted to return to the hard work and limited choices of those romanticized "Days of Homespun." Still, specialized hand skills and samples of handmade textiles were a source of personal satisfaction and pride cherished by many for a very long time. Even today, some who have preserved the tools and mastered the skills of textile production can be found wearing historic costume and demonstrating at historic sites and craft fairs where they are honored for their mastery of the craft and the accuracy of their reproductions, Elsewhere, some people with these same skills apply innovative techniques and a modern design sense to elevate their work, which is now considered fiber art.

Female Accomplishments of 1776

Portsmouth, New Hampshire, ca. 1851–1865

Among the first parade floats to illustrate the changing nature of women's work were two presented in 1851 and 1852 as part of floral processions on the Fourth of July at Portsmouth. Seven years later, both ideas were repeated just as James Head was preparing these illustrations for *The Floral Architect.* His presentation of *Female Accomplishments of 1776* carried three women engaged in traditional useful work—one braiding a rug, one knitting, and one spinning. The spinner was apparently considered to be engaged in the most important task, for she was shown seated on a raised platform at the center. To underscore the point, the float was crowned by a tiny spinning wheel.

Female Accomplishments 1859

Portsmouth, New Hampshire, ca. 1859–1865

In contrast, Head's depiction of *Female Accomplishments in 1859* offers a very different idea about women's activities. For more than fifty years a growing number of female academies had augmented their academic

curriculum with instruction in a variety of what were termed "ornamental accomplishments": drawing, music, embroidery, tapestry work, French, and/or painting in oils, watercolor, or on velvet. Mastery of these activities offered elite young women skills that would enable them to entertain their husbands, beautify their homes, or create articles that could be sold at fairs benefitting good causes. Crowned by a vase of ornamental flowers, this float carried one young lady playing the piano, another painting at an easel, and a third receiving French instruction or engaged in conversation with a young male tutor. All of this was a sharp contrast to the earlier scene of diligent household production, clearly reflecting both the growing admiration and popular concern about the proliferation of strictly ornamental accomplishments.

This Is the Loom That Wove the Cloth for Gov. Haines' First College Suit

Levant, Maine, ca. 1913

As part of their celebration of historic hand skills, many parade planners still bring forth floats with antiquated equipment in active use. Here a large frame loom was put in some semblance of working order to serve as the centerpiece on a farm wagon trimmed with flags and bunting pulled by plumed horses as a parade entry. The antiquarian significance of this particular loom was its identification as the very one on which the cloth for Maine's governor William T. Haines' first "college suit" was woven. No doubt hundreds of yards of woolen cloth, blankets, carpet, and other goods were woven on this very basic loom in addition to that special piece used for the first dress suit made for a local boy headed off to the University of Maine at nearby Orono, later becoming a successful lawyer and politician.

Days of Homespun

Tamworth, New Hampshire, 1921

Women of Tamworth wearing costume suggesting various historic periods demonstrated several textile making processes on this village float in 1921. A full-sized woven bed covering was used as a backdrop for the large frame loom which one woman appears to be threading. The others are less actively engaged, although

the woman in the center displays a hank of yarn. The small loom at the left may be one of the handcraft looms used at the time by several skilled local weavers who produced scarves, table mats, napkins, and runners sold to Tamworth's summer visitors. It seems remarkable that this nostalgic scene does not include a spinning wheel, the ubiquitous symbol of both textile production and domestic duty, but it was weaving that brought cash to some Tamworth households in the 1920s.

Kitchen Then and Now: The Impact of Gas
Salem, Massachusetts, 1926

Passing a New England triple-decker with side porches, this classic kitchen float comparing then and now was part of the Industrial Procession during the Salem tercentennial celebration. It makes an important point: times have changed and for the better! The historic figure with her demure cap and heavy clothing holds a life-sized baby doll. The painted scene in front of her depicts a large open fireplace, the hot and dirty setting for much of the cooking, preserving, and laundry that was a large part of a woman's back-breaking daily work. Her childless modern counterpart wears simpler, lighter garments with a short skirt, high heels, and a carefully styled coiffure. She might even have chosen to use the newly available birth control. Her kitchen includes a small, clean-burning gas range, a sharp contrast to the roaring fire painted on the historic side of the panel that divides them.

A Kitchen of 1810
Eliot, Maine, August 11, 1910

A highlight of the Eliot centennial parade was this float depicting hearth cooking and spinning in *A Kitchen of 1810.* By combining a painted image of an iconic cooking fireplace with a display of heavy iron kettles and pewter chargers along with a selection of textile manufacturing tools—the great wheel and two yarn winding reels—the scene honors the major aspects of women's work in preindustrial days: the preparation and preservation of food and the manufacture and care of textiles and clothing.

Commemoration

Parades have often been a major component of New England's commemoration of local and national events. Most often these were the standard civic and military processions that terminated at meetinghouses or town commons where formal exercises included prayer, speeches, and song. The pictures of these events that have been found are dramatic and powerful, but there were few floats.

Events of local significance may be commemorated on the Fourth of July or during Old Home Week. Others are observed as distinctive occasions specific to individual communities. For example, Bennington, Vermont, still shuts down its Main Street on August 17 for the traditional Battle Day parade honoring General John Stark's victory on that day in 1777.

Many national commemorations have now been moved to the Friday or Monday adjacent to the actual date of the event being memorialized in order to establish long weekends that are very popular, but unfortunately this has resulted in diminished interest in or even awareness of the original reason for the holiday. For many years, respect for the original dates and long-standing tradition resulted in celebration of Abraham Lincoln's birthday on February 12 and George Washington's birthday on February 22; these are now combined in a single President's Day. Distinctive regional commemorations include Patriots Day in Massachusetts and Maine on April 19, Rhode Island Independence Day on May 4, and Bunker Hill Day in Massachusetts on June 17. St. Patrick's Day is celebrated in many places on March 17, and because it coincides with Evacuation Day in Suffolk County, Massachusetts, additional events are scheduled.

PATRIOTS DAY, APRIL 19

The shocking encounters between British regulars and local minutemen at Lexington and Concord, Massachusetts, on April 19, 1775, launched the American Revolution. The event was frequently commemorated well before April 19 was formally designated as Patriots Day in Massachusetts in 1894. Further, because Maine was part of Massachusetts at the time of the battle and remained so until Maine achieved statehood in 1820, Patriots Day continued to be commemorated there as it is today, having been officially designated a Maine state holiday in 1907.

Fight at Old North Bridge, April 19, 1775

Concord, Massachusetts, April 19, 1925

Members of the Corinthian Lodge of Ancient Free & Accepted Masons in Concord crafted this dramatic float to illustrate the original skirmish on the North Bridge in the Patriots Day parade in 1925, the sesquicentennial of the battle. They posed in costume with their guns raised as they stood in snow and sleet while the parade wound its way through the streets of the town on April 19.

BUNKER HILL DAY, JUNE 17

Just two months after Patriots Day, Massachusetts commemorates the ferocious battle between professional British troops and newly recruited American soldiers in Charlestown, on June 17, 1775. Although a British victory, the bravery of American troops at Bunker Hill has been honored by the city of Boston annually since 1786. Even on that first occasion, the day was celebrated with a great parade of civic and military officials, Masons, private citizens, and foreign guests. They were also celebrating the completion of the first bridge over the Charles River from Boston to Charlestown. One hundred and twenty men who had been employed in building the bridge joined the line and marched carrying their hand tools. As they reached the end of the bridge, thirteen cannon were fired from the Boston shore and an answering volley was fired from Charlestown. The event ended with a fine public dinner that concluded with thirteen toasts. Eight years later a similar procession marched to the battlefield to dedicate a tall Tuscan column as a monument to General Joseph Warren and the soldiers who died there with him in 1775.

In response to fears that the battlefield would soon be developed as a residential neighborhood, the Bunker Hill Monument Association was formed in 1823 to preserve much of the battlefield as open space and to build upon it a new and more impressive monument (*see page 58 from Chapter 2, Honor, Monuments*). After the 1843 completion of the new monument on Bunker Hill, there was a general feeling among the members of the Bunker Hill Monument Association that the farther the Battle of Bunker Hill receded into the distant past, the greater the event would become. They were certainly right, for Bunker Hill Day parades grew larger and larger. By mid-century, the official civic procession was preceded by an energetic parade of Antiques and Horribles. Even today, both of these traditions continue to be observed with enthusiasm on June 17.

As the country approached its centennial in 1876, plans were focused on commemorative events and a major international exposition to be held in Philadelphia, where the Declaration of Independence had been signed. New England, however, launched its commemorative celebrations a year earlier, marking the 1775 battles at Lexington, Concord, and Bunker Hill, and the Evacuation of British Troops from Boston in March of 1776, all of which happened before the Declaration was signed. Elaborate, expensive events marking all of these occasions drew national attention and large crowds. The following year, many people went to Philadelphia to tour the Centennial Exposition at some point during the summer and in some places less money was spent on local celebrations. In New England, July 4, 1776, saw orations and extensive displays of fireworks, but few lavish parades.

Bunker Hill Centennial Procession

Boston, Massachusetts, June 17, 1875

At the time of the hundredth anniversary of the Battle of Bunker Hill in 1875, the Bunker Hill Monument Association organized a great parade. The Ancient and Honorable Artillery Company took pride of place and men of the Massachusetts Volunteer Militia turned out in greater numbers than had been seen in many years. Prestigious military units came from many other states, including some from the Deep South. With their disciplined marching and their impressive and colorful uniforms, the Bunker Hill procession in 1875 was said to have been a display of military magnificence unequalled anywhere since the celebration of the opening of the Erie Canal in New York in 1825. Noting that President Ulysses S. Grant did not attend, *The Boston Globe* chided him on June 18: "You really should have been here, Mr. Grant. You missed the biggest show of the century."

This stereograph is one of a series of different parade views taken from the upper floor of a building at the foot of Milk Street looking toward Washington Street, with the steeple of the Old South Meeting House just visible at the upper right. This entire area had been devastated by the Great Boston Fire of 1872. Only the Old South had escaped the flames; every other building seen here had been constructed in less than three years. The only remaining vacant space, that at the lower right, provided space for an enterprising individual to erect a sales booth

and a grandstand for the comfort and convenience of a few paying parade goers.

The 1875 procession was much more than a military demonstration, however. Officers of the Bunker Hill Monument Association, invited guests, and political figures were followed by delegations of many organizations, among them the Pilgrim Society, the Massachusetts Veterans of 1812, the Order of the Cincinnati, the New England Historic Genealogical Society, the Joseph Warren Monument Association of Roxbury, the Massachusetts Charitable Mechanics Association, the Charitable Irish Society, and the Grand Lodge of Masons, most riding in carriages. In all, the Association secured the participation of more than ten thousand people for their great parade.

Trades Procession

Boston, Massachusetts, June 17, 1875

The last and ninth division of the Bunker Hill centennial procession was a display of trades in which the line

of wagons carrying local products was slow to get started and then stretched for nearly four miles. The line is seen here on Columbus Avenue moving toward Concord Square, where float Number 376 with its pyramid of framed oil paintings is followed by several displays of a carpet manufacturer. No doubt most of these spectators had been waiting several hours for the first marchers to appear.

While most people jostled on the crowded sidewalks, some viewers were able to gain privileged access to rooftops, balconies, or open windows. A few enterprising owners had sold spaces in windows on the upper floors of buildings along the route for as much as twenty-five dollars. Speculators erected temporary grandstands in front yards or across intersecting streets, renting seats and offering refreshments at inflated prices.

Triumphal Arch at Charles River Avenue

Boston, Massachusetts, June 17, 1875

This grand arch was one of several erected along the parade route in Boston and across the Charles River in Charlestown as part of the 1875 commemoration of the Battle of Bunker Hill. Crowned by flags and an eagle, the keystone of the arch bore the date of the Battle, June 17, 1775, and was flanked by trumpeting figures of Fame. The arch was further adorned with views of the battle and the Bunker Hill Monument, as well as names of the American heroes Warren, Putnam, Preston, Knowlton, Stark, and Pomeroy.

Photographer Lewis Thomas captured this moment when a horsecar stopped on street rails as it headed toward City Square in Charlestown after crossing the river on Charles River Avenue, an everyday occurrence greatly enhanced that week by this impressive tangible salute to the first major battle of the American Revolution.

BATTLE OF BENNINGTON CENTENNIAL, 1877

The Centennial Celebration of General Stark's Victory at the Battle of Bennington on August 16, 1777

Bennington, Vermont, August 16, 1877

Twelve years after the end of the Civil War, the hundredth anniversary of the pivotal American victory led by General John Stark at Bennington was the impetus for huge gatherings of veterans of both Union and Confederate troops. More than sixty thousand men camped for the week at Camp Ethan Allen or Camp Stark near the Bennington Battlefield, five miles from the center of the village. There they enjoyed daily dress parades, martial music, and convivial reunions.

In addition to the military encampment, the August 1877 celebration included church services, a banquet, a presidential visit, and three parades. Newsboys in colonial

costume sold souvenir fans and special publications to the thousands of visitors who arrived by private carriages and special trains. Hotels, boarding houses, and livery stables offered special rates for rooms and meals. Nationwide newspapers covered every detail.

Despite heavy rain during part of the procession on Centennial Celebration Day, Thursday, August 16, President Rutherford B. Hayes and Vermont's governor Horace Fairbanks rode in an open carriage near the front of the line with the president often standing to bow and acknowledge enthusiastic applause. This huge arch in the center of Bennington was embellished with a painting of the Vermont coat of arms on the keystone and Stark's famous words "You see the red coats. They are ours or Molly Stark sleeps a widow tonight." Importantly, the arch also exhibited the coat of arms of the United States as well as those of individual northern and southern states, a powerful recognition of the reunification of the country following the recent Civil War. A second motto proclaimed "Peace hath her victories no less renowned than war."

Details of the Bennington centennial show the interconnected and repetitive nature of these great civic celebrations. Invitations sent to governmental officials and military units throughout the country swelled the ranks. Marching at the head of the first division in the parade were members of the Putnam Phalanx from Hartford, Connecticut, in their uniforms of Continental style. The well-known civic decorator Colonel William Beals of Boston was hired not only to ornament the triumphal arch, but also to install arches of flags and mottoes at the entrance to the campgrounds, and ten spans of flags across city streets. In addition, he posted flags, mottoes, velvet banners, and sixty oil portraits of American presidents and military heroes on prominent buildings in the city center. Cannily, he also brought $10,000 worth of flags, banners, bunting, and other decorations that were placed with a local merchant and made available for sale or rent. The *Vermont Centennial* urged everyone to participate in decorating the city, saying "Even a 10 cent flag would be better than no decoration. Don't let President Hayes, or other guests look upon a building undecorated." Beals was an experienced businessman and a master of his craft who understood his market. His work embellished cities and towns throughout New England for special occasions over a period of nearly fifty years.

HONORING NAVAL HEROES

Kearsarge–Alabama Celebration

Portsmouth, New Hampshire, September 18, 1900

Constructed entirely of evergreen, and crowned with a naval trophy, this installation of swags and a double arch over the South Mill Pond bridge in Portsmouth was the most elaborate of a series of six arches erected as part of an elaborate celebration in September of 1900. The occasion was the launching of two new US Navy

ships named *Kearsarge* and *Alabama* at the Portsmouth Naval Shipyard. The names had been selected to honor two earlier ships that had engaged in a decisive Civil War battle on September 9, 1864, during which the USS *Kearsarge* defeated and sank the Confederate ship *Alabama* off the coast of Cherbourg, France. In the previous two years, the CSS *Alabama* had captured and either burned or sunk at least sixty-five United States merchant ships in an effort to disrupt American shipping and stimulate antiwar sentiment in the North. The thrilling 1864 victory of the *Kearsarge* eliminated what had been a major threat to American commerce during the Civil War.

The commemoration and launch celebration in 1900 included a great parade with more than three thousand men in line, including government officials from Washington, DC, the states of Maine and New Hampshire, and the adjacent cities of Portsmouth, New Hampshire, and Kittery, Maine, as well as US Navy officers and sailors from the Portsmouth Naval Shipyard, and Civil War veterans who were members of the Grand Army of the Republic.

COLUMBUS DAY

Santa Maria

Montpelier, Vermont, October 12, 1911

By 1911, many people agreed that October 12 was the right day to commmemorate Columbus' landing in the new world. This ambitious horse-drawn float depicting the Italian navigator and two officers aboard the *Santa Maria* surrounded by tossing waves was featured at the beginning of a parade that day at Montpelier, Vermont. With its masts shortened to avoid contact with the city's electrical wires, the ship was flying America's stars and stripes as well as historical versions of both the Spanish and Italian flags on the bow.

At the time, Christopher Columbus and his crew were honored for their "discovery" of America, a concept less highly regarded today when Columbus is recognized as a conqueror and indigenous people now celebrate their own vibrant cultures that have persevered through colonization.

LAFAYETTE'S TOUR

Lafayette and His Hoss

Kennebunk, Maine, probably July 4, 1925

For well over one hundred years, re-enactments of the triumphal 1824–1825 New England tour of the Marquis de Lafayette created enduring memories and stimulated positive Franco-American feelings. In this centennial example at Kennebunk, Maine, local historians William Barry and George Cousens donned wigs and colonial costume to ride in a village parade as Lafayette and his driver in a "one-hoss shay." Lafayette had stopped in Kennebunk on June 23, 1825, while en route to Portland, on the final leg of his American tour.

A LONG DAY

Company E, New Hampshire Militia
Concord, New Hampshire, October 12, 1892

After looking at so many lines of well-disciplined marching men, this rather scraggly line at the end of a unit in the parade at Concord on the first official Columbus Day, October 12, 1892, reveals a certain level of relaxation toward the end of a long day. In any case, the evident attention to a good story or an interesting conversation has not interrupted the rhythm of the march. Every man is still leading with his left foot, even as some have turned their heads toward the speaker and other are lagging behind.

Historical Vehicles

The Yankee tendency to save almost anything that might someday be useful applies well to vehicles of all kinds. Some are kept functional for summertime excursions, the occasional Sunday drive, or ceremonial occasions. Others are simply pushed out of the way—deep in the landscape or the back corners of sheds, barns, and carriage houses. Long after any possible mobility has vanished, old vehicles are still treasured as sources for parts that might be useful in repair of others. Inevitably some are stripped beyond utility or fall into total decay, but even today, New England is well stocked with treasured antique cars and worn old wagons and carriages that can be pulled out and cleaned up to be used for floats or to transport dignitaries in parades.

Among the variety of old vehicles especially popular for parades are those commonly known as chaises, the durable two-wheeled passenger carriages with folding tops, like that used by Lafayette. Even inexperienced drivers find them easy to drive, since they are pulled by just a single horse. The utility of the chaise was extolled in 1858 by Oliver Wendell Holmes in "The Deacon's Masterpiece: or, the Wonderful 'One-Hoss Shay': A Logical Story." The lengthy poem described a vehicle that had served its purpose for exactly one hundred years until it suddenly fell to pieces in a heap of useless scraps. Beyond exploring the cosmic meaning of this experience, the popular poem conferred an enduring name on a ubiquitous long-time transportation standby and perpetuated the use of the New England vernacular pronunciations *shay* and *hoss*.

From at least 1850, the antique sections in New England parades included old chaises, most often with male drivers and female passengers, both usually wearing old clothing of various dates. For the parade at Northampton, Massachusetts, in 1904, a one-hoss shay, said to be more than 150 years old, was borrowed from a farmer in Vermont, and a bony old horse was found to draw it. The committee found some difficulty in persuading anyone to ride in it, since most people preferred to appear in a more attractive and up-to-date vehicle or even an automobile, but "a public-spirited couple were finally found . . . who graced the old-fashioned ramshackle vehicle in a striking manner, and provoked much mirth and admiration by the nonchalant and to-the-manor-born air with which they carried themselves. This was one of the most popular features of the parade."

Just a few years later, at the centennial celebration in Eliot, Maine, in 1910, interest in a one-hoss shay was enhanced by the nationwide popularity of a new song. Third prize in the Eliot parade was given to a float titled, *Drive Up to Dover, One Hoss Shay, 1815*. Two men, one of them wearing a dress and "an old gray bonnet, with the blue ribbon on it" had hitched up "old Dobbin to the shay," and apparently were ready to drive over to Dover, New Hampshire, just eight miles away.

Centennial Parade

Nantucket, Massachusetts, 1895

For nearly two hundred years, parades have included similar undecorated, well-kept chaises with well-dressed passengers in costumes of an indeterminate olden time riding behind white horses.

F. P. Reed and W. S. Brown in their 'One Hoss' Shay
Manchester, New Hampshire, September 10, 1896

This newspaper sketch by John E. Coffin shows a one-hoss shay of 1776 in the 1896 semicentennial parade at Manchester, New Hampshire, an event celebrating an industrial city not incorporated until seventy years after the nation's founding. The characteristic folding hood of the vehicle has been opened over the occupants and the wheels are decorated in typical parade fashion, the spokes having been wound with fabric, or possibly crepe paper, that is undoubtedly red, white, and blue. Tall stalks of flowers rise from the horses' harness and the chaise is adorned with flags, cornstalks, and a sign commemorating the key date "1776." Behind the chaise hangs the manure bucket provided for thoughtful parade participants in case street cleaning was necessary during the procession.

STAGECOACHES

Although stagecoaches providing regular transportation service in New England had largely been replaced by railroads after the Civil War, many of the huge old vehicles were still serviceable. Hotel owners in the White Mountains and on the seashore continued to use them to transport summer visitors and their luggage to and from railroad depots as well as on sightseeing excursions. Some old coaches are still kept in good condition and used for private excursions or to carry honored guests or oldest residents in parades. Others are safely stored by public or private owners in large barns or freight stations, while some quietly sank into the soil after their last ride. In both places, imaginative children have long enjoyed climbing to the driver's seat and pretending to travel far and wide.

Stagecoach Days

Newburyport, Massachusetts, 1930

Big old stagecoaches are always impressive additions to commemorative parades or historical processions where they add a vivid suggestion of travel in olden times. The vehicles have plenty of seats on top for

honored guests to see and be seen while as many as nine more people can ride inside. Further, a stagecoach display offers well-defined gender roles with pretty young women riding on top, older women inside, a skilled male driver on the box controlling four strong horses, manly footmen riding in erect posture behind, and any number of sturdy mounted guards trotting alongside.

Here in front of the1807 Tenney-Noyes House on High Street in Newburyport, during the Massachusetts tercentennial, women riding on this stagecoach appear to have chosen a variety of Victorian summer dresses, hats or bonnets, and parasols to enhance the old-fashioned appearance of the ensemble. In contrast, the men are wearing tailcoats with shiny buttons, knee breeches, wigs, and tricorn hats, all suggesting clothing of the colonial period. At the rear of the coach, one man wears a servant's livery. The clothing of the entire group was described in the local newspaper as being both "colonial" and "of their social station." Although some of the garments may have been pulled out of attic trunks, any of them could have been rented from Hooker-Howe, a costume supplier serving theatrical companies, minstrel shows, and parade organizers across the country and conveniently located in nearby Haverhill.

RAILROADS

A Model of the First Engine in New Hampshire—The First to Draw a Train Into Concord

Concord, New Hampshire, August 20, 1903

When the first passenger train arrived in Concord from Boston on September 6, 1842, its three cars were pulled by the locomotive *Amoskeag*, built at the Amoskeag Locomotive Works at nearby Manchester. In the years after the first arrival of the *Amoskeag*, Concord had become a thriving railroad hub and a regional center for the Boston & Maine Company. This was celebrated in various ways at the city's semicentennial parade in 1903. The model engine pictured here was built for the occasion by students at the Morrill School of Mechanical Arts, a division of the Concord Public Schools where the goal was to "educate the whole boy." The parade also included a full-size replica of the *Amoskeag* drawn by six horses. That one was built by the Erecting Department of the massive Boston & Maine Railroad Shops at Concord.

The first prize for the largest number marching with any organization in the semicentennial parade was awarded to the Boston & Maine for their contribution of the entire second division in which every employee, 650 men, marched to the rhythms of the Boston & Maine Drum Corps.

***Wreck of the float bearing the* Lion**

Portland, Maine, July 4, 1898

Not every parade float is strong enough to bear its burden. As part of the trades division of a procession celebrating the fiftieth anniversary of the Grand Trunk Railway, the front left wheel of this specially built dray, (*see next page*) pulled by ten heavy work horses, collapsed under the weight of its celebrated subject, the "primitive locomotive" *Lion,* believed then by the *Portland Daily Press* to be the "oldest locomotive in the country outside of the museums." Built in Boston in 1846 by Hinkley & Drury, the engine had been used for many years transporting lumber in the Maine woods. Stored in a variety of public buildings in the years after this unfortunate incident, the *Lion* has been carefully restored to its 1860 appearance and can be seen today at the entrance of the Maine State Museum at Augusta where it is identified as the eighth oldest American-built locomotive.

6

ENTERTAINMENT

Even though most parade entries are designed to catch attention and convey an idea, some are primarily intended to entertain. Whether organized on the spur of the moment to keep children busy on a summer day, planned for months to entice return visits by hotel guests, or dreamed up in secret by people whose only goal is to have a good time, the idea is to have fun in the process and to entertain the spectators.

Professional circus troupes, traveling menageries, and other itinerant entertainers deliberately formed flamboyant parades of the fanciful and attention-getting vehicles in which they moved performers, equipment, animals, and support staff from place to place as they followed a specific itinerary each season. These processions were knowingly designed to serve as impressive and enticing advertisements, giving prospective customers a hint of the rare sights and exciting performances soon to be available only to ticket holders. Having chosen not to include the parades of itinerant entertainers in this publication, perhaps this "splendid and Colossal Roman Chariot" can stand for them all.

Chrysarma or Roman Chariot

Washington, New Hampshire, 1847–1848

This drawing by Solon Newman of tiny Washington, New Hampshire, illustrates the *Chrysarma*, the fantastical bandwagon at the head of the procession carrying Raymond and Waring's "Magnificent Collection of Living Wild Beasts" in thirty wagons drawn by more than one hundred horses as they toured New England in 1847 and 1848. Not unlike the way that almost every parade is described as best the ever or the most magnificent, these lions, tigers, apes, and other specimens were claimed to be "the best, most perfect, and the largest" collection ever seen in America.

Described in advertisements as a "Gorgeous Roman Chariot," the *Chrysarma* was pulled by ten "magnificent" black horses and "literally covered with gold," fifty feet long and twenty feet high. The owners claimed that it was "the greatest mechanical and artistical prodigy of the age." Twenty men had built it over the course of nine months, using a design from an antique model recently exhibited in London. A New York newspaper described the *Chrysarma* in 1847 as "a blazing prodigy of crimson, purple, and gold, exhibiting classical figures of colossal stature, in bold and vigorous sculpture, grouped with lordly animals of the forest . . . free from all tinsel and flimsy ornament, and [it] makes a dominant impression of sumptuousness and substantial grandeur, blended with the highest compatible degree of grace and beauty."

Newman's drawing is clearly based on the image of the chariot that was printed on gigantic posters that were pasted or tacked up on fences, or on the walls of barns or warehouses, to proclaim the impending arrival of the menagerie as Raymond & Waring made their way through New Hampshire from Portsmouth, to Nashua and Manchester, and then on to Amherst in September of 1848. Whether one of the posters was displayed in the town of Washington, about forty miles from Manchester, or whether Newman saw one somewhere else in the vicinity is unknown. He may have seen the vehicle itself, but since the detail in his drawing closely replicates that in the poster, he must have made some careful sketches somewhere in the field.

Imagine catching sight of this huge, gilded vehicle emerging from a deep forest through brilliant fall foliage or descending through a rocky sheep pasture on a remote hillside, as the musicians struck up a tune and the animals in the succeeding carts began to bellow. Although it must have inspired people to buy tickets to see the animals and it surely created a lasting memory, there is little evidence that this or other elaborate traveling menageries or circus wagons inspired local builders of parade floats. Their work was usually done quickly and cheaply, making use of recycled materials whenever possible to create a stage or convey an idea.

Floral Processions

The impact of romanticism on New England parades began to be seen in picturesque floral processions first sponsored by Boston's Warren Street Chapel in 1841. Rich with literary and historical references, these were dramatically different in concept and effect from traditional civic and military processions with their vast ranks of uniformed men, colorful banners, and beating drums. Neither were they related to the strictly ornamental floral parades discussed in Chapter 7. Those began about 1880 and were presented by adults in New England summer communities. It was those later events that quickly inspired the Floral Festival at Saratoga, New York, and the Rose Parade in Pasadena, California.

Floral processions were widely presented by temperance societies and Sunday schools during the 1840s and 1850s. At first these events featured hundreds of girls and boys carrying simple baskets or bouquets of flowers, evergreen wreaths, or floral arrangements in the form of anchors, lyres, harps, or crosses. To avoid chaos, the children walked in small groups distinguished by matching costumes, usually escorted by a mother or teacher serving as chaperone and disciplinarian. On reaching their destination, usually a sponsoring church, the bouquets and floral designs were sold to support Sunday school activities or charitable purposes.

A further goal was to illustrate examples of beauty, grace, and elegance that would serve to help both participants and spectators identify the same, as well as help them develop their own aesthetic taste. Within a few years after 1840, more elaborate floral processions included floats on which the children brought to life scenes from nursery rhymes and English literature. Illustrations in various editions of James Thomson's still popular 1728 poem, "The Seasons," clearly inspired the costumed boys portraying seasonal agricultural workers such as sowers, planters, reapers, gleaners, or hay makers. Some rode on tableau floats; others walked with small farm tools, sheaves of wheat, or tall cornstalks.

Modeled after illustrations or descriptions of life in Scotland in the works of Sir Walter Scott, some groups of boys represented "Highlanders" by wearing plaid or carrying bagpipes (*see page 164*). Girls identified themselves as "Italian Flower Girls" by walking with wreaths or baskets of flowers on their arms or even on their heads. Boys in green with peaked caps and quivers of arrows were designated "Robin Hood Archers." Other costumed children appeared as the Virtues: Faith carrying a flower covered cross, Hope leaning on an anchor, or Charity extending a hand to needy women and children. Some represented characters from nursery rhymes, such as "Little Boy Blue" or "Little Red Riding Hood." Occasionally a whole crowd of children emerged from a huge shoe under the watchful eye of the famous Little Old Woman Who Lived There Too.

As time passed, additional characters such as shepherds and shepherdesses with their crooks or gardeners with rakes and tiny wheelbarrows were added to the agricultural scenes. Soon, the allegorical representations grew more complex and new topics offering more roles for girls were introduced. Flora was sometimes attended by twelve costumed girls representing the months of the year or by scenes of "Morning, Noon, and Night." Mythological scenes featured Venus, Cupid, and or the Three Graces. "The Old Oaken Bucket" emphasized the virtue of drinking only pure water and abstaining from alcoholic beverages. Most of these presentations were designed and crafted by parents and teachers, although occasionally professional help was available. At Gloucester, Massachusetts, in 1849, for example, the artist Fitz Henry Lane "volunteered his assistance, furnishing the young ladies with designs of banners, and representations."

At the time of the nation's seventy-fifth anniversary, the Jubilee celebrated in 1851, a floral procession at Salem, Massachusetts, included a tribute to internal improvements with a model steamboat and a locomotive bearing a sign that it would travel "through to Boston in 35 minutes." In contrast, at Dover, New Hampshire, the 1851 procession included "two couples on horseback in the old style, the lady on a pillion behind, as common fifty years ago." Many floral processions that year also included historical tableaux illustrating topics ranging from the landings of Columbus and the Pilgrims to the scene at Independence Hall on July 4, 1776, to battles of the American Revolution, and other touchstones in America's story.

At Portsmouth, New Hampshire, several floral processions included groups of girls designated *Nightingales* by their Juvenile Singing School instructor Thomas P. Moses, who hoped their talents might become as fine as those of Jenny Lind, the popular Swedish singer, then touring as the "Swedish Nightingale." Moses' students sometimes rode on floats or walked in floral processions with girls carrying moss baskets filled with flowers and boys carrying musical instruments. Their beautiful banners displayed mottoes such as: "The genius of wisdom will preserve our union," "Music and poetry: strong agents in freedom's cause," and "July 4th 1776: the Birthday of Liberty." At Boston in 1854, the rich cultural references in a floral procession on the Fourth of July were celebrated as "a genial, rational, appropriate, and elevating celebration of the nation's birthday."

Not all Fourth of July activities for children were as picturesque as the floral processions. One can readily understand that after being up all night celebrating the Fourth of July by firing cannons, setting off firecrackers, ringing bells, relocating fences, or tipping over outhouses, before watching their fathers and slightly older brothers prepare to march in disciplined military groups or cavort in the processions of Antiques and Horribles, many young boys would have resisted carrying bouquets of flowers or wearing classical robes in floral processions. No wonder more masculine roles soon appeared. An extreme example was the "daring and reckless" youth riding on a locomotive at Bath, Maine, in 1865. He was impersonating Young America, the popular symbol of the Democratic Party's economic policies supporting internal improvements and free trade. More often, the mid-century floral processions eschewed politics and presented ranks of uniformed school boys organized in companies of patriotic Young Volunteers or Continentalers. Dressed in quasi-military uniforms and armed with little spears or wooden guns, they stepped off in true martial style, keeping time with the music, serving as military escorts for the teachers and groups of children immediately following them. In 1851 at Portsmouth, the Continentalers marched in an unbroken line, each with a hand on the shoulder of the lad in front of him, representing the union of the group as well as of the nation. Similar units appeared for more than a decade at Salem, Marblehead, and Worcester, Massachusetts; New London, Connecticut; Machias, Maine, and probably many other places as well.

During the 1850s, many of the kinds of representations that had walked the streets in long floral processions a decade earlier moved indoors in some communities where they were combined with musical recitals in the form of floral concerts. With the costumed children out of the scorching sun or drenching rain and no longer subjected to the rigors of a long march, the efforts of mothers and teachers were thus presented to admiring audiences in a more controlled environment and less exhausting format. Before the Civil War, the once popular floral processions mostly faded away until the 1920s when they were seen again as part of the tercentennial celebrations at Salem and elsewhere, mainly in Massachusetts.

The Flora Testimonial

Portsmouth, New Hampshire, ca. 1861–1865

James Head included twenty designs for floats suitable for floral processions in *The Floral Architect.* Among them were representations of the months of the year, the four seasons of life, a flower garden, a fairy fountain, a floral queen, *The Old Oaken Bucket,* and individual floats for each of the four seasons. Some of the designs appear to have been actually constructed and were described in Portsmouth newspapers as part of the floral processions that were held as early as eight o'clock in the morning on the Fourth of July during the 1850s. However, some of the designs appear too large, too vague, or too complex to have been realized and there is no documentary evidence that all were actually built.

The Flora Testimonial epitomizes Head's designs in this category, highlighted by a plaster statue of the goddess Flora "on the summit of a pedestal, which is richly embellished with paintings and flowers." Head specified that her attendants were to be "four young ladies of good form and features" wearing wreaths of greenery and lilies atop their short curls. Their costumes were to be "white dresses cut low in the neck and skirts long enough to trail." Each attendant held a pretty bouquet and pointed toward a painted wooden tablet with suitable poetic text.

Autumn
James Thomson, The Seasons

Images that appeared in popular engravings and illustrations for children's books may well have guided the young mothers and schoolteachers who created costumes and arranged parade floats. Perhaps most influential was James Thomson's long 1726 poem *The Seasons,* which was published in multiple illustrated editions, often showing the very sowers, reapers, hay makers, and gleaners featured in floral processions.

Silk ribbon badge
Maker unknown, mid-nineteenth century

This printed silk ribbon was probably pinned to the costume of a child appearing as "A Jolly Haymaker" in a floral procession sometime between 1840 and 1860. Although most people in the street-side crowds would have immediately understood the representations of each costumed group, some children wore ribbons like this to clarify the topics. Although ribbon badges were undoubtedly treasured by proud mothers or boastful participants, most have disintegrated or disappeared over time.

Thomas Bailey Aldrich in Uniform of the Continentalers

Portsmouth, New Hampshire, 1846

Thomas Bailey Aldrich, later editor of *The Atlantic Monthly*, first marched as a nine-year-old with a troop of twenty boys called the Continentalers in floral processions at Portsmouth in 1846. Five years later in 1851, he was promoted to captain of the group, which by then numbered thirty-eight. The boys wore uniforms inspired by those of the Revolutionary War era: cocked black tricorn hats; long, blue military-style coats with buff facings; yellow vests; buckled knee breeches; and black shoes with large, shiny metal buckles. One suspects that by 1851 Aldrich had outgrown the uniform he is seen wearing in this 1846 daguerreotype. It seems strange that he is shown holding an Abenaki war club instead of musket or a sword, but no contemporary explanation has been found. What happened to the club is unknown, but the uniform is preserved in the Aldrich Memorial Collection at Strawbery Banke Museum.

Honor to Whom Honor is Due

South Danvers, Massachusetts, October 9, 1856

These young ladies look very much like some of the groups of "Italian Flower Girls" described as participants in New England floral processions during the 1850s. Dressed alike in close bonnets, full skirts with white aprons, long-sleeved chemises, and dark-colored fitted bodices with short peplums over the hips, their clothing is loosely derived from rustic or European peasant garb depicted in popular prints and book illustration of the period. On this occasion, the young women carry three Roman-style banners welcoming the Danvers-born philantropist George Peabody.

Zouave

Bangor, Maine, July 4, 1865

Far from the traditional tricorn hats and the buff-and-blue coats worn by the Continentalers, this young man wears a version of the exotic oriental cap, white jacket, baggy red pants, and tall, laced leather boots that identified brave Zouave units during the Civil War. He was one of a group of boys aged eleven to fourteen at Bangor, Maine, who adopted the Zouave uniform and practiced marching and drilling together for several days before participating in the jubilant peacetime parade on the Fourth of July in 1865.

Annie Martin, a Little Zephir
Bangor, Maine, July 2, 1866

> *"Pretty little Zephirs we,*
> *Swiftly through the air we bound*
> *Throwing blossoms all around."*

John Martin's charming watercolor of his young daughter tossing flower petals from a basket while wearing a leafy crown and a white party dress trimmed with garlands and flowers for her role in a floral concert gives us a good idea of the kind of costume worn by the girls in floral processions.

The Antiques and Horribles

As the old militia Training Days disintegrated into drunken and disorderly chaos in the 1830s and 1840s, a new parade tradition began to emerge in large cities and small towns throughout New England. Groups of men and boys from all levels of society began secret planning to appear as early as five o'clock in the morning on the Fourth of July, determined to entertain themselves and anyone who turned out to watch. News of their activity was passed by word-of-mouth or carefully leaked to the press in order to ensure large numbers of spectators. Sometimes printed broadsides pasted to buildings or nailed to trees and fences announced the details, usually in veiled language. The Bungtown Invincibles, the Kite-Enders, and a few other groups published annual newsletters describing their activities, printing long rambling speeches, and praising individual members.

These men paraded streets dressed in old military uniforms, beat-up hats, and/or scraps of clothing found in the far corners of the attic or extracted from the rag bag. Turning social norms upside down, they were frequently masked and sometimes dressed as women. Some racist expressions involved blackface and mimicked presentations in minstrel shows. Some rode oxen, mules, or bony old horses, drove rickety old vehicles, or limped along in extra-long shoes. Despite the early hour, there were people of all ages cheering and laughing along the way. Setting out to make as much noise as possible with loud drums, tin whistles, cowbells, and a variety of make-shift instruments, the marchers were sometimes joined by bands of musicians, often known as Calithumpians. Those groups were renowned for discordant music made with broken-down horns or by banging sticks or large metal spoons on dilapidated brass kettles, or playing a cowbell organ.

Among the first of these processions was a caricature military parade at Worcester, Massachusetts, in 1835. Within the next fifteen years, others formed on college campuses in Burlington, Vermont, and Hartford, Connecticut. In the Merrimack Valley textile-manufacturing towns of Lowell and Lawrence, Massachusetts, large populations of young factory workers were happy to try their hands at creative expression and social commentary, to mock the establishment, and, above all, to have a jolly good time. The basic idea of these processions spread quickly to cities and towns throughout the region where individual creativity and provocative local topics made them a highly anticipated feature of holidays.

Men in the earliest parades of Horribles organized themselves into quasi-military companies with officers, cavalry, infantry, quartermaster, and ambulance corps equipped with a motley assortment of disreputable uniforms, worn-out old vehicles, and exaggerated weapons of all kinds. Their musicians were noted for their music of great pretension and huge noise. The groups were known variously as Invincibles, Fantastics, Grotesques, Fusileers, Squizaleers, Odds and Ends, or just the Horribles. In Worcester, Massachusetts, they were the Studlefunks, in Lynn the Kite-Enders, in Beverly the Bean Kiln Invaders, in New Bedford they were variously the Shanghai Volunteers, the Squawbetty Rangers, or the Bungtown Invincibles who used clever forms of "humbugerie and partialietie" to amuse the crowd and generate hearty laughs. Perhaps the most bizarre name was chosen at Pittsfield, Massachusetts, in 1859 when a group appeared as the Bungomungo Knockneed Ruribustah Rapscallions under the command of Young America, Esq.

A parallel parade tradition emerged in 1851, as the nation prepared to celebrate its Jubilee, marking seventy-five years since the signing of the Declaration of Independence, as well as anniversaries of towns more than two hundred years old. In 1852 residents of Danvers, Massachusetts, caught the celebratory spirit and planned an Antiques parade to mark the one hundredth anniversary of their separation from the much older town of Salem. Their parade included both a regiment of young boys dressed as Continentalers and a division with floats designed to show contrasts between past and present. Not surprisingly, the chosen topics included the schoolhouse, shoemaking, marketing, a quilting party, spinning, and other domestic employments. Members of families who had lived in Danvers for generations searched trunks and attics for their ancestors' old clothing and made a few necessary repairs to the old carriages in their barns. On June 16, wearing an odd assortment of garments, they either walked in procession or rode in old vehicles pulled by ancient horses, no matter how emaciated or wobbly. A full-page illustration of their efforts published in the popular *Gleason's Pictorial Drawing Room Companion* (*see pages 214–215*) undoubtedly inspired many of the subsequent Antiques processions organized as commemorative occasions multiplied.

The Danvers people's intended honor to the past had an unanticipated result, however, as the old clothes, decrepit vehicles, and bony horses caused amusement among the crowds of spectators. As the 1850s progressed, the Antiques also became a regular fixture of the new satirical Fourth of July processions of Fantastics, Grotesques, or Horribles, which before long were known everywhere as the Antiques and Horribles or simply the Horribles, as they are usually referred to in this book.

Today the name Antiques and Horribles is frequently described by academic historians and in the popular press as having been inspired by the elaborate uniforms and public marching of Boston's venerable Ancient and Honorable Artillery Company, but no early evidence of that connection has been found. It seems the name Horribles reflected many popular parade traditions that merged well before 1876.

From their beginning Horribles parades were characterized by rowdy behavior, good-natured humor, gross exaggeration, and biting satire. Their dramatic use of gender and racial stereotypes mocked authority, current events, and social norms. As early as 1843, a group of Fantastics appeared at a Muster Day at Belfast, Maine. Among them were brave soldiers in "abominable looking dress" along with insulting and degrading characterizations "from the dingy blackamore, or copper Mohawk, to the pale dandy" giving the general impression that "scarce a class seemed without a representative."

Participants marched alone or in groups, rode in carts or on skeletal horses, acted in short skits, or tried to remain stationary on wobbling wagon beds. The topics presented were in all imaginable variety, both ancient and modern, serious and hilarious. No one was spared. Some of the popular features were characteristic of holiday traditions featuring misrule in England and on the Continent that date from medieval times. People impersonated historical figures, classical statues, and characters from Shakespearean plays, especially Falstaff and his rag-a-muffin army. Employing disreputable costume, masks, burnt cork, slovenly posture, and exaggerated gestures, Horribles poked fun at themselves at the same time that they ridiculed racial groups, women, men well known for their pompous attitudes and sense of self-importance, and politicians. One could always count on seeing Clowns, Harlequins, Indians, Punch and Judy, Giants, Tramps, a Fat Person, a Fool in a tall, pointed hat, and at least one animal or freak from Barnum's Museum among the Horribles. At Providence, Rhode Island, in 1858, a man wearing a "Cradle of Liberty on his back and Bunker Hill Monument on his head was sufficiently PATRIOTIC." By 1867 commercially made waxed gauze masks that ranged in price from five to fifteen cents offered anonymity and comic disguise. Masks and wigs of many colors and textures could help to transform anyone into "a Clown, a Negro, Punch or Judy, a Devil, or Fat Man, or a Chinaman."

Among the most popular hits, year after year, were those that used exaggeration and disguise as a form of political expression, questioning authority and challenging accepted social norms. Women's rights and suffrage advocates, drunken alcoholics, and temperance advocates were targeted for decades before the ratification of Constitutional amendments related to women's suffrage and Prohibition. Public improvements and new municipal building projects were often targeted for excess expenditure or graft. Police and fire departments, water commissioners, broken-down streetcars, unreliable railway timetables, local and national politicians, governmental officials, old-maid school teachers, deceptive traders selling watered-down milk, summer people, and the blue laws were always good for a laugh.

Timely topics might be featured just a year or two, only to be replaced by new ones. Men dressed in the "bold and laughable costume" of the Bloomer Girls in the 1850s. The Emperor of Japan appeared soon after Admiral Perry's successful visit in 1859. *Brigham Young and His 900 Wives* marched with the *Bungtown Invincibles* in New Bedford in 1859 and appeared elsewhere on foot or in covered wagons again and again all through the 1860s and 1870s. The long line of *Bummers* at Augusta, Maine, in 1865 included a representation of the capture of Jefferson Davis as well as the *Deacon's One Hoss Shay* with a cannon protruding through the roof. Men costumed as Oklahoma's Modoc Indians were seen in several Horribles parades while the Modoc War was raging in 1872–1873.

When a group at Lynn, Massachusetts, focused on local corruption in 1874 by hoisting a banner with the motto "No Bribes Taken and Equal Rights for All," some of them wore police uniforms and carried a rum bottle in one hand and a well-filled purse in the other. Horribles parades in the centennial year of 1876 saw both Boss Tweed and Queen Victoria along with the Pilgrims John Alden and Priscilla Mullins. "The Highly cultivated and most profound Building Committee of the Franklin County Courthouse" appeared at St. Albans, Vermont, in 1877 in a "Trundle-Bed with nursing bottle," drawn by forty-seven "Mudturtles with stand-up collars—latest style." Buffalo Bill was popular for years, while his Wild West Shows toured the country. Men appeared in aesthetic dress in 1881. Carrie Nation stormed along with her axe in 1902 at Gloucester, the Gold Dust Twins danced in the street at Orange, Massachusetts, in 1906, and Teddy Roosevelt's Rough Riders marched again in 1907. Comic book character Happy Hooligan appeared in many places in 1909. Radio personalities Amos and Andy arrived in their Fresh Air Taxi during the 1930s. Some of the topics were just good-natured joshing of well-known stereotypes like the codfish aristocracy, the hen-pecked husband, or the country cousin. Others, however, expressed political opinion and mocked ideas that threatened to disrupt the status quo, especially the smart-minded woman, the Bloomer Girl, the blue stocking, and the city slicker.

Although seldom, if ever, seen in other parts of the country, less than twenty-five years after the first of these processions stepped forth, the Antiques and Horribles were accepted as an integral part of Fourth of July celebrations in some, but not all New England cities and towns. Northern soldiers familiar with the idea carried their Horribles tradition into Union army camps during the Civil War where they clearly enjoyed poking fun at their own officers and suppliers as well as Confederates and local residents, especially Jefferson Davis and impoverished plantation owners. On Thanksgiving Day in 1862, members of the Massachusetts 5th and some other New England regiments held prisoner at New Bern, North Carolina, organized a mock dress parade in which the major appeared in an undress uniform of red flannel, which was probably his long underwear. Other men wore their clothes inside out and their haversacks on their heads. Several impersonated Falstaff and one made a side-splitting oration through the door of an army stove worn as a suit of armor. Further afield, New England missionaries in Hawaii presented parades of Antiques and Horribles there in 1867 and 1868, one featuring the "broom rangers."

Although parades of all kinds are usually described as having been "the best ever," when it comes to Horribles sometimes the whole thing falls flat. On a few occasions Horribles parades were criticized for being too short, too small, falling short of expectations, not entertaining, stale, or not as good as last year. At Portland, Maine, in 1898, the Fantastics were described "as a long line of young men and boys disguised in various ways, all of which fell far short of being funny. . . . The favorite costume was a ragged dress, and the popular method of transportation was a decrepit horse." In other words, the standard hits had become boring. Sometimes the satire went too far—hits were criticized for being too conspicuously partisan or personal or, on the contrary, so general that no one really understood the intention. Some presentations, especially those in blackface or featuring cross-dressing, often strengthened gender and racial discrimination instead of relieving social tension. No doubt those would be considered thoroughly offensive today.

Success depended on carefully thought-out presentations that were not mean-spirited, but readily understood by everyone and universally perceived as clever as well as funny. A good parade of Horribles was both ludicrous and entertaining, full of variety, and presented by a motley-looking crew of young and middle-aged white men who were acutely aware of contemporary culture. No doubt they had a wonderful time in planning, preparation, and presentation, expecting to fulfill their oft-expressed intention to astonish viewers and provide public amusement. They hoped to remain anonymous, disguised to such an extent that even their own mothers, wives, and children would not recognize them. Surprisingly, in some places the organizers and participants were not young working-class men, but the civic leaders, doctors, lawyers, newspaper editors, and others who held powerful positions in the community, men who rushed home or to a hotel afterward to remove street dirt and makeup, change their clothes, and find their place on the rostrum in time to lead the formal civic exercises, read the Declaration of Independence, or present the oration central to the day's official observance.

Enthusiasm for Horribles parades has ebbed and flowed over the years, not unlike that for traditional parades. Some are quickly thrown together from materials at hand, but a successful narrative presentation takes a lot of planning and hard work. Some features are expensive. Some places never skipped a year, but others paused occasionally when volunteers or funding were hard to obtain. Most often, groups of friends and neighbors worked together year after year to bring forth troops of Horribles on main streets or within neighborhoods, often relying on familiar stereotypes as well as the same old jokes and ratty old costumes, but almost always bringing forth at least a few screamingly funny new ideas and creative presentations.

New England's rowdy parades of Horribles continue in a few places, still providing an approved, municipally sanctioned stage for expression of discontent and political advocacy. Some of the presentations are truly disgusting, many are blatantly offensive, and nothing is politically correct. The hour is still early, the music is truly horrible, the participants proclaim they prefer anonymity, and at least one of the floats falls apart before it is all over. No matter, they always find an enthusiastic and appreciative audience.

Horribles now appear on the Fourth of July in New England towns ranging from Foster, Rhode Island, and others just south of Boston, to places as far Down East as Eastport, Maine. A strong Horribles tradition exists today in Nahant, Peabody, Salem, Beverly Farms, Manchester-by-the-Sea, and Gloucester, Massachusetts, among others, while upright citizens living as few as ten miles away may say that they've never heard of such a thing. Nationally, and even in New England, many people are totally unaware of it. For such an outrageous and visually powerful act of social criticism to remain largely unknown after 175 years is truly astonishing.

Again they come, the brave 'Antiques'
And 'Horribles,' with dress unique!
Of every style and every hue,
And many 'rigs" entirely new.
In vain may Fancy ever try,
Her present effort to out vie!
. . . patient toil and practice hard,
Now meets a sure, deservd reward;
Still by the same old leader led,
It proudly standeth at the head!

The Kite-Ender, Lynn, Massachusetts, July 4, 1874[8]

Antique Procession

Danvers, Massachusetts, June 16, 1852

The old clothes brought forth and worn by people in Danvers and other New England towns for celebratory processions in the nineteenth century often dated from the time of the American Revolution (*see following pages*). In the 1850s, these cocked hats, knee breeches, and flowing wigs were only seventy-five years old, garments once the military uniforms or everyday garb of grandfathers and great grandfathers. In contrast, judging by this illustration and many others, the clothing worn by most of the women who rode along was not so old; their flowing skirts and huge bonnets probably had been worn by their mothers and the styles were not far from those of the current day. Or, perhaps these huge bonnets conceal male faces at a time when some considered it unseemly for women to participate in public events of this kind. We simply don't know.

Parade ribbon badge

Hingham, Massachusetts, February 15, 1855

Ensign Jeheil Stebbings of Spunkville, more frequently known as Jeheil Stebbins, was a fictional character publicized by Benjamin Shillaber, editor of the *Boston Post* and *The Carpet Bag*, the latter a short-lived Boston humor magazine. In 1852 Stebbins was promoted as a candidate for president by the *Post*. (*see page 216*)

Ostensibly a hero of the bloodless 1839 Aroostook War concerning the northern boundary of the United States between Maine and Canada, Stebbins reportedly

GOV. ENDICOTT'S
DESCENDANTS
INDUSTRY WILL PROSPER

appeared in a satirical parade at Boston in 1851, riding on a buffalo, bearing the stars and stripes, and displaying the motto "Our Country and nothing else."

This hoax was a perfect subject for New England's parades of Antiques and Horribles, where mockery of the old militia system and politicians of every stripe were popular with men whose stated goal was mainly to have a good time. Stebbins was featured in many Horribles parades in the 1850s, even riding on a donkey at Providence in 1858. Nowhere was he more prominent than at Hingham, Massachusetts, where long speeches attributed to him were published in the *Spunkville Chronicle* and he reportedly appeared in parades as leader of the Stebbins Life Guards or the Spunkville Invincibles. At Hingham in 1854, "Colonel Stebbins" was promoted as a candidate for president of the United States, as well as reported to have been presented with an engraved silver tea service in gratitude for his leadership. Four years later he was reputed to have been the subject of a statue seven feet tall with a head cast from that of the "editor of the *Boston Herald*, Job Sass."

Although reports of Stebbins' activities faded away during the Civil War, the Stebbins Light Guard reportedly marched again at Hingham on July 4, 1876, a good joke that was part of the celebration of an Old-Time Fourth on the occasion of the nation's centennial. All of these reports were completely bogus, composed and published by newspaper men in Boston and Hingham.

4th of July

Keene, New Hampshire, July 4, ca. 1872–1876

On the Fourth of July, sometime between 1872 and 1876, Keene's well-known photographer J. A. French mounted the newly erected "music stand" in Central Square carrying his stereographic camera with double lenses. From that elevated vantage point, he was able to capture this image of a large crowd of men wearing masks and an assortment of mismatched and patched rag-tag garments. The rowdy bunch gathered on the west side of the Square in front of the Ashuelot Bank was undoubtedly an assembly of Antiques and Horribles but it seems impossible to determine the exact date.

In 1875, the *Cheshire Republican* reported on July 10 that the Fourth had been celebrated in Keene "principally by a procession of Ancients and Horribles in the forenoon, . . . [which] was quite a success in point of extent and the absurd grotesqueness of the costumes and equipages . . . the crowd of spectators which filled the streets to witness it was very large, not only comprising all kinds of Keene people, but a large contribution of humanity from the neighboring towns."

Usually, the Fourth of July crowd at Keene assembled near what is now known as the bandstand at midday for formal exercises that included musical selections, a reading of the Declaration of Independence, and a patriotic oration. Sometimes, they also gathered again at some point to hear one of the Horribles deliver a long address like that described in 1875 as having been "in keeping with the company and occasion" and in 1876 as delivered by "the Great Unknown." Undoubtedly, once the Horrible orator mounted to the podium, people drew near to hear his outrageous jokes, heckle him, and cheer those who were awarded prizes for their horrible contributions to the festivities.

A Company of Horribles

Stoddard, New Hampshire, July 4, ca. 1866–1868

Most companies of Horribles were organized by young men, but in Stoddard, New Hampshire, in 1866 and 1870, it was a woman, Sarah Gerould Blodget, who partnered with her neighbor, John Nelson Jr., to enlist the participants and gather the masks and costumes in which they would march on the Fourth of July. Here they stand in the stable yard behind Nelson's store in the center of the village. At the left, a small band in street clothes carries two drums, two clarinets, an ophicleide, and a couple of tin horns. In the front row, three of the men carry swords, one as long as that carried for decades by Colonel Pluck. They are wearing old militia

uniforms, perhaps those once worn by their fathers or grandfathers as members of the Stoddard Fleetwoods or the local Grenadiers. Two wear plumed militia caps and the third stands tall under a chapeau de bras. They are joined by others, many wearing masks and all of them in worn and decrepit, probably dirty, clothing. One man has stuffed a pillow of some sort under his long coat to form a huge belly, but since he is not wearing women's clothing, he is not mocking pregnancy. At the right of the line, a young boy tightly clasps a man's hand, perhaps seeking confidence from his father. At the extreme right, people dressed as a couple with their baby are seated in a one horse chaise with the top folded down and a thin, bony horse harnessed in front.

Because the two flags or banners are moving in a light breeze, we cannot read their message, but the stationary banner with a graphic image of a lynching is hard to miss. No records of lynchings in New Hampshire at this date have been found, but the image is a powerful statement of white supremacy, at once reassuring to whites and terrifying to Blacks.

The Fantastics

Bryant Pond, Maine, possibly July 4, 1875

Writing about Saturday morning, July 4, 1875, in the very small town of Bryant Pond, Maine, a newspaper reporter noted that "the day opened pleasantly with the usual demonstrations from the Boys. The Fantastics were out in full force at the hour appointed and created quite a sensation. Their comic dresses and grotesque appearance added much to the hilarity of the day." If this is truly they, the group was not large, but, the straw-stuffed figure of a female giant and abundance of masked characters are typical of processions of Horribles and Fantastics all over New England at that time. The couple "Bound for the Black Hills" appears to have packed all of their worldly goods into a chaise with wheels of two different sizes; they will have a wobbly trip, but their hit was timely. Gold had been discovered in the Black Hills of South Dakota in 1874 and the rush was on.

Parade of the "Antiques and Horribles"

Charlestown, Massachusetts, June 17, 1875

Very early in the morning on June 17, 1875, crowds of excited people from throughout the Greater Boston area began to move toward Charlestown on foot, in carriages and horse-drawn omnibuses, or by railroad. Anticipation of the centennial commemoration of the Battle of Bunker Hill was intense and many people had stayed up all night in order to reserve a spot along the sidewalk in order to see the first event of the day, a procession of Charlestown's renowned Antiques and Horribles. People who had worked for weeks, or even months, to prepare the costumes, vehicles, and displays for the procession were busy with finishing touches. Groups from nearby Chelsea, Lynn, Everett, and Nahant hurried to find their places. At 5:00 a.m., right on time, the line began to move with bands deliberately playing out of tune, tin horns wailing, and drums beating irregular cadence. The early morning procession was described in the *New York Times* as "not only the first, but the most enjoyable feature of the day . . . greeted everywhere with laughter and applause." This illustration from *Frank Leslie's Illustrated Newspaper* gives us a sense of how it all looked with the line moving below swirling flags and pennants and the excited spectators crowded on sidewalks as well as in windows and balconies overlooking the festive street.

First in view was a very stern-looking masked "woman" driving a horse-drawn tumbril, the kind of dump cart used during the French Revolution to carry condemned prisoners to their death on the guillotine. In New England such a vehicle was more commonly used by farmers to carry manure to their distant fields. Within the cart a tall-hatted man in formal dress accompanied a group of smiling and waving men wearing frilled feminine caps and masks painted with handlebar moustaches. They were escorted by a man in a fat suit and a fire helmet carrying a very long sword like that carried by Colonel Pluck, which was clearly marked "The Sword of Bunker Hill." Immediately following the cart, a band struck up their miserable music on extremely long horns, a tuba, and numerous ophicleides. The musicians wore matching costumes composed of masculine masks, straw hats, and long, curled feminine wigs of blonde hair, as well as matching knee-length striped summer dresses with bustles, striped stockings, and pointy-toed shoes.

At the time, the most successful things in these processions were said to have been those that brought to life familiar images from popular magazines like *Harper's Weekly* or *Leslie's.* Sure enough, the long parade of *Ancient Antiques and Horribles* headed toward Bunker Hill included items featured in recent issues, including Black Hill Gold Miners, a woman suffragist proving "the superiority of the feminine intellect to that of the tyrant man," and musicians in aesthetic dress. Third in line was a four-wheeled passenger wagon

WOODHULL
FREE LOVERS
THE SWORD OF BUNKER HILL

escorted by a devil and a skeleton, each mounted on horseback. The canopy of the wagon presented the slogan "Woodhull Free Lovers," referencing continuing public interest in Victoria Woodhull, the first American woman to run for president of the United States. Her unsuccessful candidacy representing the Equal Rights Party, three years earlier in 1872, advocated an eight-hour workday, a graduated income tax, social welfare programs, and free love. Woodhull had gained additional notoriety when she was arrested for publishing obscene literature, specifically the story of Brooklyn preacher Henry Ward Beecher's notorious affair with his parishioner, Mrs. Thomas W. Tilton. Not surprisingly, the 1875 Charlestown procession concluded with men representing both the Reverend Mr. Beecher and Mrs. Tilton, who "came on expressly from Brooklyn to join in the occasion's festivities."

We may wonder why the Horribles tradition developed in conjunction with commemoration of significant historical events like the Battle of Bunker Hill or the celebration of patriotic holidays like the Fourth of July. Indeed, some people still wonder the same thing as the annual cycle of holidays rolls by and the Horribles emerge in all their ridiculous glory.

Horribles. July 4, 1876.
Kilburn Brothers, Littleton, New Hampshire

A masked driver, one passenger in blackface, and another in a donkey mask are all ready to depart for a parade of Horribles on the Fourth of July in the nation's centennial year. Their flag-crowned horse will not have an easy time pulling the old cart that has been fitted with one wheel larger than the other. There is no question that the men are hoping to remain anonymous and get some laughs with their wobbly ride.

Fourth of July, ca. 1886

Alfred Cornelius Howland, oil on canvas, ca. 1886. High Museum, Atlanta, Georgia.

Ever since it was shown at the 1893 World's Columbian Exposition at Chicago, where it could have been seen by as many as twenty-seven million people, this painting has been heralded as a perfect picture of a patriotic holiday in small-town America (*see previous page*). Alfred Howland depicted marching musicians, soldiers, and patriotic citizens cheered by a lively group of little boys under the stately elms on the Town Common in the picturesque Connecticut River Valley town of Walpole, New Hampshire, on the Fourth of July. But look closely at the details: men wearing a variety of tattered old uniforms, minimal music, an old chaise drawn by a skeletal horse, and a man dressed as an "Indian Squaw."

Walpole's first parade of Horribles, on July 4, 1874, was described on July 9 by the *Sentinel* in nearby Keene in a way that suggests a very different interpretation for Howland's painting. At Walpole, the "variety of horribleness included a dilapidated, hospitable 'one hoss shay,' . . . Mr. Blodgett, dressed as a strong-minded woman and bearing a banner, 'Woman's Rights' riding on an ox, an Indian on horseback, and a full complement of military characters. . . . Old and emaciated horses, rickety vehicles, different styles of garments worn by the members of the troop, the fragments of old uniforms, long gone by, the tattered suits covered with many-colored patches, and the dilapidated teams with their more dilapidated occupants." It seems clear that Howland's beautiful, but deceptive, painting distilled the elements of one of New England's parades of Horribles in a way that illustrates patriotism, but also targets Yankee frugality, economic woes, racism, pompous soldiers, governmental officials, and concerns about women's rights. Walpole is a small New Hampshire town in the Upper Connecticut River Valley, a long way from Boston, but its citizens were well aware of contemporary issues and they had no problem expressing their concerns in this dramatic fashion on America's great holiday.

Roswell Blanchard (1829–1887)

Probably Walpole, New Hampshire, 1876

Roswell Blanchard was one of the men who posed for Alfred Howland's painting of the Fourth of July procession in Walpole. We can be sure that he had no trouble deciding what to wear, for this tintype shows him in his usual Horribles costume of loose trousers and a long-tailed shirt along with a tall hat featuring a face with a long, hooked nose. Blanchard's outlandish dress and tall, unlit torch help to confirm the understanding that Howland's painting actually illustrates a Horribles parade in Walpole rather than an idealized civic procession.

THE DARKTOWN FIRE COMPANY

Between 1884 and 1894, Currier & Ives published over seven thousand different scenes as prints that were often framed and displayed in middle-class homes or in public spaces like taverns and fire houses. The most popular sold as many as seventy-three thousand copies, carrying the images and ideas to wide audiences. These images reflect American scenery and romanticize local cultures as well as popular activities and attitudes. A small percentage of the total satirized Irish and Italian immigrant traditions or political activity. Among the best-selling were those in the Darktown series, which presented racist stereotypes of minstrel shows or of happy Blacks imitating "white folks' ways," playing football and baseball or attending horse races. A number of Darktown prints focused on narrative scenes of firefighting, showing uniformed men fumbling with their equipment, arriving too late, or ignoring the instructions of officials. The men were depicted as physically grotesque, dishonest, sly, or demonstrating low intelligence. Not surprisingly, the action-packed Darktown firefighting scenes became popular topics for blackface presentations in parades of Antiques and Horribles until recent years when their ugly racism is no longer acceptable.

Darktown Fire Brigade at the Conclusion of the Calithumpian and Horribles Parade
Concord, New Hampshire, July 4, 1891

Eighty members of the Concord, New Hampshire, fire department, wearing their traditional red shirts with blue trousers and white helmets, all of them in blackface, brought to life their own version of the bumbling firemen illustrated in Currier & Ives' popular prints of the Darktown Fire Brigade in this grand prize–winning feature of the city's Calithumpian and Horribles Parade on July 4, 1891. The center of attention was this wheeled hotel, a ramshackle building with smoke emerging from the siding. It was covered with suggestive inscriptions such as "Baths with soap 50 cts.," "Female help only," and "In case of Fire follow Red lights." The men paused twice during the march to send water cascading down on spectators and the police as well as the smoky building. This picture captures the moment at the end of the parade when they offered a bit of street theater after stopping in front of the New Hampshire State House. The hotel was removed from its sledge, placed on the pavement, and set on fire. Company members then tried all manner of ridiculous strategies to quell the flames. Several men held an outsized white balloon hose from which trickled only a weak stream of water while a skillful tillerman guided an improvised horse-drawn ladder truck into place beside the burning building. Although they worked valiantly for over an hour, their efforts were ineffectual. The entire building, the white hose, and all the ladders of the firemen were burnt to ashes as laughing spectators stood by. The men were awarded both the first prize of $30.00 and an additional special grand prize of $50.00 for their detailed preparation and vigorous efforts.

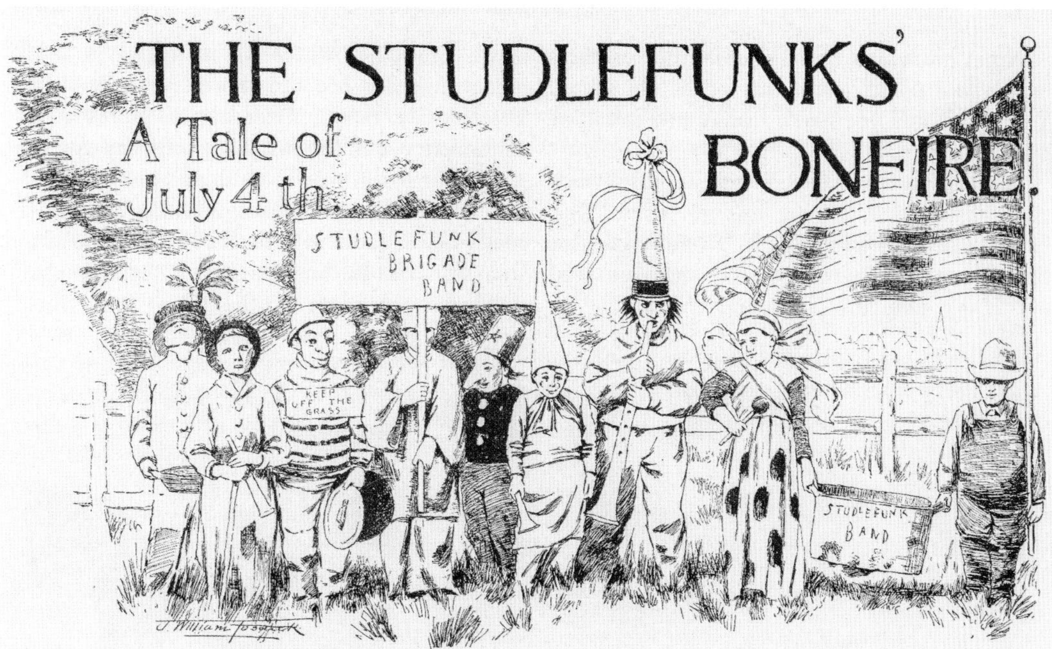

The Studlefunks' Brigade Band—A Tale of July 4th
Illustration from St. Nicholas, an Illustrated Magazine for Young Folks, 1894

Beginning in 1872 and continuing for at least fifty years, highly entertaining parades of "Studlefunks" appeared on the Fourth of July at Worcester and nearby towns. In many ways they were similar to processions of Antiques, Burlesques, Fantastics, and Horribles elsewhere, but the Studlefunks were usually praised for their avoidance of "a certain coarseness" that appeared in many of the others.

Led by yet another fictitious military character, Brigadier General Simon Studlefunk, the line of march included burlesque military units, flying artillery, and a drum major ten feet tall who wore a feather duster as a cockade atop his tall hat. Their hits in 1872 included Victoria Woodhull and Henry Ward Beecher as well as a tribe of "Indians, Hiawatha, Minnehaha, and the other hahas," local politicians, and a sewer construction project. In 1892, both "Colonel Hard Tack and an outrider wore Indian masks" and it took a "motorman, conductor, and carpenter" along with numerous passengers to keep an electric trolley car on the tracks of the "Boaster, Blister, & Spent All Road."

Studlefunk parades seem to have been particularly impressive, for when the phenomenon spread to several nearby towns, the Worcester originators offered to issue copyrights on certain popular characters. In 1894, the children's magazine, *St. Nicholas,* published a story about the activities and misadventures of an imitative *Studlefunk Brigade* organized by a group of boys in rural Worcester County. The illustration on the masthead (*above*) shows their masked characters, typical of those in any parade of Horribles—the discordant musicians, the clown, the fool, the soldier, and the well-fed farm boy standing in his overalls and straw hat as his flag billows in the breeze.

The Bedford Simplex

Bedford, Massachusetts, 1904

This extraordinary vehicle was featured in the Horribles section of the 125th Anniversary parade at Bedford. Although signs proclaim it to be a "Bedford Simplex, The Car That Will Climb (DOWN) Any Hill. Ask the Grocerman," the vehicle has no internal source of power. Its extended body is suspended over four large wagon wheels, and a long tow rope is coiled beneath a large light or horn on the hood. The driver holds a simulated gear shift as he sits behind a steering wheel located on the right-hand side of the car, in what is now the English manner. A wooden frame fitted with side curtains and trimmed with a little bunting encloses the seats on which sit three couples ready to enjoy their ride. Actually, they may have had to walk the car forward, for how it moved through the streets is otherwise unclear.

Calithumpian Band

Location unknown, ca. 1900–1910

These thirteen men wearing masks, blackface, and a few huge false noses identified themselves as a Calithumpian band when they lined up for a photograph before making a lot of noise with fifes, triangles, horns, a tambourine, a snare drum, and a few unique homemade instruments in a Horribles procession. Their scraggly clothing adorned with colorful patches, fluttering ribbons, and shiny metal discs certainly attracted attention, but not one of them represents an identifiable character.

Raucous, discordant Calithumpian music had its roots in early eighteenth-century England and was first seen in America during the 1830s. The tunes were nothing but noisy and, as for the instruments, anything goes.

Horrible Musicians

Andover, Massachusetts, 1909–1914

It must have taken many days to convert this two-wheeled cart into such an impressive entry for a parade of Horribles sometime in the early 1920s. The wheels were embellished with logs and a metal coffee pot, the hood of a wicker baby carriage has been attached at the rear with an umbrella unfurled over it, and a long pole, almost like a rudder, extends forward to the hand of a masked clown. Next to him the masked driver in a silly hat holds a single thin rope, which may have enabled him to direct the donkey they expect to pull them through the streets of Andover, Massachusetts. The two men sit behind a bank of curved pipes embellished with ropes, a drum head, and numerous metal vessels. The clown seems to sit behind a mounted whistle, and he holds a short metal rod with which he might be about to beat a rhythm to add to the clanking of the various tin cans and old pots hanging around them. At some point, someone had to draw on the tight-fitting pant legs at the rear of the donkey, harness him, hitch him to the cart, and figure out how to secure his hat. If we only knew the year the picture was taken, we might be able to find out if they won a prize. They certainly deserved it!

Columbus Day

Barre, Vermont, October 12, 1911

In an inspired version of "Every Man for Himself," these five people chose a variety of costume elements when they prepared to ride as a troupe of Horribles in the Columbus Day parade at Barre in 1912. Wearing wigs, masks, hats, devil's horns, a parasol, a union suit, and a truly admirable donkey head, their characterizations are as hard to discern as their personal identity.

Their open touring car was a 1906 Nash Rambler equipped with right-hand drive. They were certainly well prepared for travel on the muddy road, for there is a strong tow-rope coiled in front of the radiator. Below it a whiffletree hangs ready in case horsepower would be required to pull the vehicle out of a ditch or a deep puddle.

A Couple of Horribles

Portland, Maine, July 5, 1920

Part of the official program for the Maine centennial celebration at Portland on Monday, July 5, 1920 was a parade of Horribles and Antiques. Prizes were offered in a variety of categories, including the "Best Couple," "Most Original Costume," and "Funniest Female." We have to wonder if this couple qualified for all three with their mismatched shoes, blank-faced masks, and miscellaneous old clothes. Apparently the woman was inspired to display real antiques, not only with her hoop skirt and tattered parasol, but also with a small antique clock hanging from a ribbon around her neck.

Parade of Horribles

Augusta, Maine, July 4, 1929

Not to be denied participation in New England's traditional Fourth of July festivity, tuberculosis patients who were not bedridden at the Western Maine Sanatorium in Augusta used materials at hand to create an array of fantastical costumes and an elephant for their own parade of Horribles on July 4, 1929.

Truly Horrible

Andover, Massachusetts, ca. 1930–1935

By 1930, some of the floats in New England's distinctive parades of Horribles had lost their focus, and this horse-drawn wagon loaded with old washtubs and buckets, tin cans, a 1915 Massachusetts license plate, a washboard, and a burned-out teakettle can only be described as truly horrible. The teetering load was embellished with cloth streamers in many different colors and topped by a broken umbrella and a chamber pot. A tiny sprig of evergreen served as a crowning touch. Two masked men peered out with interest as the driver smoked a fat cigar. Both he and the horse wore old hats, while a fringed table runner was fashioned into a sort of bib for the horse. Undoubtedly, this impressive pile of junk attracted plenty of attention as it creaked and rattled along the streets, but here it is only the children who are looking intently; the two smartly dressed women appear more interested in their conversation with each other.

Floral and Coaching Parades

The 1880s saw several new kinds of parades that were more ornamental than patriotic. These events usually marked the end of the summer season in mountain villages or seaside towns where there were expansive summer hotels or large colonies of seasonal residents. The beauty and creativity of these parades almost immediately inspired floral parades and festivals in Santa Barbara, California; Saratoga Springs, New York; Newport, Rhode Island, and elsewhere. In some places, these beautiful and extravagant events are popular again today.

The simplest of the new summertime parades consisted of private carriages owned by upper-class women who ornamented them with greenery and blossoms from private gardens or nearby meadows. Sometimes the women chose dresses in colors that would coordinate with the large bouquets they carried and trimmed their large hats with even more flowers. Although some drove their own carriages, others chose to be driven by their usual uniformed grooms or chauffeurs. A few sent their children off in decorated carriages that were both driven and supervised by governesses.

Some of the grooms and drivers moved seasonally from city to country along with cooks, governesses, housekeepers, and other members of the live-in household staff. In many households, local people were hired annually to augment the servant corps as laundresses, maids, gardeners, or stable hands. Although most indoor servants were white women, it was not unusual for urban grooms and coach drivers to be Black men. Traditionally, all those who cared for the horses and carriages were housed separately in rooms within the stables or coach houses, while indoor help shared rooms in the main house.

Tub Parade

Lenox, Massachusetts, September 22, 1886

As early as 1886, floral parades organized by summer residents in wealthy summer communities like Bar Harbor, Maine; Newport, Rhode Island; and Lenox, Massachusetts, had evolved into a special format in which adult women drove single horses pulling two-wheeled carts that were lavishly ornamented with garlands of greenery and flowers. In Lenox, the vehicles were called "tubs."

Although other towns in the area had similar events, *Harper's* proclaimed the one in Lenox the leading tub parade of the area. Held annually from 1883, these parades marked the end of summer and celebrated the beginning of the fashionable fall social season in Lenox until shortly after World War I. In 1990, the tub parade was revived in Lenox as a tribute to a bygone era and it continues to this day.

A Most Beautiful Tub

Lenox, Massachusetts, 1894

Bostonian Marian Lawrence Peabody's description of a summertime event observed at Bar Harbor when she was a girl is well illustrated by this image of a lady and her groom preparing for a tub parade at Lenox, in 1894:

"Those were the great days of the flower parades—of ladies driving their own phaetons completely covered with flowers, from the horse's ears to the groom's seat at the back—including the lady herself who wore a dress to match or contrast with the flowers she had chosen for decoration."[9]

Isabella D. Williams with her Coachman, Frank Joy, with his Two Sons

Northampton, Massachusetts, June 7, 1904

Enthusiasm for displays of lavishly decorated carriages continued, and extended to a growing number of automobiles at the turn of the century. Parade planners at Northampton made sure to include both in their anniversary celebration in 1904. The first division included fourteen decorated private carriages while the sixth division at the end of the line was devoted exclusively to twenty-one decorated automobiles, some driven by chauffeurs and others by their owners, all of whom were men.

Henry and Isabella Williams, who lived in this house at 76 Bridge Street, were actively involved in planning and preparing for the Meadow City's semicentennial celebration, serving on committees, decorating their property with flags and bunting, and opening their doors to local dignitaries and family members from Boston. A prosperous business man and civic leader, Williams mounted his favorite mare shortly before eight o'clock on parade day to take his place as marshal of the first division, leading a group of dignitaries ranging from the governor to the oldest lady living in Northampton, all riding in carriages.

Before leaving home to join him in the first division, Mrs. Williams posed for this picture in their two-seated brake, which had been decorated with the same white paper roses and green leaves that adorned their handsome pair of black horses. The driver was Frank Joy, the Williams's regular coachman. The presence of Joy's young sons, Frank and Charles, on the driver's seat reflects a close relationship between the Williams family and their servants. Undoubtedly, the boys were excited to be objects of attention as they rode near the beginning of the long line, but also thrilled by the music of the marching bands and the opportunity to be close to the handsome floats.

We might infer that Mr. Williams may have been specially interested in coaching, since a "brake" is a vehicle used for training horses in preparation for driving large coaches. The open door of the carriage house at the left of the dwelling gives no indication of his involvment in such a hobby, but there may have also been a larger barn on the property to accommodate additional horses and the larger vehicles.

COACHING PARADES

In New Hampshire's White Mountain towns, primarily Bethlehem and North Conway, a different ornamental parade tradition evolved at this time. Guests at huge summer hotels in the area often arrived by train and stayed for a month or more, savoring a respite from the heat of cities, enjoying healthful mountain air, abundant "home-cooked" food, and a host of planned activities. The hotels owned large stagecoaches and solid carryalls which they used to transport guests and their voluminous luggage to and from railroad stations as well as for sightseeing excursions to view scenic vistas, roaring waterfalls, and other picturesque features of the mountain landscape.

Since late August in the White Mountains can be decidedly chilly, hotel owners developed novel and exciting activities to entice their guests to stay longer and extend the season. Most impressive were the elaborate parades of decorated stagecoaches and mountain wagons that competed for prizes during the last week of August beginning in 1887. Nationwide newspaper publicity served to advertise the beauties of the White Mountains and swell the number of guests throughout the season.

As we have seen, coaching was a favored activity of the very wealthy at this period, but, of course, it was expensive to own and maintain a team of horses, coaches, grooms, and stable hands. Patrons of most of the White Mountain summer hotels were generally middle-class people of more modest means, but participation in the extravagant hotel parades gave them their own distinctive way of participating in the current craze.

Parade Day showing the Sinclair Hotel

Bethlehem, New Hampshire, August 29, 1891

Planning and preparing the decorations for parade day was a collaborative effort. Local committee members and hotel guests worked together for weeks to create thousands of tissue paper flowers, crepe paper ornaments, special costumes, huge arches, and painted decorations to illustrate a theme, win a prize, and impress the spectators. Inevitably a strong and competitive team spirit developed at each hotel and guests turned out on parade day to join local citizens and day-trippers and to cheer their favorite.

The decorated coaches in the White Mountain parades reflected many of the same ideas that had been illustrated in parades throughout the nineteenth century. There were scenes from literature, history, and mythology as well as depictions of morning and night, the muses, or the seasons. Groups of young women rode on top of some coaches, sometimes singing or shouting the songs or cheers of the individual hotels. One year the list of prizes to be awarded included one for the hotel with the "prettiest load of the fair sex." Clearly that was a huge mistake, for it generated jealousy, complaints of unfairness, and all kinds of hard feelings. Not surprisingly, in subsequent years the prize categories were limited to less controversial ideas such as the best float, the finest horses, the liveliest spirit, the greatest distance traveled to participate.

A Gorgeous Oriental Vehicle

North Conway, New Hampshire, August 9, 1894

In 1894, this *Gorgeous Oriental Vehicle,* entered by the Kearsarge House in the East Side Parade at North Conway won the first prize for a decorated coach. Described in the *Portland Daily Press,* as "a dazzling glimpse of the Orient, a luxurious representation of the wealth of the East, combined with American arts in arrangement," a golden canopy five feet high had been built on top of an old stagecoach. Teetering above that, a gilded onion dome reached another four feet into the air. The rumble seat behind was decorated like a harem in which reclined a woman identified as the "Sultan's favorite." Veiled women in Turkish costume rode in the canopy, some reclining on pieces of oriental embroidery or tiger skins as they scattered flowers among the crowd. An account in the Worcester, Massachusetts, *Daily Spy,* indicated that the decorations of this one coach cost over two thousand dollars, but does not indicate whether the hotel or the guests paid the bill. Someone, however, was willing to pay whatever it cost to capture the prize.

Empire Bridal Coach

North Conway, New Hampshire, August 9, 1894

The second prize winner in the same parade at North Conway was this *Empire Bridal Coach* entered by the Wentworth Hall Hotel, which still operates in nearby Jackson. Declared "a model of grace, beauty, and artistic decoration," the coach was decorated with pink, white, and silver crepe paper, gauze, and satin along with silver and pink butterflies, silver rain [tinsel], and ten thousand paper roses made by hotel guests with plenty of time on their hands. This "superb creation" drawn by six milk-white horses carried women dressed as a bride and her attendants, all in white with silver and pink accessories. One might wonder if the local stage driver enjoyed wearing a white wig and an eighteenth-century-style costume of white satin and silver trimmed with pink ribbons.

Cleopatra's Barge

North Conway, New Hampshire, August 9, 1894

This elaborate representation of *Cleopatra's Barge* was sent by railroad from Portland, Maine, to North Conway to appear in the 1894 coaching parade and represent the Casco Bay Steamship Company. On its arrival, the barge was placed on a horse-drawn float painted by a Boston scenic artist to resemble water. Eight oarsmen and eighteen young ladies in "Grecian costume" rode in the barge with Cleopatra reclining in the bow. The float was intended as a gesture of appreciation to the Maine Central Railroad, which carried many tourists between Portland and North Conway each summer.

Queen Mab

Greenfield, Massachusetts, 1897

If you think the elaborate floats concocted by the guests of White Mountain hotels in the 1890s are somewhere beyond fanciful, consider this confection created in Greenfield, Massachusetts, for a coaching parade of the Franklin County Agricultural Society in 1897! While most processions at agricultural fairs featured displays of farming equipment, livestock, and vegetables, parade planners in Greenfield decided to imitate the splendor and imagination of the recent parades of decorated coaches at Saratoga Springs, New York, which, in turn, had been inspired by those in the White Mountain resort towns.

The entries at Greenfield included another representation of Cleopatra's Barge, a fairy riding a bicycle, and this delightful representation of Queen Mab. Riding in a shell chariot pulled by two plumed white horses, she grasped ribbons held by six gauze butterflies that appeared to be pulling her forward. Known as the Queen of the Fairies in English folklore, Queen Mab also appears somewhat salaciously in Shakespeare's *Romeo and Juliet* as a symbol of freedom, a woman having the power to deliver men their most secret wishes.

Decorated Coach with Ladies

West Boylston, Massachusetts, July 16, 1908

These young ladies in Oakdale, Massachusetts, were able to commandeer an old stagecoach for their parade entry in the centennial celebration at nearby West Boylston in 1908. They covered the coach and its wheels in shirred white crepe paper and outlined the body of the coach as well as the windows and doors with pink crepe paper flowers and leaves. Carrying parasols and dressed in summer white, they rode atop the coach as it was escorted by at least one mounted groom clad in white. The simple design and long hours of work by the Oakdale ladies won them the second prize in the category of "a four or six horse float or decorated coach." The idea was really nothing new, but clearly the judges were impressed by the coach with its top-heavy load. No doubt the excited ladies had a fine time planning, preparing, and participating in the celebration.

Winter Carnivals

Winter has always given people special opportunities for outdoor fun. During the Gay Nineties some cities and towns in northern New England organized winter carnivals that featured civic decorations and parades as well as bonfires, skating and snowshoe races, polo games on ice, figure skating demonstrations, the crowning of a snow king or queen, even the occasional ice castle. Owners of fine horses and expensive sleighs vied for the prizes awarded to the most beautiful turnout or the oldest sleigh. By the 1920s, dog sled races were introduced, and some people challenged each other to auto racing or driving trick cars on frozen lakes.

The winter parades followed the usual hierarchy of participants. Often, cash prizes were offered for the best or the largest teams, the most beautiful horses, the largest number of horses or oxen driven by one man, best team driven by a lady, best decorated sleighs, most comical team, participants coming from the longest distance, and, of course, for the concept and design of the floats. Among the topics presented were snow-covered scenes of hunting camps and rustic lodges surrounded by taxidermy specimens of woodland animals, literary scenes such as this "Court of the Storm King," as well as commercial displays of new kinds of furnaces, incandescent light bulbs, and electric streetlights. In several places, comic subjects filled the usual place of the Horribles, but the prizes offered in Concord, New Hampshire, in 1893 for the "best female personations" went unclaimed, since no one showed up in drag.

Subfreezing temperatures could be counted on in February and winter carnivals scheduled during that month continued to take place for many years. Even as funding for bands and elaborate prizes dried up during the Great Depression, the days and nights were cold, the sleighs were still in the barns, most people had warm winter clothing, and it didn't have to cost much to carry on the time-honored tradition. Editorial space in newspapers could be counted on to help attract a crowd and then report the event in detail, the lengthy accounts rewarding the participants one year and stimulating interest for the next.

Boston Heaters

Concord, New Hampshire, 1891

Remarkably, Concord, New Hampshire's first winter carnival was on a Wednesday. On February 4, 1891, even though the temperature was ten degrees below zero, the parade drew plenty of spectators. The line included a trades division in which many of the floats advertised seasonal products. Although any of Concord's four stove and furnace dealers might have entered a float mounted on a sled in the parade, it was Daniel L. Mandigo who showed these examples of the cooking ranges and hot air furnaces offered for sale in his shop at 9 Warren Street, corner of Main. One can't help but notice that there is no smoke coming from the chimney on the float, so it must have been painfully cold inside. It may have been Mr. Mandigo's own wife and daughter who stood there shivering in their heavy white capes and bonnets as they rode through the snowy streets. Fortunately, the little girl had a fur muff to keep her hands warm and there were heavy curtain panels that could have been drawn together to deflect the wind or if snow had begun to fall.

Darktown Fire Brigade

Capitol Street, passing behind the New Hampshire State House, Concord, New Hampshire, 1895

Presiding over Concord's winter carnival parade in February 1895 was King Momus, the Greek god of ridicule and satire. Not surprisingly, the line included a division for comical teams organized by men who certainly understood the concept of New England's Horribles parades. Their entries included a three-legged

policeman, Sitting Bull, Democratic president Grover Cleveland on a donkey, and the Agony Band. The first prize winner was this Darktown Fire Company, yet another interpretation of the racist prints made by Currier & Ives in the 1870s. The group of forty-one men from the nearby town of Hopkinton wore blackface and pinned round badges on their rag-tag costumes. Their equipment included an old hand tub and a sledge pulled by a young steer. The concept, their appearance, and their antics were considered by the *Concord Evening Monitor* to have been highly entertaining.

The Jolly Snowman

Manchester, New Hampshire, 1924

This float sponsored by the Manchester Traction, Light, and Power Company in the January 1924 Winter Carnival featured flags and four pretty girls in fashionable outdoor sportswear. They flanked a disc showing a jolly snowman that served as the logo for the event. This entry must have been placed near the end of the line, for there is little snow left on the pavement over which their runners scraped.

Winter Carnival float of the Amoskeag Manufacturing Company

Manchester, New Hampshire, 1924

Employees of various textile-making divisions of the massive Amoskeag Manufacturing Company at Manchester competed against each other for prizes in the annual winter carnivals in the city. In 1924, the Amoskeag Textile Club created this float with a Snow King seated opposite a ski jump, one lad with a Flexible Flyer, another seated on a toboggan, and four young women clad in fashionable ski sweaters, woolen knickers, and other winter gear. We see them in the millyard with four horses wearing heavy blankets as they wait for the signal to move.

Children's Parades

Children have always loved to mimic adult activities, so it is no surprise that they often form small, usually noisy, parades within their own neighborhoods. Depending on the amount of parental involvement, these efforts are met with varying degrees of success. Some attempt to copy the features of civic processions, complete with swirling flags, marching soldiers, musicians, costumes, and floats. Others feature decorated doll carriages, express wagons, or bicycles. Some are truly artistic and reflect many hours of careful preparation. In the best examples, the children wear costumes that illustrate broad themes or the idea behind their individual vehicle decorations. Others are more spontaneous with no more than a scraggly line of boys and girls waving flags and banging spoons on upturned pots and pans.

In 1924, the Playground and Recreation Association of America urged city recreation officers and playground managers to sponsor organized, competitive parades of doll carriages or decorated bicycles as part of their regular programming. The Association reported that these events became widely popular, reporting in their publication that even children "in the foreign section of the city" who had no doll carriages of their own participated by improvising with gaily decorated cardboard or wooden boxes mounted on wheels. Competition for the prize ribbons was intense on playgrounds everywhere.

Wigglesworth Family Parade

Cambridge, Massachusetts, July 4, 1890

It doesn't take much for even a few children to have a parade. In this example, (*see next page*) Miss Liberty waves two flags as she leads two girls with musical instruments, two carrying a banner, and two more dressed as firecrackers with a small group of followers in their Sunday best as they enjoy their very own parade on the Fourth of July in 1890. Standing by to keep order is a man in a police uniform.

Mayflower

Location unknown, 1904

While this may have been part of a sequence of historical floats, by 1904 the importance of the *Mayflower* as a symbol of New England's beginnings could stand alone in any parade. Somewhat surprisingly, in this parade celebrating the anniversary of a Sunday school, the one intrusive little brother and this group of girls attending their wheeled *Mayflower* are not dressed in stereotypical Pilgrim costumes. In all likelihood, however, any one of these children could have told the story of the landing of the Pilgrims, recited a portion of Longfellow's poem, "The Courtship of Miles Standish," or been part of a play depicting the first Thanksgiving at home, church, or school.

The Winners

Doll carriage parade, Portland, Maine, 1924

The three girls at the front of this long line were the prize winners at a doll carriage parade held at Deering Oaks, a park in Portland, Maine, on Saturday, August 30, 1924. Each received a large doll to honor her presentation. The winners were the girl with her carriage transformed into a swan (as suggested by a Dennison crepe paper craft booklet illustrated here), the center carriage and its owner both adorned with crepe paper roses, and the girl at the left in a Japanese-style kimono, with an umbrella and her doll, even though her carriage itself appears to be undecorated.

A Swan Carriage of Crepe Paper

Design from Dennison Manufacturing Company instructional booklet, 1923

Children's Parade Participants and Spectators

Charlestown, Massachusetts, June 17, 1937

Four little boys dressed as an American Indian, a baseball player, a delivery man, and a drum major stand beside a line of girls with crepe-paper decorated doll carriages, in front of a group of anxious mothers, as they wait to join the Bunker Hill Day parade on June 17, 1937. A red, white, and blue tradition that began during the Depression, the Bunker Hill Day Doll Carriage Parade continues to this day.

Decorated Tricycles

Kennebunk, Maine, 1930s

Two Indians, two clowns, and a paperboy lined up with their decorated tricycles for a children's parade at Kennebunk, Maine, sometime in the 1930s. None of these young boys was very skilled at winding crepe paper through the spokes of his vehicle, but they all seem proud of their efforts. The mothers of the two clowns outdid themselves with the costumes, but the balloons took one entry over the top.

7

ADVOCACY

Almost everyone in a parade is hopeful that both spectators and fellow participants will recognize their position in the line and their chosen identity. Many also hope that people will take action in response to a specific message. Politicians advocate for decisions about choice of party, candidate, or platform. Merchants, manufacturers, and professionals seek to influence expenditures on goods and services. Reformers draw attention to causes of conscience and use moral suasion to promote social change and the adoption of good habits such as temperance, abstinence, or heathy living. Philanthropists seek financial support and volunteers. At times of national emergency, the community is asked to prepare for the challenges ahead or to participate in the common defense. Inevitably, the reaction to social change is intense, and unfortunately it can be negative as well as positive. Some of these ideas are cyclical; others have their moment and then fade away.

Politics 1840–1872

Political processions have long been a familiar sight as people proclaim their allegiance to particular candidates and parties. When a presidential candidate arrives, or large numbers come from far and wide to assemble in convention, select candidates, and affirm a platform, the processions are the largest. Few of these events include floats, but large banners naming candidates and symbolizing key ideas are legion. Whether created by professional sign painters or enthusiastic volunteers, the powerful images and stirring slogans on painted banners carried through the streets are both impressive and influential. These deserve a much wider treatment, but the following selection may give an idea of the general appearance of political banners and daytime events in the years before the nation's centennial in 1876.

Whig Gathering, Song and Chorus Respectfully dedicated to the Whigs of the United States (detail)

Boston, Massachusetts, 1840

A small uniformed marching band leads a procession of Whigs through the cobbled streets of Boston's Dock Square in support of their 1840 presidential campaign. Instead of focusing on the popular log cabin and hard cider motifs of the 1840 Whig candidate William Henry Harrison that inspired the lyrics of this song, the artist Benjamin Champney has focused the cover image on a procession in the historic area of the city. The men are shown passing between the decrepit, nearly two-hundred-year-old building known as the Old Feather Store and Faneuil Hall with the new Quincy Market in the distant background. The first banner illustrates Faneuil Hall itself. Known even then as the "First Cradle of Liberty," in the 1770s the building had been the site of vigorous American protests against taxation without representation as well as influential speeches by patriots Samuel Adams, James Otis, and others.

A Challenge from Four Veterans

Kennebunk, Maine, July 4, 1840

The York County Whig celebration on July 4, 1840, was described as "unquestionably the largest political gathering ever before witnessed in Maine." This naïve but powerful painted banner carried that day by men identified as "Four Patriots of the Revolution" sought to convey an inspiring patriotic message to the younger generation. Clearly the banner was not painted by a professional artist and one cannot help but wonder who made the necessary edits to the text!

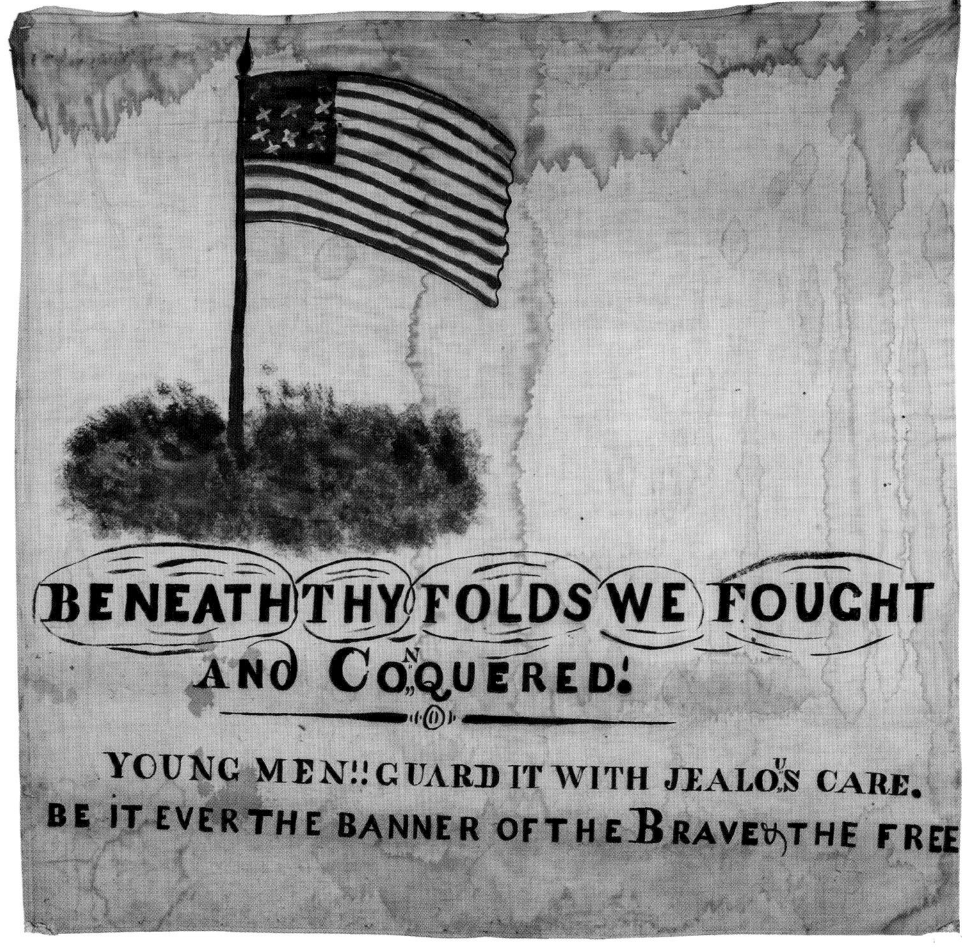

Whig Mass Meeting, Return of the Procession
Boston, Massachusetts, September 19, 1844

Four years later, anticipating another presidential election, thousands of Whigs from all over the country assembled in Boston on September 19 at nine o'clock in the morning to form a procession. Each ward, town, county, and state delegation was invited to carry a banner, many of which are visible here. Under the leadership of Josiah Quincy IV, the long procession wound through the oldest parts of the city, honoring sites associated with the birth of the nation

and pausing at the birthplaces or former residences of patriots Joseph Warren, Samuel Adams, John Hancock, Paul Revere, and Benjamin Franklin, the scene of the Boston Massacre, the sites of the Liberty Tree and Green Dragon Tavern, Faneuil Hall, "and all other spots where Whigs have contended for Liberty." After their return to the Boston Common, the weary men settled down on the ground between the Great Elm and the State House to hear long addresses by Daniel Webster and other distinquished Whigs, which continued until four in the afternoon. Although their presidential candidate, Henry Clay, opposed the expansion of slavery and the related issue of the annexation of Texas, he was defeated by Democrat James K. Polk in November, setting the stage for continuing controversy.

The banners legible in this image show that Whigs had come from Louisiana, Delaware, Kentucky, Ohio, North Carolina, Vermont, and "Old Plymouth" and "Old Essex" (both in Massachusetts). One banner proclaimed that "Liberty's Voice Calls Her Sons to New Life" and another that "Our Fathers Met At The Green Dragon To Oppose Tyranny." Many banners of this type were painted on silk. As a result they were fragile and not easily repurposed for use in support of another candidate in subsequent years. Not surprisingly, it seems that none of the Whig banners of 1844 exists today.

CIRCULATE THE DOCUMENTS.
YOUTH IS THE TIME FOR ACTION
THE CONSTITUTION AND THE LAWS!
NO ABUSE OF POWER.

No Abuse of Power—A Message for All Time
Boston, Massachusetts, 1848

A powerful political statement that is still relevant today, this banner of the Boston Young Men's Whig Club shows a professional man, possibly a lawyer, standing with a workman holding a carpenter's square, a tool used to create right angles and assure accurate measurement. Together they hold a scroll with long text titled "The Constitution and the Laws." Above them is a ribbon that proclaims: "Circulate the documents. Youth is the Time for Action." Most important is the statement beneath them: "NO ABUSE OF POWER." The other side of the banner proclaims "Our cause is just, our union is perfect." It is dated May 1, 1848, a time when potential presidential candidates and tensions over extending slavery to Western territories were being hotly debated in advance of the party's national convention in September.

Fremont and Lincoln campaign banner
Manchester, New Hampshire, 1856, reworked 1860

In 1856, some New Hampshire members of the newly formed Republican Party commissioned this banner to support their unsuccessful presidential candidate, General John C. Fremont, known then as "The Mustang Colt." The banner shows Fremont in uniform on a white horse while intercepting a

Augusta
DEPOT
Sept 6th 1872

wooden "Cincinnati Platform" on which his distraught opponent James Buchanan has fallen to his back in his attempt to reach the White House, toward which he appeared to be carried by four running Black men clad only in white breeches.

The amazing thing is that four years after Fremont lost the election, the banner was used again in 1860 by the same party, disregarding the imagery showing the uniformed equestrian General Fremont and the slaves carrying Buchanan. Apparently, a thrifty Yankee cut out an arc of stout white cotton and stenciled it with the new Republican slogan "Honest Old Abe is Bound to Win." Someone stitched that over the original words "The Mustang Colt is Bound to Win," which had been Fremont's 1856 slogan, and also the title of a campaign ditty sung to the tune of "Camptown Races."

Mottoes on the reverse of the banner were also updated in 1860 for the successful new candidates, replacing "Fremont and Liberty forever/ Buchanan and Slavery Never" with "Lincoln and Liberty Forever/ Breckinridge and Slavery Never." Apparently, no one was concerned that Lincoln, the humble rail-splitter, had never worn an officer's uniform like that depicted on Fremont, the rider shown heading for the White House in 1856 and still going in 1860.

Grant–Wilson Political Rally at the Augusta Depot

Augusta, Maine, September 6, 1872

The fall days leading up to the presidential election of 1872, were tumultuous. Ulysses S. Grant campaigned vigorously for a second term, but his Republican Party was divided and many of its liberal members had decided to vote for Horace Greely, the Democratic nominee. The contest was further complicated by the Equal Rights Party candidacy of New York suffragette Victoria Woodhull, the first female candidate to run for president of the United States.

In September, Grant brought his campaign to Maine, where he was met in Augusta on the sixth by a brass band and a huge crowd of supporters at the train depot. Local bookseller, diarist, and artist John Martin captured the frenetic scene in this sketch, showing the depot in the corner, next to a massive arch painted with the names "Grant" and "Wilson." Crowds of cheering men and women as well as numerous military companies filled every street in support of Grant's re-election effort. Seven of the houses along the parade route are shown with flags and decorative bunting, the one exception being the "Democrat House [with] no illumination" at the center of the picture. The artist has even captured some of the shouts of the crowd: "Three Cheers for the Illumination" and "Three cheers for the Triumphal Arch." The Republicans' hopes were fulfilled on November 5, when Grant captured all seven of Maine's electoral votes by a margin of nearly 68 percent.

Temperance and Prohibition

Hard cider, ale, and beer were daily fare for men, women, and children in most New England households during the colonial period and the first decades of the new nation. Social occasions of all kinds included alcoholic beverages as a matter of course. Taverns and stores sold rum and other alcoholic beverages by the glass to travelers and local patrons alike. Patriotic toasts using alcohol, numbering at least thirteen, were offered at political gatherings, militia Training Days, and on national holidays. Election Day and militia Training Days were notorious for excessive drinking and drunken brawls. Drunkenness was certainly frowned upon, but it was hardly unknown.

This all began to change about 1825 when active efforts led by clergy and groups of determined men and women sought to dissuade people from over-indulgence or, ideally, to persuade them to abstain from drinking any alcoholic beverage whatsoever. Formal organizations and an expansive publishing effort promoted the cause. The dangers of drink were vividly dramatized in illustrated juvenile books and religious magazines where intemperance was identified as both wicked and sinful. On the Fourth of July temperance advocates began to toast the nation with lemonade instead of rum. Many participated in public processions with the distinctive banners and badges of an expanding number of organized groups, among them the Sons of Temperance, the Washingtonians, the Rechabites, the Father Matthew Temperance Society, the Independent Order of Good Templars, the American temperance unions, and boisterous groups of boys and girls wearing the badges of the Cold Water Army. Temperance advocacy became a highly visible part of New England culture. For more than one hundred years the effort continued, with ongoing campaigns sometimes achieving total prohibition in a town, or even statewide, only to have it quickly repealed or simply ignored by local officials. Even the Eighteenth Amendment to the federal Constitution failed to completely control the sale or significantly reduce drinking before it was repealed in 1933, just fourteen years after its adoption. There are still some dry communities where alcohol cannot be sold, but the battle to control alcohol consumption is now more often fought in group meetings or on an individual level than by the broad public campaigns that characterized earlier times.

Cold Water Army Pledge

July 4, 1842

So here we pledge perpetual hate
To all that can intoxicate

Cold Water Army badge, ca. 1830–1840

Founded in Boston in 1826 by the American Society for the Promotion of Temperance, the Cold Water Army reached nearly one million members in just ten years. Upon taking the pledge affirming their intention to completely abstain from alcoholic beverages of all kinds and to drink only pure cold water, both adults and children were enrolled in the Cold Water Army.

Closely aligned with Sunday schools, Cold Water Army members attended temperance rallies and marched in long processions with banners as they sang temperance songs. They sometimes wore ribbon badges like this with its printed images of a well and a fountain, both revered as sources of pure water, their preferred beverage.

Banner of the Cold Water Army
Hampton, New Hampshire, ca. 1841

An unknown New Hampshire artist created this banner to be mounted to two tall poles and carried in processions by temperance advocates. The image suggests that the young men enlisted in the Cold Water Army marched from villages as far away as New Hampshire's White Mountains all the way to Hampton by the sea to attend a large outdoor rally. There, in 1841, they organized the Rockingham County chapter of the Washingtonian Total Abstinence Society, which flourished for about a decade, having additional major conventions at Hampton in 1844 and 1849. At their first meeting, the Washingtonians persuaded the proprietor of one Hampton tavern, the Railroad House, to transfer his entire stock of alcoholic beverages to them and they promptly poured it all onto the ground.

Founded in Baltimore in 1840, the Washingtonian movement spread quickly throughout New England

and continued to combine active promotion of total abstinence with convivial fraternity and structured social occasions for its working class members. After 1842 women were enrolled in subsidiary groups known as Martha Washington Societies, from which they provided sympathetic help and material support to drunkards. Some Washingtonian parade entries included wagons carrying disheveled men acting out the horrors of intoxication. Women were more restrained in their appearance, but some wore badges with the threatening motto, "Tee total or no husband." Lacking a highly educated leadership or coordinated strategies, the movement gradually lost focus and faltered in the face of a multiplicity of new temperance groups and as public attention shifted to other causes, especially advocacy for the abolition of slavery.

Young Men of the Cold Water Army (detail)

Banner of the Maine Charitable Mechanics Association

Portland, Maine, ca. 1841

The temperance pennant flying over the hull of this ship under construction proclaims one of the primary goals of the Maine Charitable Mechanics Association for which this banner was painted in 1841. MCMA members strongly opposed the consumption of alcohol, especially the long-standing maritime tradition of issuing grog, a hearty alcoholic beverage usually made with rum, to sailors at 11:00 a.m. and 4:00 p.m. each day.

Grand Mass Washingtonian Convention

Boston, Massachusetts, May 30, 1844

Newspaper accounts tell us that on May 30, 1844, more than forty thousand people assembled near the Great Elm on Boston Common to participate in the Grand Mass Washingtonian Convention. This was a rally of reformed drinkers and total abstinence advocates who came from all over New England to hear well-known orators and share personal stories with fellow members. The highlight of the day was the great parade. Following a carriage full of dignitaries and the marching members of the Washington Light Infantry, the Washingtonians moved along several streets in the center of the city, carrying painted banners with emblems of the temperance movement and singing

temperance songs while 250 of the children marched as members of the Cold Water Army.

Grand Mass Washingtonian Convention (detail)

Boston, Massachusetts, May 30, 1844

In the 1844 Washingtonian parade, one group pulled a float with an open boat that appeared to be rowed by sailors, some of them cheering their recent successful efforts to reduce liquor consumption among New England's sailors. In addition, the South Boston Total Abstinence Society brought a float featuring a well furnished with an old fashioned sweep, the tall, diagonal pole seen here that made it easy to raise a bucket of water from a well. This float was certainly inspired by Samuel Wadsworth's popular 1817 poem, "The Old Oaken Bucket." With its nostalgic references to beloved "scenes of my childhood" and "the moss covered bucket which hung in the well," "The Old Oaken Bucket" was sung for decades by temperance groups, all of which advocated drinking pure cold water as one's primary beverage.

Silk banner of the Washingtonian Total Abstinence Society
Dennysville, Maine, 1841

Almost as far Down East as you can get, in tiny Dennysville, Maine, with its population of only about forty families, people came together in 1828 and formed a temperance society. In 1841, having already pledged moderation in the consumption of alcohol, they went even further and formed a local Washingtonian Society, now pledging total abstinence. Local women raised funds and commissioned John Regan, a local fancy painter, to create this banner, which they presented to the Dennysville Total Abstinence Society on the Fourth of July in 1842.

The Dennysville temperance banner offers a dramatic illustration of the dangers of alcoholism and the rewards of sobriety. It features a gold-domed temple supported by thirteen visible pillars representing the original states that ratified the Constitution of the United States and symbolizing the solid foundation of the nation. To the left of the temple is an image of a well-dressed citizen, apparently sober and happy, brandishing a sword under stars and the words "Moral Suasion." In the detail below is a smiling man in patched and tattered clothing who is holding broken shackles, apparently rejoicing that he has broken free from the bonds of his own intemperance. Moldings on the base of the temple are inscribed with mottoes of the Washingtonian Society: "Temperance & Charity" and "Never Forsake a Brother." The entire design is enhanced by a gold border with ribbons and sheaves of wheat suspended by eagles.

Rum—Here It Goes!
Boston or Salem, Massachusetts, ca. 1836–1850

These are at least two surviving examples of this modest temperance banner with a large woodcut showing two boys chopping open a barrel of rum and emptying a wine bottle on the ground. Both were printed on inexpensive cotton in Boston or Salem sometime after 1836 and hundreds more may well have been printed for use by various temperance organizations. We know that one was used by the Reverend Samuel May, an uncle of Louisa May Alcott, who was a well-known abolitionist and temperance advocate in Norwell, Massachusetts. The other (illustrated here) was one of many different banners carried in processions by students of the Boston Asylum & Farm School for Indigent Boys, located on Thompson's Island in Boston Harbor. In 1850, the school served one hundred resident boys sent there by their poor families or by the courts. At age fifteen they were apprenticed to local farmers or tradesmen. Apparently the boys received stern warnings about the evils of drink as part of their education. Whether or not youth in either community actually chopped open rum barrels is unknown, but it is true that many temperance advocates supported organized activities of this kind rather than condemning them as vandalism.

Efforts to control alcohol consumption resumed after the Civil War and many went so far as to advocate total abstinence and its natural concomitant: the absolute prohibition of both the manufacture and sale of any kind of alcoholic beverages. The presentation of these messages in parades, began to be seen in ambitious floats instead of the traditional marching groups with their banners.

The Old Oaken Bucket

Portland, Maine, July 5, 1886

Although it was supposed to represent the "old fashioned well of 1786," clearly this historical tableau in Portland's centennial procession was another float inspired by Wadsworth's popular poem. The idea of an old, moss-covered bucket rising from the depths of the well, pulled by a long old-fashioned well sweep, and full of pure cold water endeared the image and the poem to the Washingtonians and other temperance advocates. As early as the 1840s, the poem was published in McGuffey's readers and recited by thousands of children across the country. Images of many different Old Oaken Buckets appeared on sheet music covers, embroidered bookmarks, and popular prints—especially those of Currier and Ives that were published in 1864 and reissued in 1872. Combining nostalgia and an appeal to virtue, similar vignettes appeared in New England parades for at least one hundred years.

19 Prohibition States

Northampton, Massachusetts, June 7, 1904

At Northampton in 1904, the local chapter of the Women's Christian Temperance Union adapted an old parade tradition when they selected nineteen young women to dress in white and wear diagonal sashes, each identifying a state where Prohibition laws had already been enacted. For more than a century, New England floats had carried groups of girls dressed in white and identified as personifications of either the original thirteen colonies or the number of states that had joined the Union before the date of the parade. In this case, the symbolism went further as the women celebrated partial success in their drive to establish a national ban on liquor sales.

WCTU, the national Women's Christian Temperance Union, was founded by the dauntless suffrage and temperance advocate Frances Willard in 1874. Members were mainly Protestant women who worked in local chapters across the country to promote abstinence and purity in order to secure "a sober and pure world." From the beginning they worked in public schools and Sunday schools, developing classroom activities, and publishing cheap illustrated leaflets and storybooks, all designed to instill fear of the evils of drink in members of the rising generation and their parents. Although most of these women were born at a time when it would have been considered unseemly to participate in large public events, by 1900 WCTU members did not hesitate to climb aboard parade floats to advocate the cause.

We Must Save Our Boys

North Bennington, Vermont, July 4, 1914

Members of the Women's Christian Temperance Union of North Bennington entered this symbolic nautical float in the Fourth of July procession in 1914. Above the WCTU's broad motto, "For God and Home and Native Land," the vessel carried a crew of young boys in sailor suits under a sail proclaiming it to be a "Life Boat" with a lofty purpose: "Save Our Boys." One of the young sailors urged spectators to "VOTE NO" in the forthcoming local election, one of those held annually throughout Vermont between 1902 and 1920 to decide whether to issue licenses for the sale of alcohol within the boundaries of each town.

The increase in advocacy for Prohibition in the

early twentieth century certainly must be recognized, at least in part, as a response to the growing number of immigrants from countries where drinking was a cultural norm. Not surprisingly, opposition to German beer drinking became near hysteria by 1916.

No Cigarettes and No Liquor for Us
Worcester, Massachusetts, 1915

Some members of the large Swedish community in Worcester, Massachusetts, were proud to illustrate their alignment with Yankee Protestant values such as frugality, honesty, industriousness, clean living, and, of course, temperance. To make their point white-clad children and members of the Swedish White Ribbon Society, a local chapter of the WCTU, rode in this rather awkward float in the traditional Swedish *Midsommar* festival parade in 1915.

Mock Funeral for John Barleycorn
Boston, Massachusetts, January 16, 1920

More than one hundred years of temperance advocacy was ultimately successful on the national level. On the very day that the Eighteenth Amendment prohibiting the manufacture, distribution, and sale of all alcoholic beverages was to take effect at midnight, Boston Prohibitionists celebrated with a mock funeral for John Barleycorn, the legendary English folk hero long associated with the enjoyment of alcohol. Both men and women paraded through the city streets following a motor truck carrying a black casket adorned with signs urging people to join them at the Morgan Memorial in the South End, at 7:30 p.m. At the head of the parade was a tank truck full of what else but water, carrying an official of the Morgan Memorial dressed as Uncle Sam. Once inside the Memorial's Church

of All Nations, services were conducted by the secretary of the Massachusetts Bible Society and other clergymen. The procession turned into a joyride, with people laughing all the way and singing the old song written by Scottish poet Robert Burns, "John Barleycorn Must Die!" All in all, Old John had a great sendoff.

There's Still Work to Be Done

Concord, New Hampshire, 1923

Before the Eighteenth Amendment to the federal Constitution became effective on January 16, 1920, many private citizens stocked their cellars with alcoholic beverages of all kinds. Private clubs did likewise, and then raised their dues in order to be able to give their members free drinks. Under the new law drinking was not illegal, but prohibition of the manufacture and sale of alcoholic beverages had a substantial impact on consumption.

The years after 1920 saw both aggressive enforcement of liquor laws and flagrant abuse. Despite the WCTU's continuing efforts to discourage drinking, the roaring twenties were largely fueled by alcohol consumption and the popular perception of drinking as an enjoyable, if daring behavior. Although much changed in 1933 when the Prohibition amendment was repealed, the battles against alcohol consumption continued.

Business and Industry

As a result of increasing industrialization, the old parade tradition of workmen walking together while carrying illustrative banners and the tools of their trades changed in the 1840s. The long lines of men largely gave way to wheeled floats on which merchants and manufacturers displayed tools, machinery, and products as they celebrated the thrifty and progressive enterprise of the community, the creativity and skill of the workers, and the high quality and fashionable appearance of their products.

Civic leaders soon realized that trade and mercantile processions were an inexpensive way to expand a celebration and attract more visitors. Merchants and manufacturers eager to advertise their products and display their new equipment took on many of the costs. They mobilized their employees to create and ride on floats that carried the message to enthusiastic onlookers. Some utilized their entire fleets of delivery vehicles. Active demonstration of hand skills and complex machinery attracted additional attention. Parade planners encouraged businesses to send as many floats as possible, underscoring their belief in the potential for limitless expansion of American innovation and industry.

Since every successful businessman owned horses and wagons to move raw materials into the workplace and to deliver products, it was easy enough for an owner to clean them off, load them up, and enter them in a parade. After the Civil War, parades included more and more delivery vehicles loaded with employees and products. As we have seen, at Boston's Bunker Hill Day parade on June 17, 1875, the trades were represented in the ninth division, which was nearly four miles long, took a long time to appear, and was described by one exhausted spectator as "interminable."

The task of maintaining order and avoiding gaps in the line fell, as always, to the Chief Marshal who had hard work to keep the advertising teams moving at steady pace and maintaining a respectful distance from each other. In some places the number of units entered by a single business owner was limited, but pressure to include everything was powerful and is still felt today.

The Railroad Jubilee (details)

Boston, Massachusetts, September 19, 1851

As shown in Chapter 4, the highlight of the Railroad Jubilee was the grand procession by which the planners hoped to "provide the stranger a bird's-eye view, with what hope, and smiles, and happiness, men labor in this land of freedom" on the seventy-fifth anniversary of the United States of America. Thanks to the talented engravers who worked for *Gleason's Pictorial Drawing Room Companion*, we can clearly see some of the "variety, beauty, and magnitude" of the richly detailed floats presented by Boston's merchants and manufacturers in the massive seventh division.

Led by a plaster model of Peter Stephenson's heroic marble sculpture "The Wounded Indian," which was then on display at the Crystal Palace in London, the division included entries by fifty different industries. It featured a miniature man-of-war on wheels, an elephant from the Boston Museum, followed by a pyramid of gold and silverware "borne on the shoulders of four colored men rejoicing in the gorgeous oriental costume," huge samples of granite designated as a gift from Massachusetts for use in constructing the Washington Monument, carriages in which rode the artists of *Gleason's Pictorial Drawing Room Companion,* and the editor of the *Carpet Bag.* Further along, a large car hung

with lavish drapery carried three large square pianos.

Pyrotechnists Sanderson and Lenergan presented a model of Mount Etna emitting clouds of perfumed smoke. Beyond them was another display of fireworks by James G. Hovey, Esq., followed by a model of Quincy Market with an array of live pigs, geese, and fowl, as well as butchers at work cutting carcasses of beef under the motto "We Feed the Hungry." Elsewhere in the procession were railroad steam engines, an immense cannon called the "peacemaker," an active printing press, and examples of carpets, wallpaper, sofas and chairs, school furniture, pianos, silverware, sewing machines, stoves, India rubber goods, fire engines by Hunneman & Co., Tapestry carpet looms, roller printing machines for wallpapers, machines making crackers, and others making boots and shoes were all in operation as they rolled through the streets. Most displays were followed by marching groups of specialized workmen, as many as 350 in some cases. One agricultural equipment firm struck an antiquarian note, comparing their own modern products with the old plough used by Connecticut's Roger Sherman in 1742.

All agreed that nothing so elaborate had ever been undertaken in Boston and that the parade had successfully illustrated the extraordinary economic resources of the city. The high bar that they set for subsequent parade participants was probably not equaled until after the Civil War.

SHOEMAKING

Blind Hole Shoe Manufactory in 1789 in full Operation (detail from image on page 215)

Danvers, Massachusetts, June 16, 1852

On an oppressively hot June day in 1852, the Antiques section of the Danvers, Massachusetts, centennial procession included this small, wheeled building representing shoemaking, one of the earliest industrial activities in the town. Several men inside were actively working at cobbler's benches. Examples of their finished work hung just outside the door. Small shoe shops like this were not only located throughout Danvers but also scattered in hundreds of places throughout New England. They were known as "ten footers" because they usually measured just ten feet square.

FURNITURE MAKING

Walter Corey & Co., Furniture Makers

Portland, Maine, July 5, 1886

Portland furniture maker Walter Corey's impressive entry in the Portland centennial parade in 1886 was easy to accomplish for a man with many skilled employees, stables full of horses and delivery wagons, and an extensive warehouse full of ready-made goods. Corey's workmen built floats with tiered shelves on which to display the rich variety of furniture forms and styles produced by the firm. On parade day, they dressed in their best clothes to drive thirteen of Corey's delivery teams loaded with their own products over the lengthy parade route.

LOCOMOTIVES AND STEAMSHIPS

All the Bells and Whistles

Portland, Maine, July 5, 1886

As employees of a major industry in the city, men in the workshops of the thirty-eight-year-old Portland Company prepared this float for the city's centennial parade. Large paintings on each side highlighted their construction of locomotives, steam boats, and other vehicles. Examples of their production of gears, wheels, shafting, and various iron parts were displayed around the base, with bells and whistles mounted on top.

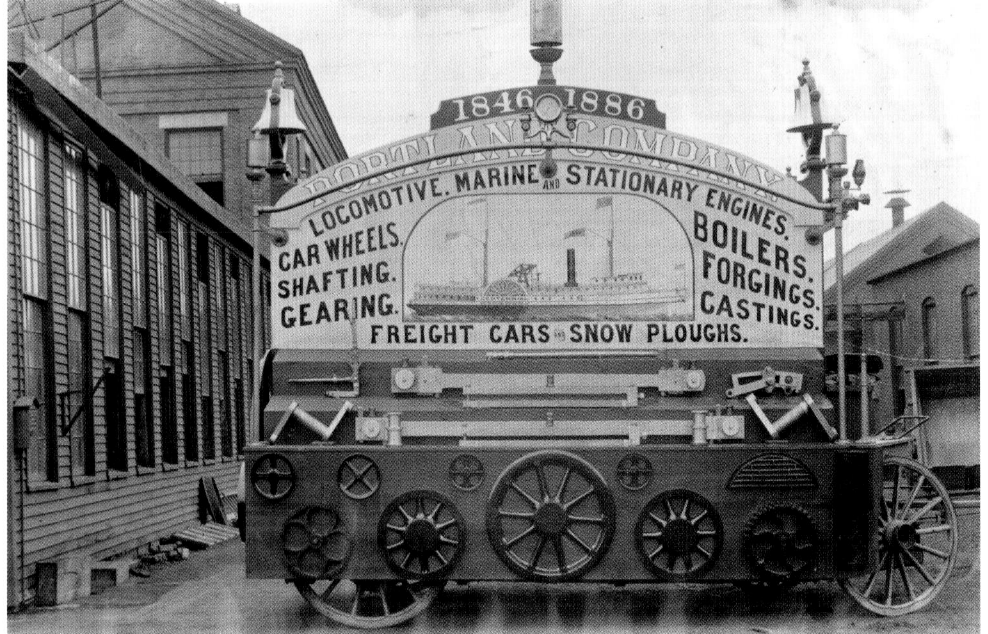

LIFE INSURANCE

Mayflower

Haverhill, Massachusetts, 1890

Photographed beside the Merrimack River, this ambitious representation of the *Mayflower* with its load of costumed Pilgrims was deemed a "very effective float" in the 250th anniversary parade at Haverhill,

Massachusetts, in 1890. Incongruously, it was placed in the fifth division with other "Floats of Societies" instead of with the business floats in the trades division. Although it was entered by members of the Plymouth Rock and Winnekenni Colonies of the United Order of Pilgrim Fathers, it did not represent a lineage society. Rather, it was a mutual insurance company that adopted the icons of New England's founders to assure customers of the honesty and integrity of their business through "a striking contrast" between the idea of the Pilgrims "seeking protections on a foreign shore and the protection given to the homes of the members" guaranteed by commercial insurance.

FARMERS

Going to the Fair

Rochester, New Hampshire, 1899

Ten yoke of oxen pulled this huge wagon with its lavish display of summer produce arranged by farm families on Ten Rod Road in Farmington, New Hampshire, on their way to the annual Rochester Fair in 1899. Four and one-half miles from their rural neighborhood, they encountered these excited crowds at Central Square in Rochester and they still had two miles to go before reaching the gate of the fairgrounds.

Work Cattle

Sandwich, New Hampshire, 1898

Dressed in their Sunday best, these farmers, goad their teams of oxen and young steers beneath newly installed telephone wires in a village parade during the Sandwich Fair in 1898. They were part of a long-standing New England tradition that began as early as 1811 in Pittsfield, Massachusetts, at the first Berkshire County Cattle Show where sixty yoke of prime oxen connected by chains, and drawing a plow were led in the public street parade by "the two most ancient farmers present." Today, adults and children of both sexes proudly display the health and discipline of their ox teams in the annual parade at the Sandwich Fair in early October and at many others throughout the region.

GROCERS

Garden of Eden

Manchester, New Hampshire, September 9, 1896

This bountiful display of fruits and vegetables appeared on a float in the Firemen and Merchants Parade of the semicentennial celebration in the textile-manufacturing city of Manchester on September 9, 1896. Although the city had only been formally incorporated in 1846, Manchester's civic leaders made sure to participate in the wave of anniversary celebrations that swept the country in the years after the World's Columbian Exposition in 1893.

LONG-ESTABLISHED BUSINESSES

Wilson's Pharmacy
Brunswick, Maine, 1889

Advertising "Fancy Toilet Articles," "Pure Drugs," and "Perfume" in addition to medicines and medical supplies, Wilson's Pharmacy had been in business in Brunswick for fifty years. Their float in the city's 1889 sesquicentennial parade featured a massive mortar and pestle, the traditional emblem of apothecaries and drug stores.

CREPE PAPER

Venetian Gondola

South Framingham, Massachusetts, 1900

In 1900, the Dennison Manufacturing Company used masses of its primary product to create this Venetian gondola with six golden oars as its entry in the city's bicentennial parade. Hundreds of crepe paper roses formed garlands that extended over the canopy of the Queen, looped over her attendants, and drooped over the sides of the boat. The entire base of the vehicle was covered in crepe paper, bordered with fringes and additional crepe paper flowers. Not surprisingly, the young women wore crepe paper headdresses and costumes described as soft and clinging.

First introduced in the 1890s, crepe paper was inexpensive and easy to manipulate. It quickly became popular for decorating spaces for public and private parties, display windows, and parade vehicles as well as for costuming children's theatrical performances and tableaux for all ages. By 1904, Dennison's illustrated booklet, *Art and Decoration in Crepe and Tissue Paper,* with its helpful instructions and patterns for things as diverse as lampshades, doll clothes, fancy dress, and artificial flowers, had grown to ninety pages in its sixteenth edition.

HARDWARE

Preston Brothers Hardware

Norwich, Connecticut, September 4, 1901

The huge windmill entered by Prestons' Hardware Store in the Old Home Week parade at Norwich on September 4, 1901, was embellished with one thousand examples of merchandise sold by the firm. From guns and knives of various types to every possible kind of hand tool, hinge, or hasp, the glittering items on the Preston Brothers float drew attention from an admiring crowd. Spectators peering from second story windows undoubtedly had the better view.

MILLINERY

"The Seasons"—Mrs. L. E. Theoret, Milliner

Sanford, Maine, July 4, 1903

Louise E. Theoret operated a millinery shop in Sanford between 1902 and 1907 before moving to nearby Somersworth, New Hampshire, where she continued to operate her business well into the 1920s. Although unmarried, she observed the contemporary convention by which respectable women in business referred to themselves as *Mrs.* She must have been a smart and frugal woman, a good marketer as well as a fine milliner. For the Sanford Fourth of July parade in 1903, Sanford's undertaker, Luther A. Hurd, put on his best suit and a tall silk hat to drive the decorated carriage in which Mrs. Theoret and three other women displayed some of her most successful hat designs. The women seated closest to the curb wore winter styles, while the others showed summer hats. Both the striped bunting swathing the carriage and the horse blankets bearing the name of the business could easily have been used for other parades. To preserve the moment and enhance its impact, this photograph was taken with the carriage parked directly in front of Mrs. Theoret's Millinery Rooms, so that her name, her sign, and her hats would all be clearly visible.

WOMEN TEXTILE WORKERS

Japanese Pagoda and Tea Garden

Northampton, Massachusetts, June 7, 1904

Reflecting popular interest in Japanese culture and calling on every stereotype in the book, employees of the Nonotuck Silk Company mill at Leeds, Massachusetts, designed and decorated this elaborate red and gold Japanese pagoda and tea garden with huge umbrellas, snarling dragons, and paper lanterns for the 1904 quarter-centennial parade at nearby Northampton. On the upper deck, girls in kimonos were busy with their embroidery or serving tea. Below them, four "Geisha girls" posed with ornamental umbrellas and others busied themselves reeling silk. The name "Corticelli" on the horse blankets refers to the primary brand of silk thread produced by the Nonotuck Company.

No doubt they were proud of what they believed to be an informed representation of a culture that was considered both fascinating and exotic at the time. Such a production today would probably be condemned as disrespectful cultural appropriation.

BANDBOX MAKING

Mrs. Marion A. Poole as Hannah Davis, "Bandbox Maker"

Jaffrey, New Hampshire, August 12, 1923

Long remembered in New Hampshire, Miss Hannah Davis (1784–1863) and her famous bandboxes were represented with her horse and wagon in the semicentennial parade at Jaffrey in 1923. Miss Davis was a successful maker of stout, oval wooden boxes which she covered with colorful wallpapers, lined with newspapers, and identified with printed paper labels bearing her own name that she pasted inside the lids. Known as bandboxes, her products were both carried by travelers and useful at home for storing many things, especially fragile articles of apparel, such as muffs, and large bonnets. Miss Davis sold her products locally, but she also traveled alone by horse and wagon to Lowell, Massachusetts, Manchester, New Hampshire, and other mill towns where she sold her colorful and durable bandboxes primarily to girls and women who were earning cash wages as employees of large textile factories. By the time of this parade, original Hannah Davis bandboxes were prized by collectors of New England antiques, as they are today.

WAR MATERIEL

General Electric Company

Lynn, Massachusetts, November 11, 1928

Through most of the last century the General Electric Company was a huge employer in Lynn. This float was created ten years after the 1918 Armistice to commemorate the company's contributions to World War I. Amidst the patriotic stars and stripes, the eagles, the impressive machinery, and pretty girls in the dusters and slacks that were their work clothing, are signs documenting both the company's employment of over sixty-five thousand people and production war materiel ranging from motors and airplane components to incendiary bombs. Special notice was given to the 2,416 General Electric Company employees who enlisted during World War I, of whom forty-two died, sixty-eight were disabled, fourteen were cited for exceptional bravery, one was captured, and one was still missing in 1928.

HOME OWNERSHIP

Why Pay Rent? Build A House

Concord, New Hampshire, 1927

The American dream of private home ownership was fostered in this tidy cottage entered by the Concord Lumber Company, in the 200th Anniversary parade at Concord, New Hampshire, in 1927. Plumed horses like these continued to be used to pull floats long after motorized trucks and cars were available, especially in parades commemorating community anniversaries and historical events.

BATHROOM FIXTURES

Bedford Hardware and Plumbing Co.

Bedford, Massachusetts, 1912

This float in the 1912 Old Home Week parade at Bedford bravely exhibited something seldom seen in public: all the components of a modern sanitary bathroom. There is even a flush toilet combining a porcelain bowl with a wooden tank and seat, both having a shiny finish on dark wood. Beside a steam radiator, a footed enamel bathtub is equipped with an overhead shower and white curtain, a porcelain sink stands on three legs against the wall with a mirror above. Although it is unclear if the walls and floor are tiled, they are certainly white like all the fixtures in this very up-to-date and easy-to-clean space. Even the horses are white.

THE POWER OF THE PRESS

Another popular subject for both floats and toasting was a salute "To the Press and to Freedom of the Press, hoping to spread the benefits of Freedom."

The Valley Times

Pittsfield, New Hampshire, 1908

Following a parade tradition that extends back centuries, the owners of Pittsfield's newspaper, *The Valley Times,* mounted their new Golding "Pearl" job printing press on the back of a decorated wagon. In this photograph, the printer himself appears ready to press the foot pedal and begin striking off handbills for the two young boys to hand out to spectators along the route of the Old Home Week parade in 1908. (*Another image from this parade appears on page 149.*)

The Sanford News

Sanford, Maine, ca. 1912–1914

With the arrival of the first automobiles, many business owners abandoned their long-time use of horse-drawn wagons for floats and began to drive their families or employees in decorated automobiles. Here in Sanford, Maine, about 1912, Everett Averill, publisher of the *Sanford News,* has printed a few simple signs and mounted some flags on his Model T Ford to carry his wife and children along with the minister of the Unitarian Church in the city's Fourth of July parade.

FLORAL DESIGN

P. H. Vose Co., Grand Carnival Parade Float

Bangor, Maine, June 18, 1912

After a huge fire destroyed much of the commercial center of Bangor on April 30, 1911, local businessmen and civic officials planned a "mighty trades procession" the following spring. They believed that the event would demonstrate the resourcefulness of local citizens in the face of tragedy and encourage people from neighboring towns to take advantage of the resurgent commercial strengths of the city. Declared "decidedly novel" was this huge, steaming, green teakettle made of sweet-smelling cedar trimmings with a white rectangle having the name VOSE composed of fresh daisies on the side. The float was entered by Prescott H. Vose, the operator of a large stoneware factory as well as a retail crockery and glassware business on Main Street in Bangor.

NEW ENGLAND PRODUCTS

The Giant Tricycle

Concord, New Hampshire, 1896

This huge tricycle with rear wheels measuring eleven and one-half feet in diameter was manufactured by the Boston Woven Hose & Rubber Company to advertise its Vim Cycle Tires. Weighing 1,900 pounds, the machine required eight men to propel it along flat surfaces and additional help was often sought when going up steep hills. Not surprisingly, the trike easily rolled downhill all by itself. The vehicle is seen parked beside the arch in front of the New Hampshire State House on Main Street in Concord, where it was one of the star attractions of a bicycle parade held during the 1896 Merchant's Week. For more than a decade, the Vim Tricycle appeared in many New England parades and torchlight processions sometimes having been ridden as many as sixty miles from The Hub.

Moxie

Bellows Falls, Vermont, October 1, 1912

This liveried coachman was accompanied by a little girl who was supposed to wave her flag as they rode in a horse-drawn carriage in the Third Annual Street Fair at Bellows Falls on October 1, 1912. Their display features a huge model of a bottle of Moxie, a beverage first sold about 1876 as an alcohol- and cocaine-free tonic called Moxie Nerve Food. The remarkable popularity of the strong-flavored beverage led to popular use of the word "moxie" to describe a person having a determined character or nerve, someone with exceptional strength who is unlikely to give up.

Moxie's distinctive flavor was originally derived from gentian root, which grows abundantly in northern New England. After soda water was added about 1884, sparkling Moxie quickly became one of the first mass-produced carbonated beverages. Currently a Coca-Cola product, Moxie is still a favorite New England beverage despite its bitter aftertaste.

Green's Clothier
Houlton, Maine, July 4, 1914

The novelty of flight captured the imagination of the men who provided this moving airplane to advertise Green's Clothing Company in the Fourth of July parade on Main Street at Houlton, Maine, in 1914. One man walking inside the fuselage provided propulsion for the plane while another hurried alongside, steadying the wing.

Mantel Clock
Hartford, Connecticut, October 12, 1935

Connecticut has been known as a center of clockmaking since the time of the American Revolution. Skilled craftsmen used innovative design, inexpensive materials, and interchangeable parts along with a far-flung distribution system to dominate the market and bring reliable timekeeping to hundreds of thousands of homes throughout the country. The long-lived Seth Thomas Company built this huge model of their classic mantel clock to enter in the Connecticut tercentennial parade in Hartford on October 12, 1935, where it truly did appear to float. The crowds seen here must have been typical of the day, for newspaper accounts indicate that 400,000 people viewed this parade, which took more than three hours to pass any given point along the way.

Lydia Pinkham's Vegetable Compound
Location and date unknown

Long after the introduction of Lydia Pinkham's Vegetable Compound in 1873, the herbal product with its alcohol base is still praised as a panacea for women. First marketed as a cure for women's "hysteria," weakness, and general disability, these were actually coded messages suggesting the product's effective treatment of menstrual and menopausal disorders and discomfort. Although the formula has been modified over time, thousands of women have given testimony to its transformational impact on their general health or their specific complaints. If you would like to try it, you will have no trouble finding it even today.

A Merry Christmas, Santa Claus Parade

Boston, Massachusetts, Thanksgiving Day, 1938

As part of New England's expanding commercial culture, Boston's Jordan Marsh Department Store sponsored parades in the heart of the city on Thanksgiving Day, beginning in 1927. They hoped to launch a robust Christmas shopping season and to stimulate business, especially in the toy department. At the time, giant helium-filled balloons were an innovative parade feature, first introduced in New York in 1927 by Macy's, one of that city's largest department stores, which had been sponsoring Thanksgiving Day parades since 1924. Nantucket puppeteer Tony Sarg designed many of these popular balloons, among them figures of a musical pig and a rabbit, a kangaroo, a caterpillar, trains, clowns, and a double-headed giant. Here a huge balloon representing a policeman is controlled by men in striped prison uniforms as it flies above Beacon Street in Boston on Thanksgiving Day in 1938. Ironically, Jordan Marsh is now Macy's.

Women's Clubs and Charity

From the earliest days of the American Republic, women's benevolence in peacetime has focused on modeling charitable behavior and helping poor women and children, especially the widowed and fatherless. Informal donations of food, firewood and candles or coal and lamp oil, clothing, bed linens and blankets, and/or cash provide essential support at times of birth, illness, mortality, or other special need. In times of war, women also provide special help to soldiers, especially those departing from home or suffering from illness or injury. At the same time, additional assistance is given to the newly widowed and those families whose breadwinners leave to join the fight.

Informal sewing circles within the family, the church, or the neighborhood offer women opportunities to socialize while doing necessary and helpful work, such as sewing layettes and bed linen for expectant mothers or garments for poor families. Inevitably their conversations lead to serious consideration of ways to increase the impact of their charitable efforts and improve their own lives. Over time, many of these have led to more public efforts to effect social change by establishing sewing classes in which poor women could learn skills that might be used to make clothing for their own families or sold to earn needed income. They also organized nurseries to provide day care, kindergartens, and English classes for new immigrants. Further, some women participated in groups organized to support Sunday schools and hospitals or to advocate temperance, governmental and educational reforms, or women's suffrage.

Some women chose to focus on self-improvement through support of local libraries or participation in reading and discussion groups in which they listened to invited speakers chosen for their special expertise in topics like child health and development, antique collecting, fine art, travel, or gardening. In many women's groups, the charitable sewing and knitting continued during meetings, for in New England idle hands are deplored.

In the first half of the twentieth century, organized club work appealed to prosperous women, many of whom were college educated and could employ help with housekeeping or childcare, and who neither needed nor chose to work for wages. For them, women's clubs taught leadership skills and offered activities imbued with purpose as well as opportunities to socialize with others of their religion, ethnicity, race, or class. Many of these clubs pursued charitable work, even sewing. Others chose activities of less lofty purpose such as playing bridge or golf with regular partners. Sometimes nothing more than a regular weekly or monthly luncheon meeting was an approved excuse to get out of the house, or to display one's cherished tableware, floral arrangements, and culinary skills, while enjoying feminine companionship.

Beginning in the 1840s, public school and Sunday school teachers often walked in floral processions to escort and discipline their pupils. Often women were the creative forces behind the elaborate floats and costumes that enhanced parades everywhere, but it was not until very late in the nineteenth century that women's groups began to appear as independent units in civic processions and parades.

FEMALE CHARITY

An Errand of Mercy, 1812

Concord, New Hampshire, 1927

Two officers of the Concord Female Charitable Society pulled some old clothes out of their attics and dusted off the Walker family's old chaise to participate in the parade commemorating the two hundredth anniversary of the settlement of the city in 1927. Stopped in front of the church of St. John the Evangelist on South Main Street, these ladies commemorate the long tradition of women's benevolence in the city of Concord by reenacting an "errand of mercy" as it might have appeared in 1812, the year the organization was founded. The group's written records detail thousands of practical gifts of food and clothing made over the year, before they disbanded in 1991. Notably, one donation was a new gown to a poor woman who had not had one for eight long years.

The old bonnets chosen by these two women for their appearance in the bicentennial parade would have been fashionable in two different eras as much as fifty years apart—perhaps unintentionally illustrating the old New England adage that "we don't buy our hats, we have them."

WOMEN'S CLUBS

Broom Brigade

Hinesburg, Vermont, ca. 1885–1890

These thirteen young women wearing matching costumes have probably practiced for weeks to participate in a "broom brigade," a snappy marching demonstration somewhat resembling that of a military drill team. It is probably no coincidence that the group numbered thirteen, the number of the original colonies, long associated with unity. Sometimes broom brigade demonstrations were standalone activities; some symbolized the women's desire to clean up local politics; others were part of official civic processions. Indeed, the 1888 monster procession at Burlington, Vermont, that celebrated Benjamin Harrison's election to the presidency, included a broom brigade.

These callisthenic activities were part of a short-lived, but nationwide fad that began as early as 1881 and died out soon after 1895. When Mark Twain described the phenomenon in *Life on the Mississippi* in 1883, he called the broom brigade a "complex manual done with grace, spirit, and admirable precision . . . everything which a human being can possibly do with a broom, except sweep."[10] Ironically, these young ladies illustrated women's growing participation in public life by their adoption of activities long considered the exclusive purview of men. At the same time, their effectiveness relied on a powerful symbol of domesticity, the common household broom.

CONGREGATIONAL CHARITY

Wesley M. E. Church, Ladies' Aid

Bath, Maine, 1907

This white "boat of the ancient Roman type," trimmed with red and green, carried members of the Ladies' Aid Society of the Wesley Methodist Episcopal Church in a parade at Bath in 1907. It was part of the huge celebration of the three hundredth anniversary of the establishment of ship building on the banks of the Kennebec River in 1607, an event that coincided with ceremonies honoring the first English settlement at Jamestown, Virginia, thirteen years before the landing of the Pilgrims at Plymouth.

The stern of the craft was marked 1796, the date of the founding of the church. There under a canopy sat Love, a young girl dressed in white with her hand on the tiller, guiding the boat. Seven additional girls and women held aloft white parasols and banners representing various charitable organizations of the congregation. One wore a severe black bonnet and gown to suggest her role as a deaconess, while another wore a Japanese costume to represent the Foreign Mission Society. In a reference to classicism, two little girls in white held cords attached to a banner entitled "Mother's Jewels," referencing the ancient story in which the noble Roman matron, Cornelia, identified her children as her only jewels.

Southbridge Woman's Club
Southbridge, Massachusetts, July 4, 1916

Riding within this Doric temple in the centennial parade in 1916 are eight members of the Southbridge Woman's Club. Their matching headdresses and loose, toga-like garments suggest the enduring classical nature of their lofty principles. On the broad ribbon sashes worn across their breasts, can be discerned five areas of their interest and public service: art, music, education, conservation, and motherhood. The shield behind them makes it clear that the overarching goal of their club work was to promote progress.

Founded only two years earlier, the Southbridge Club was affiliated with the General Federation of Women's Clubs, a national group founded in 1890. GFWC members still work together as volunteers to support the arts, advance education, encourage civic involvement, promote healthy living, preserve natural resources, and work toward world peace and understanding.

WAR WORK

The Bee—Workers in Four Wars

Cambridge, Massachusetts, April 27, 1918

Many New England cities and towns still have sewing circles, usually groups of upper- or middle-class women who meet as often as weekly to make garments and plan other kinds of relief for the needy. The earliest continuously operating example may be the Fragment Society, established in Boston in 1812.

The Bee was one of these sewing circles, begun by sixteen teenaged girls in Cambridge, Massachusetts, who met weekly during the Civil War to work together for the benefit of Union soldiers. Their first projects were sewing blue flannel shirts and knitting blue socks with red and white striped cuffs. After the war they continued to meet regularly in each other's homes, enjoying tea or dinner, gossiping, storytelling, or even tipping tables—always with busy hands sewing bedding, towels, and or nightclothes for patients in the new Mount Auburn Hospital or providing garments for needy families. During World War I they again busied themselves knitting for soldiers: especially sweaters, pairs of socks, mufflers, and the fingerless gloves that made shooting easier in cold weather. The Cambridge women continued these kinds of work until the group was formally disbanded in 1923.

After all those years of close collaboration and generous support for soldiers and the needy, it is no surprise to see that members of the Bee participated in the April 27, 1918, parade in Cambridge supporting the Liberty Loan program. One patriotic member engaged this large truck and furnished it with rugs and easy chairs to make a homelike setting not unlike their usual meeting spaces. A large sign identified the riders as members of *The Bee—Workers in Four Wars.* Not much effort was expended in creating an elaborate float for this down-to-earth group; the Bees preferred to use their time and money more productively in support of their mission. Ten members just bundled up against the cold and kept on knitting.

THE AMERICAN RED CROSS

The Mobilized Humanity of the World

Portland, Maine, July 5, 1920

This float carrying a large red cross and a uniformed nurse in the centennial parade at Portland in 1920 celebrated the work of women in the American Red Cross during the recent Great War. The thirty young women who escorted the float represented their joint efforts by holding crimson streamers extending from the huge cross. Each wore a distinctive costume intended to identify one of the countries served by Red Cross nurses during the conflict. Closer to home, there were more than one hundred Red Cross units active in Maine in 1920. Their peacetime activities included public health nursing, working with needy families, organizing home nursing classes for both local citizens and the foreign-born, and operating public health centers in urban and rural areas.

Thought and Work Club

Salem, Massachusetts, July 7, 1926

Garlands of wisteria totally concealed this truck when it appeared as ninth in the line of more than one hundred floats in Salem's Floral and Historical Parade on Friday, July 7, 1926, the sixth day of the city's week-long celebration of its three hundredth anniversary. Float Nine won first prize in the floral section for its sponsors, the Thought and Work Club of Salem. Club members not only had gathered and arranged the flowers, but also wore matching lavender gowns and hats trimmed with the same flowers. Three women riding high above the cab "provided orchestral accompaniment" to others riding on the float who were singing as they moved through the city streets on their fluttering confection.

The Thought and Work Club was typical of many upper middle-class women's organizations early in the twentieth century, with activities that reached well beyond the typical sewing circles of previous generations. Their motto "Lofty Thoughts and Kindly Deeds" summarized their goal "to encourage women in all departments of literary work, to promote home study, and secure literary and social advantages for members." Members held classes in history, languages, and literature. Like a lyceum, they also sponsored lectures, concerts, and dramatic presentations for members and their guests. In the wider community they worked to improve conditions in schoolrooms and advocate for clean streetcars, to elect women to the school board, and they successfully campaigned to win a half holiday for retail store clerks, most of whom were women.

The Club's entry in the tercentennial parade was part of a concerted community effort hailed by the editor of the *Salem Evening News* as proof that Salem was "a wide awake modern town with energy to devote of civic causes."

"We Keep Clean"—Little Nurses

Kennebunk, Maine, May 1928

Imitating adult role models and proclaiming an important rule for good health, these little girls dressed as Red Cross nurses and pushed their doll carriages with their "patients" in a health parade on a spring day in Kennebunk. Most of the dolls were also dressed in white and wore nurses' caps.

The Greatest Mother in the World

Bedford, Massachusetts, 1929

This towering float is one of many in the years during and soon after World War I that were inspired by a popular and influential 1918 poster designed for the American Red Cross by Alonzo Earl Foringer. Rather than exhibiting an exact personation of the original design with its Madonna-like figure holding a wounded soldier, the postwar float in Bedford emphasized women's role in compassionate civilian care. It featured a seated mother figure in white wearing her Red Cross cape and cap while holding a baby and accompanied by two girls in white. Not surprisingly, they were all placed in front of American and Red Cross flags.

Preparedness

In 1916, as America's participation in the Great War began to seem more and more inevitable, there was a conscious effort to reassure citizens that the country was ready for the conflict. As part of this effort, many communities sponsored "preparedness parades" on Memorial Day, the Fourth of July, or the official Preparedness Day, July 22. Impressive long lines of uniformed soldiers and sailors moved through the streets, thrilling the hearts of patriotic citizens, and tugging at the heartstrings of many mothers and sweethearts who were forced to contemplate the rapid buildup of the armed forces. Enlisted men were joined by organizations such as the Sons of Veterans and the Women's Relief Corps, the American Red Cross, and many others determined to raise money and assist in the noble work of supporting the war effort.

On the Fourth of July at Newport, Rhode Island, there was some criticism of a preparedness parade as "monotonous," no doubt because of the endless lines of marching men. For most people, these parades were both a thrilling sight and a sobering suggestion of the hard work and sacrifice that lay ahead.

U. C. USINKEM

Nantucket, Massachusetts, April 13, 1917

The name of this float modeled as a United States Navy submarine, the *U. C. USINKEM*, suggested an appropriate action in response to the growing concern about the dangers of German submarines along the east coast. With war having been declared on April 2, 1917, feelings were running high on April 13 when Nantucket launched its third Liberty Loan parade. The submarine float was a creative part of the effort to build public support and increase available funds to support the allied cause by selling government bonds.

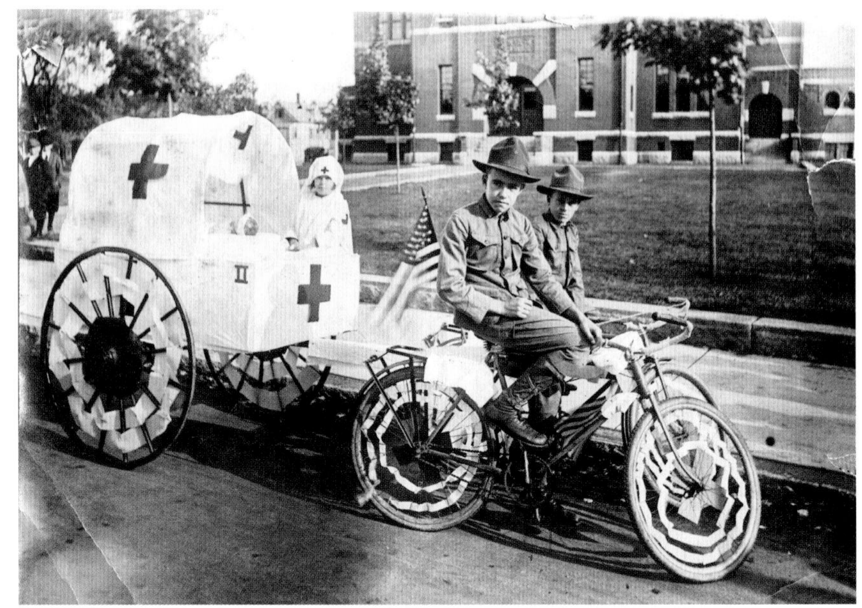

Red Cross Ambulance

Biddeford, Maine, 1917

Part of the preparedness effort focused on the need for widespread citizen participation. Two Maine boys dramatized one aspect of the work with their entry in the Biddeford Motorcycle Club parade in 1917. They dressed as doughboys and trimmed their bicycles with flags and crepe paper before using them to draw a cart turned into a Red Cross ambulance. Two more children rode in the wagon, one dressed as a nurse and the other as her suffering patient.

Liberty and Future Generations

Pittsfield, Massachusetts, undated (1918 or later)

This bold, self-propelled float summarized the rationale for American participation in the Great War. At the rear of the platform, a threatening man in a German imperial helmet, a young boy, and three girls wrapped in dark, hooded cloaks stood next to a "Barrier of Democracy" erected between two large cut out figures of the Statue of Liberty. A group of adults and a cluster of young children in white stood toward the front, representing the future generations for whom Liberty and Democracy were defended from German imperialism as a result of the successful war effort.

Progressivism

Today the multifaceted aspects of early twentieth-century progressivism are seen as having had both positive and negative connotations. The movement sought to counter problems caused by industrialization, immigration, urbanization, and government corruption by raising awareness of inequality and social injustice as well as promoting specific political and social reforms. There was considerable middle class support for women's suffrage, Prohibition, (discussed earlier in this chapter) and promotion of sanitation and public health, as well as for establishing protective labor laws, developing guidelines for fair wages and antitrust regulation, improving public schools, preventing vice, and limiting use of fireworks to ensure a safe and sane Fourth. At the same time, strong nativist forces resulted in dramatic growth of fraternal groups like the Improved Order of Red Men and the Ku Klux Klan, as well as Americanization classes and immigration quotas to deflect perceived cultural threats from immigrants arriving from a broad range of countries.

Although many of these issues were publicly promoted by people marching with signs or painted banners in processions dedicated to specific goals or as part of more comprehensive civic events, the ideas were infrequently represented in floats. Widespread support for reform movements was centered among the working class, whose employment responsibilities limited their participation to weekends or evenings.

WOMEN'S SUFFRAGE

As public activity promoting women's right to vote strengthened early in the twentieth century, after more than fifty years of effort, advocates of the cause organized massive parades of supporters in New York, Baltimore, the District of Columbia, and other large cities. In the spring of 1914, the energy was high and in many New England towns some women decided that they could not stay away. They packed their bags, bought train tickets, and traveled by ones and twos to Boston, proud to represent their hometowns and thrilled to be part of the action.

SONG SHOP
THOS. A. ELSTON CO. INC.

Suffrage Parade

Boston, Massachusetts, May 2, 1914

On Saturday, May 2, 1914, more than nine thousand people joined the first Boston parade exclusively dedicated to support women's suffrage. The sight of so many women dressed in white and marching in unison underscored the power of the movement.

Throughout New England, most suffrage advocates were well-educated, white, upper- and middle-class women for whom public support for any controversial topic was a bold new activity. Their white dresses, bouquets of daffodils or yellow roses, and ribbon sashes accented with the signature purple and gold of the movement, boldly proclaimed their goal of "Votes for Women!"

For the most part eschewing narrative floats, the women and their supporters walked in processions, rode in carriages, or sat in decorated automobiles, carrying banners proclaiming their support for women's suffrage. A small number rode saddle horses, a few even astride! Observing the convention of riding sidesaddle or being driven by a man in a carriage or chauffeured in an automobile apparently did not seem incongruous as it would today. Still, the goal was to be recognized as equal participants in the body politic seeking full voting rights.

Organized public activity supporting the suffrage movement intensified across the country and benefitted greatly from President Woodrow Wilson's Spring 1918 decision to add his support. After both the House and the Senate passed the Nineteenth Amendment to the United States Constitution a year later, it was sent to the states for ratification. When Tennessee became the thirty-sixth state to ratify it on August 18, 1920, the fight was over. Very simply, restriction or abridgement of voting rights of citizens on "account of sex" was made illegal after more than seventy years of advocacy.

This great surge of support for women's suffrage in 1914 came at a time when there had been years of active opposition by formally organized anti-suffrage groups as well as determined individual men and women who feared a devastating impact on family and community life. Perhaps not surprisingly, the opposition was sometimes expressed by men in drag, costumed horses, or men in blackface, usually within parades of Horribles. These two striking examples appeared before the groundswell of support that precipitated the 1914 marches.

Votes for Women

Andover, Massachusetts, July 4, 1912

When the parade of Horribles moved out at six o'clock in the morning in Andover on July 4, 1912, the entrants were competing for a prize of two dollars offered by the *Andover Townsman.* That newspaper reported later that women's suffrage was advocated in the parade by a

number of "willow plumed, hobble skirted girls" who had to split the prize with the Andover Remnant Band.

Surprisingly, the suffragists and their patriotic escort seen in this picture do not seem to be attracting much attention from people walking on the sidewalk or the young clown crossing Main Street behind them. What the newspaper account does not mention is that those "prize winning hobble skirted girls" were actually men in drag. Their long skirts, broad hats, and veiled faces created an effective disguise, but their manly arms and broad strides suggest a different story. Cross-dressing changes the message and undermines the purposeful words on the billowing banner. In all probability, this group is actually promoting the anti-suffrage cause.

Votes for Women, 1912
Hamilton, Massachusetts, 1912

This satirical entry was part of the annual Summer Parade and Field Day at Hamilton, Massachusetts, also in 1912. The decorated sulky was pulled by a horse named Jerry wearing trousers on his front legs and being driven by the well-known local postmaster, Hap Daley, who wore a dress and a hat with a tight veil that obscured his face and hair. The banner on the vehicle shafts calls for "Votes for Women" and portrays two women waving rolling pins of the type then sold commercially with labels reading "We Have Had the Big Stick. Now Let's Have the Big Rolling Pin. Roll Out the Opposition and Roll In Votes For Women." Since the cross-dressing and the garments on the horse are special effects often seen in Horribles parades, it may be that this example used satire to present an anti-suffrage point of view. From a distance of more than a century, it is hard to tell.

Still Seeking Votes for Women
Biddeford, Maine, September 16, 1916

The tercentennial procession at Biddeford on September 16, 1916, included a special section for decorated automobiles which were praised for their unique ideas, artistic designs, and abundant use of flowers.

A group of local suffragettes took a place in the line with this vehicle and conveyed their larger purpose with pennants on the doors that read "Votes for Women." Trimmed in greenery and the suffragettes' chosen yellow, the car carried the president, vice president, and two other members of the Biddeford Women's Suffrage League sharing large, flower-trimmed parasols. Their driver may have been a member, but he was not married to one of the passengers. The group received an honorable mention for their modest efforts.

League of Women Voters

Concord, New Hampshire, 1927

In the 1920s, women were proud of their hard-fought victory to obtain voting rights. These members of the League of Women Voters expressed both sisterhood and patriotism by riding in an open car swathed in red, white, and blue bunting as part of Concord's city anniversary in 1927. The League had been formed at the National Women's Suffrage Association Convention in 1920, shortly before the ratification of the Nineteenth Amendment. Membership in the League supported and promoted women's civic engagement at the local as well as the national level. Importantly, it still provides a non-partisan forum for women's political discussion and for planning strategic campaign strategies to influence voters and advance women's initiatives.

HEALTHY LIVING

At the beginning of World War I, the discovery of widespread malnutrition and generally low levels of general health and physical fitness among men drafted for the armed forces prompted serious concern about the nation's public health in general. Numerous public and private efforts sought to improve nutrition, secure dental health, publicize methods of disease prevention, and reduce child mortality. Liberal reformers, women's clubs, religious organizations, and even the Daughters of the American Revolution joined in the work. Unfortunately, even the best intentions reflected the class and racist issues seen widely in the twenties as some activists displayed patronizing attitudes or excluded specific groups.

Herbert Hoover founded the American Child Health Association in 1923 to identify and campaign for initiatives that would improve child health generally. Early efforts focused on securing safe milk supplies and developing a health curriculum for public schools. To expand its impact, the Association recommended organizing children's health parades that would dramatize the principles of good health and strengthen the health lessons being taught in public schools. Since children love to dress in costumes and pretend, the parades were a huge success at the time, but they only continued for a little more than a decade in most places.

Heralding Modern Health Crusaders

Portland, Maine, May 1924

As early as 1915, the American Lung Association began to involve children in successful campaigns to combat tuberculosis and promote healthy living. Seizing on children's love of playing soldier, elementary

schoolchildren were enlisted as "crusaders" for good health. Outfitted with special caps and capes, reciting slogans such as "Crusaders band for health we stand," and singing "With hands and bodies clean and hearts all brave and bold, Prepared our country's flag and honor to uphold," the children competed for points that would earn them the progressive honorific titles of Crusader, Knight, Knight Banneret, and Knight of the Round Table. More than three million children were enrolled by 1919. Who could resist?

Brush Thoroughly Twice a Day

Portland, Maine, May 1924

Children's health parades almost always included a segment promoting dental hygiene, especially brushing teeth often. Massive equipment demonstrated by these three caped crusaders underscored the ideal of brushing teeth twice a day. At the conclusion of many health parades, certificates were given to those children who had perfect teeth. These rewards were intended to inspire good dental habits in even more children who hoped to receive such a certificate the next year.

Kennebunk Health Parade

Kennebunk, Maine, May 1928

Beginning in 1924, the Kennebunk Public Health Association sponsored a yearly children's health parade. Their popular event was cited as "one of the best in the state" and continued for more than a decade. Variously dressed as nurses and doctors, milkmen and farmers, fruits and vegetables, healthy teeth, or other characters, children carried signs or banners articulating the primary topics in the federally mandated health curriculum of the period.

This long line of costumed children with their decorated wagons, bicycles, and doll carriages was part of the healthy living initiative at Kennebunk. The organizers must have enjoyed strong municipal support, for, astonishingly, the children are not only walking in the middle of a street, but they are walking right up the middle of US Route One, the main highway from Maine to Florida, now notoriously choked with traffic.

Each side of the street is lined with parked cars of remarkably similar appearance, reminding us of Henry Ford's comment that customers could have whatever color they wanted, as long as it was black! There are people on the sidewalks and although a small group of boys appears to be quite intrigued by the sight of the parade. Only one adult seems to be paying any attention to the well-disciplined line of march!

You Need Milk

Kennebunk, Maine, May 1928

This young man, wearing his uniform cap, clean white shirt, and knickers, pulled his wagonload of milk bottles to represent one of the primary goals of local health parades: building awareness of the importance of safeguarding milk supplies and promoting greater milk consumption by city children.

Farmers with a Load of Fresh Vegetables

Kennebunk, Maine, May 1928

On the same day, these two young children in matching overalls promoted fresh vegetables as a component of a healthy diet. Since Children's Health Day was usually held during the first week of May, this cargo must have been difficult to assemble. With the possible exception of a few dandelion greens, fresh local produce would have been unavailable in Maine, so the vegetables seen here must have consisted of the remains of someone's root cellar or the expensive products of railroad shipments from Florida or California.

Cleanliness Is One of the Foundations of Good Government and Good Living

Boston, Massachusetts, 1930

This float was designed and produced for the Boston Tercentenary Parade by the New York firm of Messmore and Damon. It was sponsored by the Launderers' Union to promote their business as well as express the contemporary concern for cleanliness as a fundamental aspect of good citizenship. By illustrating historical activities such as boiling soiled clothing and household linens over a blazing fire, displaying a clothesline for drying laundry in the open air, and the old reliable spinning wheel for good measure, the costumed people aboard the float imply that these practices have been employed in America since Pilgrim times and further suggest that newly arrived immigrant groups should do likewise.

THE KU KLUX KLAN

New England membership in the Ku Klux Klan began to rise about 1915 and continued through the 1920s, after which it largely faded away until its recent unfortunate stirrings. The appeal of the Klan's nativist message differed in response to social and economic conditions in various places. Especially in Maine and New Hampshire, the Klan's anti-immigrant feeling was especially appealing in areas where long-simmering intolerance of Catholic French Canadians dated from the Know Nothing movement in the 1840s. More broadly, in the 1920s the Klan appealed to middle- and lower-class whites who felt threatened by newly arrived non-white and non-Protestant people from southern and central Europe whom they vilified as not 100 percent American.

Membership in the Klan, with its secret rituals, uniforms, and honorary titles, gave its members a welcome sense of identity and belonging that was very much in the manner of other fraternal organizations. Members took pride in celebrating the traditional Protestantism and family values that they believed were under attack. However, their activities were not limited to private rituals, public picnics, parades, and baseball games. The KKK in New England was aligned with the Republican Party, and its activities offered members both political agency as well as a step up the social ladder.

Within the sheltering group and protected in public by the anonymity of masks and their distinctive white hoods and robes, Klan members expressed their bigotry and felt free to threaten and intimidate people, sometimes in violent confrontations. With American flags flying and banners reading "America First" or "Preserve Racial Purity" they marched together in their own parades, openly expressing their ugly message of intolerance and hatred of immigrants, Blacks, Catholics, Jews, and labor unions.

First Parade in N. E. States of Ku Klux Klan. First Daylight Parade in U. S. A.
Milo, Maine, September 3, 1923

Many people were surprised when the Ku Klux Klan began recruiting members in Maine during the spring of 1923. The group held large rallies throughout the state and enjoyed a certain level of popularity for about five years.

The Declaration of Independence, the Constitution of the United States: the Bedrock of American Society
Portsmouth, New Hampshire, August 1923

Moving under a banner that proclaims, "Christ Our Home Our Country," members of the Ku Klux Klan presented this simple red, white, and blue float in the parade celebrating the New Hampshire Tercentenary in August 1923 at Portsmouth. Perhaps their appropriation of the basic symbols of Christianity and patriotism rendered the letters KKK less intimidating than the sight of marching men in pointed hats and long white robes would have been, but time would prove this to be a false comfort.

AMERICANIZATION

Liberty and Uncle Sam with Americanization Class Members Ready for a Parade
Portland, Maine, 1926

In the decades after 1900, formal Americanization efforts were organized in many places as a Progressive response to the increase in perceived threats to America's cultural identity from the arrival of millions of immigrants. Formal lessons in English and civics that were offered to newcomers focused on knowledge of American history and the duties of citizenship. These were augmented by classes that communicated knowledge about American holidays, heroes, and traditional American values and customs. The overt goal was to prepare people for the citizenship examination, but clearly there was a parallel attempt to detach immigrants from the culture of their homelands.

8

PATRIOTISM

The Second Continental Congress approved a resolution on June 14, 1777, specifying the colors and design of the United States flag with its thirteen alternating red and white stripes and thirteen stars on a solid color field, the latter representing "a new constellation." Soon blue became the standard background for the field of stars and from that time forward the colors red, white, and blue, the silouetted white stars, and the number thirteen have been essential in expressions of American patriotism.

As early as 1776, civic occasions and political gatherings were often enhanced by thirteen hearty toasts honoring the original thirteen colonies that became the United States of America. On many occasions thirteen young ladies, usually dressed in white to symbolize their innocence and virtue, appeared on parade floats, each wearing a sash or cap printed with the name of one of the thirteen colonies that became the original states. As the country grew, an increasing number of young women symbolized the growing number of states in the Union and even new American territories such as Alaska (1867), Hawaii (1893), and the Philipines (1898). Joining the colonies and states as patriotic symbols were individual representations of America, Uncle Sam, Columbia, Liberty or Independence, all personified by community leaders or young people.

Toward the middle of the nineteenth century, retail outlets ranging from country stores to specialty shops in urban areas and, later, large mail-order retailers like Montgomery Ward and Sears, Roebuck, and Company, offered parade supplies such as striped bunting, badges, hats for Uncle Sam and members of the Grand Army of the Republic, wigs, masks, costumes, flags, torches, fireworks, and noisemakers. The growing textile industry produced large quantities of cheap cotton cloth printed with various patterns of red and white stripes with bright stars on a dark blue ground.

Coarse woolens were woven in red, white, and blue stripes. Some of this cloth was used for building, fence, and bridge decoration or by commercial costume manufacturers. It was also used by skilled dressmakers and creative home sewers for float decorations and an increasingly wide variety of patriotic parade costumes worn by people of all ages.

With the exception of religious processions and some funerals, parades of all types include commonly understood symbols of patriotism. The lines are never without a flag, a group of civic officials, uniformed soldiers, a patriotic song, or a martial drumbeat. Often, there are multitudes of each. Repeated year after year, national symbols have been shaped over time and continue to evolve even as they are questioned. Whether focused at the beginning or spread throughout the line, these symbols stir the heart and promote personal feelings of loyalty and patriotism among both participants and spectators.

Colonies and States

Enduring emblems of the federal Union have been featured on parade floats for more than two hundred years. In 1800 in a parade at Augusta, Maine, held on February 22, George Washington's birthday, the sixteen states of the growing Union were represented by sixteen young ladies in white dresses, each wearing a scarf bearing the name of a state. They also wore black hats and cloaks to represent the nation's sense of mourning and loss after the death of the first president just two months previously.

As the country grew, more and more young ladies were invited to participate in these features. On the Fourth of July in 1811 at Pawlett, Vermont, seventeen young ladies in white represented the states and were praised in a subsequent toast as "emblems of innocence and purity—the only sure basis of all republics. When thus represented, our rights and liberties are safe."

Easy to produce, floats with these ideas were repeated again and again in many different places. They are still seen occasionally in parades to this day. In 1851 at Portsmouth, New Hampshire, "thirty one little misses, each carrying a miniature national flag" represented the states in the procession celebrating the nation's Jubilee, seventy-five years after the signing of the Declaration of Independence. At Springfield, Massachusetts, that same year, thirteen girls wore wreaths on their heads and carried bouquets instead of flags; at Lowell a similar group wore broad-brimmed gypsy hats trimmed with wreaths and streamers printed with the names of different states. At Salem, Massachusetts, the floral procession of 1851 ended with a "band of thirty-one Bloomers" carrying banners of the thirty-one states. These daring young women were wearing the shocking knee-length skirts and loose-fitting trousers gathered at the ankle that were popularly known as bloomers and were all the rage that summer. In 1854 at West Stockbridge, "the pleasantest feature of the celebration was a vehicle load of young ladies—beautiful Berkshire girls—32 in number, each representing a state of the Union, including the latest addition, Nebraska, all dressed in white with fresh twined wreaths of Berkshire flowers about their heads." At Peterborough, New Hampshire, in 1859, this feature was described as "the crowning glory of the procession." With their neat white apparel, heads decked with garlands of flowers, and sashes bearing the names of individual states, the girls elicited showers of compliments from observers everywhere.

Finding young women to represent the growing number of states was never a problem, for this feature was considered one of high status. There was always an abundance of prominent businessmen or politicians with daughters or nieces vying for a position on this important float. The real problem became providing sufficent space for everyone and making sure they were both visible and safe while moving over the parade route.

Columbia and 37 States

Rochester, New Hampshire, July 4, 1876

As part of the American centennial celebration at Rochester on July 4, 1876, this stepped platform float was considered an especially attractive feature. The design enabled spectators to see all of the thirty-seven rather solemn-looking children dressed in white with matching caps. Each one held an American flag and represented a single state of the Union. Above them was a mature woman holding fast to a tall flagpole and wearing a gown printed with stars. She represented Columbia and served as chaperone for the group. One has to wonder how the girl in the front row managed to obtain such a prominent position from which to display her high button shoes and colorful striped stockings amid the sea of white.

The Goddess of Liberty and Her Thirteen Colonies

Nantucket, Massachusetts, 1895

As the number of states in the Union grew, some parade organizers abandoned the idea of inviting a girl to represent each one. Such seems to have been the case on Columbus Day at Nantucket in 1895, when this float sponsored by the GAR carried just thirteen young ladies representing the original thirteen states. Each carried a patriotic shield ornamented with stars and stripes and the name of a state. Towering over the group, holding a large American flag, stood the goddess of Liberty wearing a red, white, and blue shawl. All fourteen of the women wore soft Phrygian caps, probably red, in the distinctive conical shape that slumps at the top and has been worn since Roman times to represent Liberty.

Uncle Sam and the States

Keene, New Hampshire, September 7, 1898

A new and popular feature of the annual Cheshire County Grange Fair in Keene in 1898, was an exhibition of decorated bicycles. Among them was this line of fifty-four girls in "becoming light colored costumes" enhanced by red, white, and blue sashes, who rode together following Uncle Sam. In an amplification of the old parade tradition, each girl wore the name of a state or territory of the United States,

At the time, many women were unaccustomed to moving alone through public streets. They all wore long skirts and close-fitting garments that impeded physical activity and proclaimed their modesty. As late as 1890, few, if any, self-respecting women would have appeared in public in ways that invited public observation and judgement but cycling brought women into public thoroughfares. Female cyclists began to wear more informal clothing, sometimes with fuller and slightly shorter skirts that revealed their heretofore concealed ankles. Such garments offered the kind of greater comfort found in other sportswear of the period, such as clothing worn for playing tennis and golf. Active women, especially cyclists, were widely admired for their graceful appearance and skillful movements. Almost as soon as cycling skills were mastered, women rode their machines in organized excursions or participated in competitive activities such as races and parades. Whether competing for a prize or proclaiming their support for a public cause, engaging in these activities was truly something new. So dramatic was the impact of this change that by the turn of the century the bicycle had become an emblem of women's rights.

America

Springvale, Maine, July 4, 1907

This ambitious float appeared in two towns on the same day! It was the first feature of a grand patriotic parade at eight-thirty in the morning at North Berwick, Maine, that included Horribles as well as "fancy floats" like this. Later they all returned twenty-two long, hot miles through Sanford to appear in a more traditional civic celebration at Springvale in the afternoon. The six strong horses with plumed headdresses and tasseled fly-nets were guided by white-clad grooms in blackface, a dramatic expression of racism in small town Maine. The float itself was fitted with a stand of bleachers, palm

trees, and a large sunshade, all trimmed in red, white, and blue. On board were Uncle Sam and Columbia as well as the usual thirteen young ladies in white dresses and patriotic sashes. As they rode, the girls sang patriotic songs composed by a local woman.

Miss Liberty and Her Thirteen Colonies

Newport, Rhode Island, 1916

In direct contrast to the forward-looking social statement made by the Keene women on their bicycles, this patriotic float carries women representing traditional domesticity as well as the original thirteen colonies. Liberty stands above them, extending her benefits to all. The most prominent item on their decorated wagon is a spinning wheel with a large hank of unspun flax hung on its distaff, symbolizing both feminine industry and domestic skill, a far cry from the cyclists' assertion of women's rights.

Uncle Sam

The patriotic character Uncle Sam began to appear in literature as a personification of the United States even before the War of 1812. The idea was based on an actual Massachusetts-born Yankee named Samuel Wilson who supplied provisions to the army in barrels marked "U. S." That mark soon became recognized as a symbol of the United States instead of that of the owner of the shipping containers. Even before hostilities ceased, Uncle Sam was a widely beloved symbol, but it was not until the centennial of American Independence in 1876 that he began to appear in Independence Day parades, often escorting the young ladies impersonating Liberty, Columbia, the original thirteen colonies, or the increasing number of states. Occasionally, a costumed Uncle Sam served as the orator at the concluding ceremonies of parades of Horribles. At Keene, New Hampshire, in 1892, Uncle Sam receive a prize of $5.00 for being the "best Horrible on foot." At Greenfield, Massachusetts, on the Fourth of July five years later, he rode in a chaise reputedly dating back to his boyhood. There he was reported to be in both good health and spirits, pleased at the way the town was celebrating his birthday.

Uncle Sam's clothing and appearance seem to have

become formulaic well before the publication of John Montgomery Flagg's well-known "I Want YOU!" troop recuitment poster of 1917. Although there have been many minor variations in the patterns of stars and stripes on his clothing, the character usually is a vigorous, but elderly white man with long white hair and beard, wearing a top hat, vest, striped trousers, and a tailcoat.

Uncle Sam and Lady Liberty

Lancaster, Massachusetts, July 4, 1890

Sanford B. Wilder trimmed his buggy in red, white, and blue, and donned a long white wig and a tall hat with a starry hatband before driving his grandaughter, in her costume as Lady Liberty, in a local parade on the Fourth of July. A well-known local figure, Wilder used this vehicle for many years working in his role as village lamplighter until the first electric street lights were installed in Lancaster about 1905.

Charles Bartlett Folsom

Pittsfield, New Hampshire, 1909

Uncle Sam was not always represented by an elderly person. Here is young Charles Bartlett Folsom dressed as Uncle Sam and ready to drive his flag-bedecked goat cart in the Old Home Day parade in Pittsfield, New Hampshire, in 1909.

George Cousens as Uncle Sam

Kennebunk, Maine, 1920

Once a person learns to ride a high-wheel bicycle, the temptation to show off the skill by riding in parades appears to be irresistible. Spectators look forward to seeing the wheels and their skilled riders return year after year to weave along on the Fourth of July or Old Home Day. People in Kennebunk, Maine, looked forward to such appearances by a well-known local "character," George Cousens. Seen here dressed as Uncle Sam and standing beside his wheel, he can also be seen riding on US Route One during the Kennebunk centennial parade. (*George Cousens also appears on page 188, riding with "General Lafayette."*)

These distinctive bicycles first appeared around 1870, replacing earlier machines called variously "bone shakers" or velocipedes. With a front wheel measuring as much as five feet in diameter, a high-wheeler moves more than fifteen feet with each pump of the pedals and is capable of high speed. Braking is achieved by applying direct pressure to the tires with a simple hand lever and/or by reversing the pedals. Stopping too quickly or hitting a large rock might result in a dangerous forward fall, a common accident known as a "header."

People today marvel at the skill involved in riding such a bicycle, especially as an unskilled rider wobbles back and forth along the roadway. In truth, aside from avoiding hazards like rocks on the road, the real challenge here is in getting on or off the vehicle. A would-be rider must approach from the rear, step up on to a mounting bar on the rear of the frame, and then leap forward onto the seat and steady himself while maintaining both balance and forward momentum.

Beginning in the 1890s, high-wheel bicycles were sometimes called "penny-farthings." The name was introduced in England where the two wheels of different sizes were recognized as being similar to those of two coins: the large penny and the much smaller farthing. The name is sometimes still used today for these challenging, but obsolete machines. After the development of "safety" bicycles about 1890, some of the old penny-farthings remained in occasional use by people like Cousens who liked to display an arcane skill, but they were quickly abandoned for both general transportation and recreation.

Uncle Sams

New London, Connecticut, May 6, 1934

This souvenir postcard shows a pair of men in colonial costume beating drums as they lead a flock of Uncle Sams followed by friends in civilian dress as part of the tercentennial parade on State Street at New London, Connecticut.

Uncle Sam and Sailor Boys

Bath, Maine, ca. 1930s

Local 469 of the Sheet Metal Workers and Coppersmiths Union at Bath Iron Works decorated a flatbed truck to carry this winning combination of Uncle Sam and five lucky local boys dressed in sailor suits as they stood in front of a large forty-eight-star flag during a Labor Day parade sometime in the 1930s. Constructing such a float must have provided the men with a welcome diversion from building massive ships for the US Navy.

Liberty Bell

1776 Liberty 1919

Bennington, Vermont, July 4, 1919

The Fourth of July parade at Bennington in 1919, was praised for the attractive and effective floats that exemplified the spirit of the day. The centerpiece of this float was a replica of the Liberty Bell with its molded inscription "Liberty throughout the land." On board was a guard of four men holding rifles, two in colonial costume, one in an army uniform, and another in navy dress. The original eighteenth-century bell from Independence Hall had served as the logo of the Centennial Exposition at Philadelphia in 1876, and between 1885 and 1915 it had traveled across the country as a national symbol. Crowds came to see it, elderly men and women knelt before it, and miniature replicas of it sold like hotcakes.

Three Cheers for the Red, White, and Blue!

Yankee Doodle
Dedham, Massachusetts, possibly 1876

With a fife and two drums, this trio appears ready to lead a parade on a very muddy street in Dedham. Without a date on the original photograph, it is hard to be sure, but since there is very little foliage on the trees and no tall grass on the Common, it may well have been April 19, Patriots Day in Massachusetts.

The three men have dressed in a variety of old-fashioned clothes, the fifer in a frock coat and tall silk hat both of which could have been first worn as early as 1845. The others are in well-worn garments they may have considered their best for many years.

Their appearance may have been inspired by Archibald M. Willard's well-known painting, *Yankee Doodle*, which quickly became an icon after it was featured at the Centennial Exposition in Philadelphia in 1876, where it must have been seen by many of the twenty-seven million visitors. Countless others saw the painting in succeeding months during its nationwide tour. The engaging picture of a fifer accompanied by two drummers has come to be known as the *Spirit of '76*. It has inspired numerous copies, both as prints for framing, as illustrations in periodicals and advertisements, and as marching units in parades. It does so to this very day.

Spirit of '76

Concord, New Hampshire, June 14, 1916

This spirited group sponsored by Boston & Maine Railroad timekeepers marched in a patriotic parade under an avenue of stately elm trees in Concord, New Hampshire, on the first Flag Day in 1916.

Woodrow Wilson had proclaimed June 14 as a national Flag Day in recognition of the date in 1777 when the Second Continental Congress adopted a resolution specifying the colors and design of the flag. Flag Day began to be observed in many places, although it was not established as a permanent holiday until 1949.

Stand by the President

Brookfield, Massachusetts, June 14, 1917

After President Wilson called again for recognition of Flag Day on June 14, 1917, promotional posters bearing his portrait and the message "Stand By the President" were distributed to schools, courthouses, post offices, and other public buildings. In Brookfield, Massachusetts, when the day arrived, Uncle Sam stood to drive this simple horse-drawn float for children of the school at Podunk, a tiny hamlet within the town. At the center holding a sceptre stands Columbia, a tall girl or perhaps the teacher herself, wearing a white gown and a crown. She is surrounded by boys and girls waving forty-eight-star flags, the girls in white robes and wearing starry crowns. On the street behind them a division of young boys in woolen knickers, coats, and flat caps waits to join the parade once it begins to move. It must have been a very late spring, for the trees are still not leafed out on June 14.

Fred Smith and His Flag Girls

Bellows Falls, Vermont, October 1, 1912

We will never know whose idea it was for these ten young women to wear golden crowns of the type usually chosen to symbolize Columbia and dress in red, white, and blue costumes featuring stars and stripes when they prepared to march in the Gala Street Parade of the Third Annual Street Fair in Bellows Falls in 1912. Dressed in an Uncle Sam costume was their gallant escort, twenty-seven-year-old Fred Smith, a railroad "flag man" who used signal flags to direct trains at the massive Boston & Maine railroad yards in the town.

A Patriotic Neighborhood

East Longmeadow, Massachusetts, July 4, 1923

When twenty-seven rather sober-looking children crowded together on this flatbed truck before a big parade in East Longmeadow in 1923, they and their families certainly deserved a prize for their diverse interpretation of America. The costumes are familiar representations of community, history, patriotism, racism, and popular culture. Liberty, Columbia, Indians, Pilgrims, a Sailor, a Dutch boy, a Boy Scout, a Red Cross nurse, a Farmer, two boys in black masks, and two more in blackface makeup have all climbed aboard to celebrate Independence Day. The intrusive little tyke in red, white, and blue on her crepe paper-trimmed bicycle in the foreground was not about to be left out of the picture.

Ruth Fairbanks Ready for an Americanization Parade

Portland, Maine, ca. 1922

Dressing cute children in red, white, and blue for a parade always stirs patriotic feeling and entertains spectators. Two-year-old Ruth Fairbanks in Portland, Maine, certainly takes the cake!

Stars and Stripes

New Bedford, Massachusetts, perhaps November 18, 1918

This time it is a much larger, forty-eight-star flag, perhaps thirty by forty feet, carried in a large city. Six men across the head and foot with more marchers supporting each side carry this flag horizontally along

Pleasant Street in the business section of New Bedford, Massachusetts. The date is unknown, but it appears to be a cold day. With only a few bits of bunting displayed on the buildings, it could have been November 11, 1918, when the joyous parade celebrating the signing of the armistice ending World War I was held without much time for preparation or decoration.

Old Home Day Comes Every Year

Tamworth, New Hampshire, 1926

A woman dressed as Columbia and carrying a ribboned staff stands beside a patriotic man in an unusual version of an Uncle Sam costume, ready to escort a group of flag bearers in front of a yoke of horned oxen in rural Tamworth, New Hampshire, on Old Home Day in 1926.

Color Guard and Boy Scouts

Bath, Maine, 1928 or later

Although the United States flag code specifies that "the flag should never be carried flat or horizontally, but always aloft and free," many parades in the years between World Wars I and II featured this kind of demonstration. Here, a group of uniformed Boy Scouts follows their color guard on a tree-lined street in Bath. The car behind them is a Ford with details characteristic of production in 1928 and 1929.

Living Flag

Manchester, New Hampshire, November 11, 1933

Living flags were inspired by the work of Hortense Reynolds, an elementary school music supervisor in Des Moines, Iowa, who may have produced the first one when she arranged red-, white-, and blue-clad children to represent a flag in a stadium grandstand during the Spanish-American War. Her idea was widely imitated, especially during times of war or economic distress when the living flag symbolized the essential role of individuals in preserving the liberty and freedom of the nation.

This living flag in the gigantic National Recovery Act Parade on a cold and windy Armistice Day in 1933 at Manchester, New Hampshire, was an especially ambitious example of the format. Two hundred women employees of the Worsted Department of the city's massive Amoskeag Textile Mills, wearing either red or white capes or blue dresses with hats featuring white stars, took their assigned places and marched in step without ever breaking ranks over a long route. They were greeted by hearty applause all along the way, even though the flag effect was best seen from the upper stories of office buildings on Manchester's Elm Street. Here they are passing Manchester's impressive Gothic Revival city hall, built in 1844–1845.

Amidst the hardships of the Great Depression, this parade combined a tribute to Manchester's sons who had fought in the First World War as well as an affirmation of the city's faith in a national recovery program that was "designed to lift America from the slough of despond into which four tortured years had crowded her." Planners expected Manchester's parade to be the leading Armistice Day entertainment in the northeast, attracting "almost everybody of importance in the whole state," either as participants or spectators.

RICARD'S
BEN MEYER
YOUR CREDIT IS GOOD
MANCHESTER HAT WORKS
LOANS
11-11-1933
#28

For nearly 250 years, the images and ideas seen in New England parades have enhanced the shared values, knowledge of history, and honest esteem for America that has fueled individual participation in democratic government and the growth of the nation. These ongoing events reflect a rich regional culture that takes pride in its past, and at the same is also responsive to challenge and change. Although there is sometimes backlash, there is always adaptation and innovation. With ever greater diversity, new topics, and more inclusiveness, parades continue to exhibit the complexity of our society and express a wide variety of ideas and concerns. At the same time, they help to bind us together, nurture civic responsibility, and express our long-term hope for the future. Even in a time when national unity seems threatened by new and divisive forces, the powerful emotions stirred by parades can inspire us to move forward together with confidence.

Everyone loves a parade!

Acknowledgments

As I think about my experiences in studying parade traditions over the past sixteen years, I realize that I have tapped a rich vein of regional culture that is deeply meaningful to many. As a result, I must first acknowledge my indebtedness to the host of New England historians, antiquarians, collectors, librarians, conservators, and curators who have assembled, identified, and preserved vast archives of images and ephemera. It would be impossible to name them all, for they range from Jeremy Belknap and Isaiah Thomas in the 1790s, and the successive legions of staff and dedicated volunteers who have worked with this material for decades, to the latest crop of public history, library science, and museum studies graduates. Every picture in this book is here because of the perspicacity of those who saved it in the first place and the ensuing stewardship of those responsible for its care, their increasing commitment to broad access, and the technical skills of today's digital imaging specialists.

People in historical societies and libraries throughout New England have been generous beyond my expectations as I asked to see everything related to parades or sought identification of specific images. Dedicated local historians and custodians of rare ephemera have opened their vaults, shared the contents of rich personal files, and tapped their lengthy contact lists with generosity and enthusiasm. They have welcomed me for in-person visits and responded to remote research queries. Some pursued elusive information or image identifications through their Facebook networks. Once their interest was piqued, some refused to give up. Many are still sending interesting new material even as I have turned my attention to writing. In particular, I am pleased to acknowledge that permission to include material from an article I wrote for *Historical New Hampshire* about White Mountain coaching parades was kindly granted by the New Hampshire Historical Society.

The list of people who have helped bring all this together now includes more than six hundred names and, although space prohibits naming them individually, I trust they know both who they are and how grateful I am to each and every one. Much of their work has not been easy. When I began, some of this material had not even been cataloged, much less digitized. Collectors, curators, and librarians from Houlton, Maine, to the Smithsonian have told me that few if any scholars have ever approached them to study or publish their holdings on this topic and they were thrilled that some of their choice items might be brought to light. Some brought out dusty boxes of crumbling newspapers, rusty badges, and dead spiders, encouraging me to go through it all carefully, for there just might be something of interest . . . and often there was. A few struggled through snowdrifts to search for requested material in unheated buildings. Many working remotely during the Covid-19 pandemic surmounted additional difficulties to retrieve information and provide images. Skilled photographers and image technicians have made it possible to see extraordinary detail, making it possible to look into the eyes of a veteran of the American Revolution as well as those of an excited child riding high above the streets of her hometown on parade day.

Having retired from full-time employment and teaching before I began this project, I have not been the beneficiary of regular interaction with a flock of graduate students or a defined group of academic colleagues. However, I do wish to acknowledge the contributions of everyone who shared ideas and information, some after hearing me lecture on various aspects of New England parades and others who heard more than they expected when they sat next to me on an airplane or at a dinner and asked, "what do you do" or "what are you working on now?" My favorite cashier at the grocery store has developed an extraordinary enthusiasm for the topic and now asks what I have found recently and when he will be able to read the book. Usually, as we talk, others stop their own conversations and listen in with growing interest. Not only do complete strangers draw near and hear my latest discoveries, but they often tell me their own parade stories and point me to new sources of images and information, some useful and some not. Sullen teenagers even smile and always say, "Cool!" Most people have never heard of the Antiques and Horribles and are fascinated as I explain this arcane New England phenomenon. I am grateful to all of them for their interest, their questions, and their generous sharing.

I am especially indebted to the many friends, professional colleagues, and family members who served as readers of various drafts of my manuscript. Their perceptive comments, helpful suggestions, and specific corrections have greatly enriched my text and helped me avoid many mistakes. Those errors that remain are entirely my own responsibility, for which I apologize.

Howard Mansfield and Richard Candee were kind enough to read every word, and they both offered incisive comments and constructive suggestions. Margaret Spicer, Darrell Hyder, and Tom Curren each read several chapters and were able to augment information as well as suggest editorial revisions and provide helpful advice. Tom Kelliher at Old Sturbridge Village read the section on the New England militia as well as several individual entries, offering additional information reflecting his rich knowledge of New England during the years 1790–1840. Earle Shettleworth reviewed many entries and was always responsive when I had a question or needed clarification about an event in Maine. Among other things, Tom Hardiman made *The Floral Architect* and other resources at the Portsmouth Athenaeum available in more ways than one. Lauren Hewes at the American Antiquarian Society has been helpful in many ways, especially in searching for elusive examples of sheet music covers. And, as always, Lorna Condon at Historic New England has been most helpful in sorting out and identifying early visual material. John Ott reviewed text and provided information, especially about the Masons and the Grange. He and his wife, Lili, have been my most helpful and encouraging friends.

I am especially grateful to those who were instrumental in bringing the book to publication. Jane Garrett at Knopf, Jud Hale at Yankee Publishing, and David Godine all offered encouragement and suggestions. It was Howard Mansfield who suggested that it might be of interest to Sarah Bauhan, and she quickly agreed to add it to the list at Bauhan Publishing, LLC. At the same time, Brock Jobe suggested to Jim Donohue at Old Sturbridge Village that parades might serve as a useful theme for the forthcoming 75th Anniversary celebration of the museum, asserting that parades have always been central to festive culture and influential in defining community identity and values. After Jim readily agreed, the Village became co-publisher of the book, and staff there began planning the related exhibitions and public programming that will continue for several years. An important goal for all of us is to help reinvigorate parade traditions as useful bricks in the much-needed rebuilding of community, not only in New England.

Working with Publisher Sarah Bauhan, Art Director Henry James, and Editorial Director Mary Ann Faughnan at Bauhan Publishing has been an absolute pleasure. I am grateful for the interest they have taken in the whole project, their careful attention to detail, and their patience. The finished book is very much the result of their editorial and design skills. Bringing out a handsome and interesting publication has been our mutual pleasure.

Every member of my family has been part of this project from the beginning. My children Sarah, Tom, and Tim began joining me as parade spectators in their strollers, and they have become experts in pointing out both new ideas and the same old stuff. My granddaughter, Elizabeth, spent part of one summer beginning the task of securing permissions for image publication from nearly one hundred institutions. As I became focused on analysis of trends, members of three generations expressed disbelief at my reliance on banks of old-fashioned index cards to sort and track individual float topics and troops of Horribles. In the end, they had to agree that it worked.

My daughter, Sarah Rooker, is a respected northern New England historian and a great teacher who has shared many history projects with me over the years. She has been an invaluable advisor this time, carefully reading and re-reading many drafts. I am most grateful for her perceptive comments on interpretation and suggestions of appropriate language as well as her encouragement at times when I felt overwhelmed by the quantity of material and the scope of the project.

My biggest debt of gratitude must go to my dear husband, Richard, a patient perfectionist and an antiquarian of the best kind, with widespread knowledge of New England genealogy, history, and material culture. His editorial skills, photographic memory, and loving support have contributed to every aspect of my parade study and been instrumental in the completion of this book. In addition to his careful compilation of the illustration credits, he has augmented my research, read many drafts, tracked down endless details, cooked many meals, and provided both time and space for me to focus on the writing. It would have been a lesser book without him, if it had happened at all.

Notes

1. Letter from John Adams to Abigail Adams, July 3, 1776. "Had a Declaration . . ." *The Adams Papers. Adams Family Correspondence.* Edited by L. H. Butterfield. Cambridge, MA: The Belknap Press of Harvard University Press, 1963. II. June 1776–March 1778, 30.
2. George Washington Warren. *The History of the Bunker Hill Monument Association During the First Century of the United States of America.* Boston: James R. Osgood and Company, 1877, 314.
3. *Portsmouth Journal*, January 8, 1851.
4. *Mechanic's Song. . . by Franklin And the President's Chorus in Paris and London As sung at the Tremont Theater, Boston.* Library of Congress, Rare Books and Special Collections Division, America Singing. Nineteenth-Century Song Sheets.
5. M. A. DeWolfe Howe, ed., *The Articulate Sisters: Passages from Journals and Letters of the Daughters of President Josiah Quincy of Harvard University*, Cambridge, Massachusetts: Harvard University Press, 1946, 13–14.
6. *The New-Bedford Register*, New Bedford, Massachusetts, June 7, 1843.
7. *Nashua Telegraph*, Nashua, New Hampshire, July 5, 1853.
8. *The Kite-Ender.* Lynn, Massachusetts, July 4, 1874.
9. Marian Lawrence Peabody. *To Be Young Was Very Heaven: A Boston girlhood at the century's turn from the Diaries of Marian Peabody Lawrence.* Boston: Houghton Mifflin Company, 1967, 25.
10. Mark Twain. *Life on the Mississippi.* Boston: James R. Osgood and Company, 1883, 447.

Selected Bibliography and Primary Sources

As I outlined in the Preface, the information and illustrations in this book are the result of sixteen years of dedicated research in museums, libraries, and historical societies, both online and in their physical spaces, mostly in New England. The work also reflects a lifetime of deep reading, careful observation, and personal experiences that have been both vocational and avocational. One of the shared pleasures of being a cultural historian and a museum curator married to another is the opportunity to observe and identify ongoing traditions and symbols as well as patterns of evolution and change. Finding new images and unique objects contributes to broader understanding. This is never a nine-to-five obligation but an essential part of the fabric of an interesting life as well as the reason behind overflowing bookshelves and a personal cabinet of curiosities.

I began my study by reviewing parade-related materials at organizations where I knew the collections well, having once been employed as Director at the New Hampshire Historical Society, Strawbery Banke Museum, and the Society for the Preservation of New England Antiquities (SPNEA, now Historic New England). At the same time, I began broad reading on the origins and meaning of parade traditions in Europe and America over many centuries. I spent several days reviewing graphic materials at the American Antiquarian Society in Worcester and the Pocumtuck Valley Historical Society (PVMA) in Deerfield. Having long experience with New England's local historical societies, I knew that many of them hold rich collections of material that is largely unknown outside each individual community. Early on I spent full days reviewing parade materials in three selected collections: the Historical Society of Old Newbury (now the Museum of Old Newbury), the Peterborough (New Hampshire) Historical Society (now the Monadnock Center for History and Culture), and the Marblehead Historical Society (now the Marblehead Museum). I quickly realized each had materials related to one or more celebrations unique to that community in addition to scattered images mostly focused on the Fourth of July. Some had evidence of the Antiques and Horribles, others did not. Most had files or microfilm of local newspapers that amplified my study. Clearly a broader search would yield more than enough material to focus on New England, the place I know best. Doing so would permit me to dig deep in some local repositories, feeling certain that plenty of similar things can be found by others, both here in New England as well as in other parts of the country. I have now worked in more than one hundred New England collections, and I sincerely hope that my studies will prompt many more, for there is both insight and delight in looking closely at material related to these events.

As I assembled several thousand images, I concentrated on those that were visually compelling and conveyed a clear idea. It was easy to understand the ways identity, power, and patriotism were displayed, but there were some narrative floats whose meaning eluded me. Whenever I found both place and date identified, voluminous newspaper research usually made it possible to identify parade portrayals and complex details that have now lost their meaning, as well as help me to trace the way new ideas spread from place to place.

For most of the years covered by this study, newspapers published in New England's cities and towns included extensive descriptive and documentary coverage of local events. Long before there were any illustrations of small, local civic celebrations and parades, editors of weekly newspapers provided extensive coverage and detailed descriptions of children's floral processions and the individual characters marching with the Antiques and Horribles. Editors clearly understood that names sell newspapers, so it is no surprise to find long lists naming the officials and sponsors of a parade along with each separate marching group, band of musicians, engine company, occupational division, and business. The floats are usually listed with both title and sponsor, sometimes with the name of every participant, the text of the signs or banners, and detailed descriptions of the primary components. Since these sources are now readily available on several internet sites, I will not name every newspaper that I consulted. You can be assured, however, that almost every illustration in this book has been matched with a description in a contemporary newspaper, many of which are the source of quotations in the accompanying text.

Although many curators and librarians insisted that I was the first to study their collections, clearly this cannot be the case, for I found useful information and interpretation in the titles listed below. What I also found in the secondary literature, though, was a heavy reliance on the same few illustrations, a general disregard of small-town events or illustrations, and either misunderstanding or total ignorance of the importance of the Antiques and Horribles. Careful study of local collections and historic newspapers has helped me to begin to address these issues.

The following list includes most of the sources consulted for this study, but in the same way that many historic images remain to be discovered, there are countless printed accounts of civic anniversary and Old Home Day celebrations, programs, orations, poems, and ephemera that relate to the topic of parades in New England. More and more of it is being digitized, but in all probability, there will always be additional material remaining to be discovered, especially in local repositories and private collections.

Selected Bibliography

America's Parade: A Celebration of Macy's Thanksgiving Day Parade. New York: Life Books, Time, Inc., 2001.

Appelbaum, Diana Karter. *The Glorious Fourth: An American Holiday, an American History.* New York and Oxford: Facts on File, 1989.

Bell, Whitfield, Jr. "The Federal Processions of 1788," *The New-York Historical Society Quarterly* 46 (1962): 5–30.

Benes, Peter, ed. *New England Celebrates: Spectacle, Commemoration, and Festivity. The Dublin Seminar for New England Folklife Annual Proceedings, 2000.* Boston: Boston University, 2002.

Benes, Peter, ed. *New England Music: The Public Sphere, 1600–1900. The Dublin Seminar for New England Folklife Annual Proceedings, 1996.* Boston: Boston University, 1998.

Bird, William L., Jr. *Holidays on Display.* Washington, DC: Smithsonian Institution, Museum of American History in association with Princeton Architectural Press, New York, 2007.

Blancke, Shirley and Barbara Robinson. *From Musketaquid to Concord: The Native and European Experience.* Concord, MA: The Concord Antiquarian Museum, 1985.

Bremer, Francis J. "Remembering—and Forgetting—John Winthrop and the Puritan Founders." *The Massachusetts Historical Review* 6 (2004): 38–69.

Brown, Dona. *Inventing New England: Regional Tourism in the Nineteenth Century.* Washington, DC, and London: The Smithsonian Institution Press, 1995.

Burstein, Andrew. *America's Jubilee: A Generation Remembers the Revolution After Fifty Years of Independence.* New York: Vintage Books, 2001.

Candee, Richard M. *The Artful Life of Thomas P. Moses, 1808–1881: "Full of Poetry, music, painting—anything but money."* Portsmouth, NH: Portsmouth Athenaeum, 2002.

Castle, Terry. *Masquerade and Civilization: The Carnivalesque in Eighteenth-Century English Culture and Fiction.* Stanford, CA: Stanford University Press, 1986.

Chrystal, William G. "Elijah Lovejoy's Oration on the Fiftieth Anniversary of American Independence: An Essay Discovered." *Maine History* 48, no. 2 (July 2014): 300–319.

Cohen, Hennig and Tristram Potter Coffin, eds. *The Folklore of American Holidays.* Detroit, London: Gale, 1998.

Conforti, Joseph A. *Imagining New England: Explorations of Regional Identity from the Pilgrims to the Mid-Twentieth Century.* Chapel Hill, NC, and London: The University of North Carolina Press, 2001.

Curren, Thomas S. *A Bicentennial History of Bridgewater, New Hampshire, 1788–1988.* Bridgewater, NH: Bridgewater Bicentennial Committee: 1988.

———. *Old Home Day in New Hampshire, 1899–1998: Celebrating the Living History of New Hampshire's Communities.* Concord, NH: Inherit New Hampshire, 1998.

Curtis, John Obed and William H. Guthman. *New England Militia Uniforms and Accoutrements: A Pictorial Survey.* Sturbridge, MA: Old Sturbridge Village, 1971.

Davies, Wallace Evan. *Patriotism on Parade: The Story of Veterans' and Hereditary Organizations in America, 1783–1900.* Cambridge, MA: Harvard University Press, 1955.

Davis, Susan G. *Parades and Power: Street Theatre in*

Nineteenth-Century Philadelphia. Berkeley and Los Angeles: University of California Press, 1988.

Deloria, Philip J. *Playing Indian.* New Haven and London: Yale University Press, 1998.

Diamant, Lincoln. *Hoopla on the Hudson: An Intimate View of New York's Great 1909 Hudson–Fulton Celebration of 1909.* Fleischmanns, NY: Purple Mountain Press, 2003.

———. *The Diary of William Bentley, D. D., Pastor of the East Church, Salem, Massachusetts.* 4 vols. Gloucester, MA: Peter Smith, 1962.

Doderer-Winkler, Melanie. *Magnificent Entertainments: Temporary Architecture for Georgian Festivals.* New Haven, CT, and London: Published for the Paul Mellon Centre for Studies in British Art by Yale University Press, 2013.

Estus, Charles W. and John F. McClymer. *gä till Amerika: The Swedish Creation of an Ethnic Identity for Worcester, Massachusetts.* Worcester, MA: Worcester Historical Museum, 1994.

Fisher, David Hackett. *Liberty and Freedom: A Visual History of America's Founding Ideas.* New York: Oxford University Press, 2005.

Fox, Charles Philip and F. Beverly Kelley. *The Great Circus Street Parade in Pictures.* New York: Dover Publications, 1978.

Glassberg, David. *American Historical Pageantry: The Uses of Tradition in the Early Twentieth Century.* Chapel Hill, NC, and London: The University of North Carolina Press, 1990.

Goetz, Stephen H. "The Ku Klux Klan in New Hampshire." *Historical New Hampshire* 43, no.4, (Winter 1988): 245–263.

Harrison, Mark. *Crowds and History: Mass Phenomena in English Towns, 1790–1835.* New York: Cambridge University Press, 1988.

Hazen, Robert M. and Margaret Hindle Hazen. *Keepers of the Flame: The Role of Fire in American Culture, 1775–1925.* Princeton, NJ: Princeton University Press, 1992.

Heideking, Jürgen, Geneviève Fabre, and Kai Dreisbach, eds. *Celebrating Ethnicity and Nation: American Festive Culture from the Revolution to the Early 20th Century.* New York and Oxford: Berghahn Books, 2001.

Hickey, Donald R. "Notes on the Origins of 'Uncle Sam,' 1810–1820." *New England Quarterly.* 88, no. 4 (December 2015): 684–692.

Higham, John. "Indian Princess and Roman Goddess: The First Female Symbols of America." American Antiquarian Society, *Proceedings*, C (1990), 45–79.

Hill, Tracey. *Pageantry and power: A cultural history of the modern Lord Mayor's Show, 1585–1639.* Manchester, UK, and New York: Manchester University Press, 2011.

Johnson, Kathleen Eagen. *The Hudson–Fulton Celebration: New York's River Festival of 1909 and the Making of a Metropolis.* New York: Fordham University Press, 2009.

Johnson, Malcolm. *David Claypoole Johnston, American Graphic Humorist: 1798–1865. An Exhibition jointly held by The American Antiquarian Society, Boston College, The Boston Public Library and The Worcester Art Museum in March 1970.* Printed at Lunenberg, VT: The Stinehour Press, 1970.

Jung, Sandro. *James Thomson's The Seasons: Print Culture, and Visual Interpretation, 1730–1842.* Bethlehem, PA: Lehigh University Press, 2015.

Kammen, Michael. *Mystic Chords of Memory: The Transformation of Tradition in American Culture.* New York: Alfred A. Knopf, 1991.

Levasseur, A. *Lafayette in America in 1824 and 1825: Journal of a Voyage to the United States.* 2 vols. Philadelphia: Carey and Lea, 1829; Forgotten Books, 2012.

Leepson, Marc, *Flag: An American Biography.* New York: Thomas Dunne Books, An Imprint of St. Martin's Press, 2005.

Little, David B. *America's First Centennial Celebration: The Nineteenth of April 1875 at Lexington and Concord, Massachusetts.* Boston: Houghton Mifflin Company, 1974.

Lourie, Christine Arnold. "Baby Pilgrims, Sturdy Forefathers, and One Hundred Percent Americanism: The Mayflower Tercentenary of 1920." *Massachusetts Historical Review* 17 (2014): 35–66.

Lynn, Kenneth S., ed. *The Comic Tradition in America: An Anthology of American Humor.* New York: W. W. Norton & Company, Inc., 1958.

Marling, Karal Ann. *George Washington Slept Here: Colonial Revivals and American Culture, 1876–1986.* Cambridge, MA, and London: Harvard University Press, 1988.

McCullough, David. *The American Spirit: Who We Are and What We Stand For.* New York: Simon and Schuster Paperbacks, 2017.

McNamara, Brooks. *Day of Jubilee: The Great Age of Public Celebrations in New York, 1788–1909.* Illustrated from the Collections of the Museum of the City of New York. New Brunswick, NJ, and London: Rutgers University Press, 1997.

Melder, Keith E. *Hail to the Candidate: Presidential Campaigns from Banners to Broadcasts.* Washington, DC, and London: Smithsonian Institution Press, 1992.

Miller, Marla R. *Betsy Ross and the Making of America.* New York: Henry Holt, 2010.

Minor, Romie, Laurie Ann Tamborino, and the Parade Company. *Images of America: Detroit's Thanksgiving Day Parade.* Charleston, SC, Chicago, Portsmouth, NH, and San Francisco: Arcadia Publishing, 2003.

Nelles, H. V. *The Art of Nation-Building: Pageantry and Spectacle at Quebec's Tercentenary.* Toronto, Buffalo, London: University of Toronto Press, 1999.

Nemanic, Mary Lou. *One Day for Democracy: Independence Day and the Americanization of Iron Range Immigrants.* Athens, OH: Ohio University Press, 2007.

Newman, Simon P. *Parades and the Politics of the Street: Festive Culture in the Early American Republic.* Philadelphia: University of Pennsylvania Press, 1997.

Nickels, Cameron C. *New England Humor: From the Revolutionary War to the Civil War.* Knoxville, TN: The University of Tennessee Press, 1993.

Nylander, Jane C. "Coaching Parades in Bethlehem and North Conway, 1887–1896." *Historical New Hampshire: Northern New Hampshire—Through the Notches and Beyond* 62, no. 2 (Fall 2008): 79–99.

O'Gorman, James F. *Accomplished in All Departments of Art: Hammatt Billings of Boston, 1818–1874.* Amherst, MA: University of Massachusetts Press, 1998.

Parfrey, Adam and Craig Heimbichner. *Ritual America: Secret Brotherhoods and Their Influence on American Society—A Visual Guide.* [Port Townsend, WA] Feral House, 2012.

Pencak, William, Matthew Davis, and Simon P. Newman. *Riot and Revelry in Early America,* University Park, PA: The Pennsylvania State University Press, 2002.

Pfitzer, Gregory M. *Picturing the Past: Illustrated Histories and the American Imagination, 1840–1900.* Washington, DC, and London: Smithsonian Institution Press, 2002.

Roberts, Paige W. "The Floral Architect: Rules and Designs for Processions." In Dublin Seminar for New England Folklife *Annual Proceedings, 2000.* Boston: Boston University, 2002: 29–46.

Ryan, Mary. *Women in Public: Between Banners and Ballots, 1825–1880.* Baltimore, MD: Johns Hopkins University Press, 1990.

———. "The American Parade: Representations of the Nineteenth-Century Social Order." in *The New Cultural History.*

Edited by Lynn Hunt. Berkeley, Los Angeles, and London: University of California Press, 1989.

Saxton, Alexander. *The Rise and Fall of the White Republic. Class Politics and Mass Culture in Nineteenth-Century America.* London and New York: Verso, rev. ed. 2003.

Simpson, Richard V. *Independence Day: How the Day Is Celebrated in Bristol, Rhode Island.* Middletown, RI: Aquidneck Graphics, 1989.

Smith, Craig Bruce, "Claiming the Centennial: The American Revolution's Blood and Spirit in Boston, 1870–1876." *Massachusetts Historical Review* 15 (2013): 7–53.

Splendid Ceremonies: The Paul and Marianne Gourary Collection of Illustrated Fête Books. New York: Christie's Sale Catalogue, June 12, 2009.

Spicer, Richard C. "Popular Songs for Public Celebrations in Federal Portsmouth, New Hampshire. *Music and Society* 25, nos. 1 & 2 (Spring/Summer 2001): 1–99.

Stevenson, Louise L. "The Transatlantic Travels of James Thomson's *The Seasons* and its Baggage of Material Culture, 1730–1870." *Proceedings of the American Antiquarian Society,* 116, Part I (2006): 121–165.

Travers, Len. *Celebrating the Fourth: Independence Day and the Rites of Nationalism in the Early Republic.* Amherst, MA: University of Massachusetts Press, 1997.

Wade, Melvin C. "'Shining in Borrowed Plumage': Affirmation of Community in Black Coronation Festivals of New England, ca. 1750–1850" in Robert Blair St. George, ed. *Material Life in America.* Boston: Northeastern University Press, 1988. 171–181.

Waldstreicher, David. *In the Midst of Perpetual Fetes: The Making of American Nationalism, 1776–1820.* Chapel Hill, NC, and London: University of North Carolina Press for the Omohundro Institute of Early American History and Culture, Williamsburg, Virginia, 1997.

Wittmann, Matthew, ed. *Circus and the City: New York, 1793–2010.* New York: The Bard Graduate Center: New Haven, CT, and London, Yale University Press, 2012. Bangor, ME: 1870.

Withington, Robert. *English Pageantry. An Historical Outline.* New York, London, and Cambridge, MA: Harvard University Press, Vol. I, 1918 (reprinted by Nabu, 2001); Vol. II, 1926 (reprinted by Benjamin Bloom, Inc., New York: 1963).

Selected Primary Sources

A Brief History of the Town of Salisbury, Massachusetts, and Program of the [Tercentenary] Celebration. Salisbury, MA, 1938.

A Memorial of Christopher Columbus from the City of Boston in Honor of the Discovery of America. Boston: Printed by Order of the City Council, 1893.

A Record of the Commemoration July Second and Third of the Two Hundred and Fiftieth Anniversary of the Settlement of Haverhill, Massachusetts. Boston: Joseph George Cupples, 1891.

"An Historic Event. Wolfeboro Celebrates Its One Hundred and Fiftieth Anniversary." *The Granite Monthly* 52, no.10 (October 1920): 374–408.

Baum, L. Frank. *The Art of Decorating Show Windows and Interiors.* 3rd ed. Chicago: The Merchant's Record Co., 1903.

Castine State-Centenary Carnival under the Direction of the Castine Women's Club and Board of Selectmen. Program August fifth, nineteen hundred and twenty. Containing the list of Episodes of the Pageant and the Explanatory Historic Narrative. Ellsworth, ME: The American Print, 1920.

Celebration of the Centennial Anniversary of the Battle of Bunker Hill. Boston: Printed by Order of the City Council, 1875.

Celebration of the Centennial Anniversary of the Introduction of the Art of Printing in New Hampshire in the city of Portsmouth, October 6, 1856. A sketch of the proceedings, the oration, decorations, speeches, sentiments, letters, &c. &c. Portsmouth, NH: Edward N. Fuller, 1857.

Celebration of the Fiftieth Anniversary of the Adoption of the Charter of the City of Concord, New Hampshire. Official Programme. August 19th–20th, 1903. Concord, NH, 1903.

Celebration of the One Hundred and Fiftieth Anniversary of Gorham, Maine, May 25, 1886. Portland, ME: B. Thurston & Company, Printers, 1886.

"Celebration of the 150th Anniversary [of Hartland, Vermont]." *The Vermonter,* November 1913, 221–234; December 1913, 291–256.

Celebration of the Two Hundred and Fiftieth Anniversary of the Settlement of Boston, September 17, 1880. Boston: Printed by Order of the City Council, 1880.

Celebration of the Two Hundred and Fiftieth Anniversary of the Settlement of Newbury, June 10, 1885. Newburyport: Printed by Order of the Historical Society of Old Newbury, 1885.

Centennial Celebration, at Danvers, Mass. June 16, 1852. Boston: Printed by Dutton and Wentworth, 1852.

Colden, Cadwallader D. *Memoir, Prepared at the Request of a Committee of the Common Council of the City of New York, and Presented to the Mayor of the City, at the Celebration of the Completion of the New York Canals.* New York, 1825.

Cole, Aaron B. and J. L. M. Willis, eds., *History of the Centennial of the Incorporation of the Town of Eliot Maine August 7th–13th, 1910.* Eliot, ME: Augustine Caldwell, 1912.

Cothren, William. *Second Centennial Celebration of the Settlement of Ancient Woodbury, and the Reception of the First Indian Deed, Held at Woodbury, Conn., July 4 and 5, 1859.* Woodbury, CT: Published by the General Committee, 1859.

Cummings, Thomas Harrison, ed. *The Webster Centennial. Proceedings of the Webster Historical Society at Marshfield,*

Mass., October 12, 1882. With an account of other celebrations on the one hundredth anniversary of the birth of Daniel Webster. Boston: Published by the Webster Historical Society, 1883.

Eastman, Herbert W., comp. *Semi-Centennial of the City of Manchester, September 6, 7, 8, 9, 1896.* Manchester, NH: Printed by the John B. Clarke Company, 1897.

Excursion of the Putnam Phalanx to Boston, Cambridge, and Providence, October 4th, 5th, 6th, and 7th, in the year of our lord, 1859. Hartford, CT.: Published by the Phalanx, 1859.

Exeter Tercentenary Committee. *1638 Program Tercentenary Celebration of the Town of Exeter, New Hampshire, June 30th to July 4th, 1938.* Exeter, NH, 1938.

Festival of the Sons of New Hampshire: with the Speeches . . . Celebrated at Boston, November 7, 1849. Boston: James French, 1850.

Head, James H. *Home Pastimes; or, Tableaux Vivants.* Boston: J. E. Tilton and Company, 1860.

———. *The Floral Architect, and Decorators Companion. Containing Designs and Rules for Projecting Forty Triumphal Arches and Monuments, Fifty Cars and Chariots, for Floral, National, and Horticultural and Firemen's Processions, with One Hundred Useful and Elegant Ornaments in Verdure, Flowers, Flags &c. For Decorating Halls, Churches, and Public Buildings, Together With Two Hundred Descriptions of Street and Interior Decorations.* Unpublished manuscript with illustrations in watercolor and ink. Portsmouth, NH. Compiled ca. 1858–1865.

Historic Processions in Boston, 1789–1824. The Bostonian Society Publications. Vol. 6, Boston: Old State House, 1908. 65–119.

Historical Sketch of the Ancient and Honorable Artillery Company of Massachusetts Chartered 1638 and Catalogue of Members of the Company. Boston, 1914.

Historic Events of Worcester. A Brief Account of Some of the Most Interesting Events Which Have Occurred in Worcester During the Past Two Hundred Years. Worcester, MA: Issued by the Worcester Bank & Trust Company in Commemoration of the Two Hundredth Anniversary of the Incorporation of the Town of Worcester, 1922.

Hull, John T. *1786–1886 Centennial Celebration. An Account of the Municipal Celebration of the One Hundredth Anniversary of the Incorporation of the Town of Portland, July 4th, 5th, and 6th, 1886.* Portland, ME: Publication Committee of the City Council. Printed by Owen, Strout & Company, 1886.

Jones, Frederic William, A. M., M. D., comp. *Celebration Proceedings of the One Hundred and Fiftieth Anniversary of New Ipswich, N. H., August 26–28, 1900.* New Ipswich, NH: The Celebration Committee, 1900.

Litchfield County Centennial Celebration, Held at Litchfield. Conn., 13th and 14th of August, 1851. Hartford, CT: Edwin Hunt, 1851.

Masquerade and Carnival: Their Customs and Costumes. n. p. The Butterick Publishing, Co., 1892. Reprinted by Fredonia Books, Amsterdam: the Netherlands, 2003.

Medfield, Massachusetts. Proceedings at the Celebration of the Two Hundred and Fiftieth Anniversary of the Town, June 6, 1901. Boston: Geo. H. Ellis Co, 1902.

Memorial of the Inauguration of the Statue of Franklin. Boston: Prepared and Printed by Authority of the City Council, 1857.

Official Program of the One Hundred and Fiftieth Anniversary Celebration. Hancock, New Hampshire. August 21–22, 1929. Hancock, NH: The Sesquicentennial Committee, 1929.

Official Souvenir Program. Greenfield, Massachusetts. Sesquicentennial 1753 June 9, 1903. Greenfield, MA: Press of E. A. Hall & Co, 1909.

Official Souvenir Program of the 275th Anniversary of the Town of Stamford, Connecticut. Thursday, Friday, Saturday, Sunday, June Eight, Nine, Ten, Eleven Nineteen Hundred and Sixteen. Stamford, CT: Published Under the Auspices of the Publicity Committee, 1916.

Potter. C. E. *An Address, delivered before the Amoskeag Veterans, of Manchester, N.H., February Twenty-second, 1855. Together with the Proceedings of the Association on the Occasion, and the Constitution and By-Laws of the Same.* Manchester, NH: Adams, Hildreth & Company, Printers, 1855.

Pringle, James R., comp. and ed. *The Book of the Three Hundredth Anniversary Observance of the Foundation of the Massachusetts Bay Colony at Cape Ann in 1623 and the Fiftieth Year of the Incorporation of Gloucester as a City.* Gloucester, MA: Issued by the Three Hundredth Anniversary Executive Committee, 1924.

Proceedings and Addresses Commemorative of the Two Hundredth Anniversary of the Incorporation of the Town of Lexington. Lexington, MA: Published by Vote of the Town, June 25, 1914.

Proceedings at the Centennial Celebration of the Battle of Lexington, April 19, 1775. Lexington, MA: Published by the Town. Boston: Lockwood, Brooks, & Co., 1875.

Proceedings at the Reception and Dinner in Honor of George Peabody, Esq., of London, by the Citizens of the Old Town of Danvers, October 9, 1856. Boston: Henry W. Dutton & Son, 1856.

Quarter Millennial Celebration of the City of Taunton, Massachusetts. Tuesday and Wednesday, June 4 and 5, 1889. Taunton, MA: Published by the City Government, 1889.

Rhode Island Tercentenary, 1636–1936. A Report by the Rhode Island Tercentenary Commission of the Celebration of the Three Hundredth Anniversary of the Settlement of the State of Rhode Island and Providence Plantations in 1636 by Roger Williams. Published by the Rhode Island Tercentenary Commission, 1937.

Second Festival of the Sons of New Hampshire, Celebrated in Boston, November 2, 1853; Including also an Account of the Proceedings in Boston on the Day of the Funeral at Marshfield, and the Subsequent Obsequies Commemorative of the Death of Daniel Webster, Their Late President. Boston: James French and Company, 1854.

The Berkshire Jubilee, Celebrated at Pittsfield, Mass. August 22 and 23, 1844. Albany, NY: Weare C. Little; Pittsfield, MA: F. P. Little, 1845.

The Centennial at Windsor, Vermont, July 4, 1876. Being a record of the proceedings of the celebration; and containing the address and poem there delivered; also a view of Windsor as it now is. Windsor, VT: Published by the Journal Company, 1876.

The Centennial Celebration of the Settlement of Bangor, September 30, 1869. Published by the Committee of Arrangements.

The Meadow City's Quarter Millennial Book. A Memorial of the Celebration of the Two Hundred and Fiftieth Anniversary of the Settlement of the Town of Northampton, Massachusetts. June 5th, 6th, and 7th, 1904. Published by the City of Northampton, 1904.

The Railroad Jubilee: an account of the celebration commemorative of the opening of railroad communication between Boston and Canada, Sept. 17th, 18th, and 19th, 1851. Boston: J. H. Eastburn, city printer, 1852.

The Re-Union of '73. The Second Reception of the Sons and Daughters of Portsmouth, Resident Abroad, July 3, 1873. Also, an Account of the High School Re-Union, July 5, and the Great Praise Meeting on Sunday, July 6. Portsmouth, NH: Published by Charles W. Gardner, 1873.

"The Vermont Celebration." *The Journal of American History, 1912.* I, no. 1: 177–270.

Thomas, Benjamin Franklin. *Celebration by the Inhabitants of Worcester Mass. of the Centennial Anniversary of the Declaration of Independence. To Which Are Added Historical and Chronological Notes.* Worcester, MA: Printed by Order of the City Council, 1876.

Vaughn, L. F. *Vaughn's Parade and Float Guide.* Minneapolis, MN: T. S. Denison and Company, 1956.

Walker, Joseph Burbeen. *Chronicles of an old New England Farm: the House and Farm of the First Minister of Concord, N. H., 1726–1906.* Concord, NH, 1906.

Warren, George Washington. *The History of the Bunker Hill Monument Association During the First Century of the United States of America.* Boston: James R. Osgood and Company, 1877.

Wheildon, William W. *Inauguration of the Statue of Warren, by the Bunker Hill Monument Association, June 17, 1857.* Boston: By Authority of the Committee, 1858.

Credits

CHAPTER 1—CELEBRATE

Independence Day

Page 4 *Southbridge Light Infantry.* Captain Luther Ammidown (1790–1877). Ink, watercolor, and graphite pencil. 13 3/4 x 17 1/8 in. (34.93 x 43.5 cm) 1967.061. Columbus Museum of Art, Columbus, Ohio. Gift of Edgar William and Bernice Chrysler Garbisch.

Page 5 *Hinsdale Town Band.* Hinsdale, New Hampshire, July 4, 1855. Daguerreotype. Historical Society of Cheshire County, Keene, New Hampshire.

Page 6 *The Constitution and the Union, They Must Be Preserved.* James Head (ca. 1830–1869), watercolor. *The Floral Architect and Decorator's Companion, containing Designs and Rules for Projecting Forty Triumphal Arches and Monuments, Fifty Cars and Chariots for Floral, National, Horticultural, and Firemen's Processions* (unpublished manuscript). Portsmouth, New Hampshire, 1861. Courtesy of the Portsmouth Athenaeum, Portsmouth, New Hampshire.

Page 8 *Honoring Public Servants.* Marblehead, Massachusetts, July 4, 1884. Marblehead Museum Collection.

Page 9 *Car of Young Ladies Representing Thirty-Eight States.* Thomaston, Maine, July 4, 1887. Stereoview. Maine Historic Preservation Commission, Augusta, Maine.

Page 10 *Remember the Maine.* Greenville, New Hampshire, July 4, 1898. Private collection.

Page 11 *Part of Parade.* South Shaftsbury, Vermont, July 4, 1908. Real photo postcard. Vermont Historical Society, Barre, Vermont.

Page 12 *Horribles Presented by Hall Farm Owners and Employees.* North Bennington, Vermont, probably July 4, 1912. Courtesy of The Fund for North Bennington Archive.

Page 13 *Centennial Parade.* Southbridge, Massachusetts, July 4, 1916. Postcard. Digital reproduction provided by Jacob Edwards Library, Southbridge, Massachusetts.

Page 14 *If We Farmers Miss the Prize, Blame the Weather Man.* Canterbury, New Hampshire, July 4, 1916. Canterbury Shaker Village Archives, Canterbury, New Hampshire.

Page 15 *Alfred Conte's Float.* Lenox, Massachusetts, July 4, 1921. Postcard. Courtesy of the Lenox Library Association. https://ark.digitalcommonwealth.org/ark:/50959/rj430r538 (accessed March 05, 2021).

Ratification of the Constitution

Page 17 *Model of the Ship* Constitution. New Haven, Connecticut, Ratification procession, July 4, 1788. New Haven Museum, New Haven, Connecticut.

Abolition Day

Page 18 *Splendid Celebration, of the "BOBALITION" of Slavery, by the African Society.* Boston, Massachusetts, June 14, 1823. Broadside (detail). Courtesy, American Antiquarian Society.

Victory

Page 19 *Victory.* James Head (ca. 1830–1869). Watercolor. *The Floral Architect and Decorator's Companion, containing Designs and Rules for Projecting Forty Triumphal Arches and Monuments, Fifty Cars and Chariots for Floral, National,*

Horticultural, and Firemen's Processions (unpublished manuscript). Portsmouth, New Hampshire, 1861–1865, Plate 69. Courtesy of the Portsmouth Athenaeum, Portsmouth, New Hampshire.

Civil War

Page 21 *All Honor to Our Gallant Army & Navy.* Worcester, Massachusetts, July 4, 1865. From the collection of the Worcester Historical Museum, Worcester, Massachusetts.

Page 22 *The Car* America. Augusta, Maine, July 4, 1865. The Kennebec Historical Society, Augusta, Maine.

Page 25 *Reception of Company A, 14th Reg. of N. H. Volunteers and other Returned Soldiers.* Westmoreland, New Hampshire, August 17, 1865. Historical Society of Cheshire County, Keene, New Hampshire.

Peace

Page 26 *Liberty.* Lebanon, New Hampshire, October 13, 1919. Real photo postcard. Photograph by Alfred Pauze. Courtesy of Lebanon Historical Society, Lebanon, New Hampshire.

Page 27 *Victory and Peace.* Lebanon, New Hampshire, October 13, 1919. Real photo postcard. Photograph by Alfred Pauze. Private collection.

Page 28 *Columbia.* Bath, Maine, Armistice Day, November 11, 1919. Maine Maritime Museum, courtesy of the late Charles E. Burden.

Page 29 *Disarmament.* Montpelier, Vermont, November 11, 1921, Vermont Historical Society, Barre, Vermont.

Page 30 *Odd Ladies Float, Armistice Day.* Lynn, Massachusetts, November 12, 1928. Lynn Public Library. https://www.digitalcommonwealth.org/search/commonwealth-oai:tm70p6374 (accessed March 05, 2021).

CHAPTER 2—HONOR

New England Institutions

Page 33 *First Meetinghouse 1727.* Concord, New Hampshire, July 4, 1927. New Hampshire Historical Society.

Page 34 *The First Meeting House on the Rocks, 1660s.* Norwich, Connecticut, July 5 and 6, 1909. Real photo postcard. Private collection.

Page 35 *Justice in 1786.* Portland, Maine, July 5, 1886. John T. Hull, ed., *An Account of the Municipal celebration of the One Hundredth Anniversary of the Incorporation of the Town of Portland, July 4th, 5th, and 6th, 1886.* Tableaux VIII Justice. Portland, Maine: Owen, Strout & Company, 1886.

Page 36 *Inauguration of Governor George P. McLane.* Hartford, Connecticut, January 1901. The Connecticut Historical Society (2000.209.18).

Page 37 *Center School.* Center Sandwich, New Hampshire, 1899. Courtesy of the Sandwich Historical Society.

Page 38 *Ye Deestrick Skule.* Marblehead, Massachusetts, July 4, 1903. Photograph by Merrill H. Graves. Marblehead Museum Collection.

Distinguished Guests

Page 41 *View of the triumphal Arch and Colonnade erected in Boston in honor of the President of the United States, Oct. 24, 1789.* Engraved by Samuel Hill, *Massachusetts Magazine* II, no. 1 (January 1790): 3. Boston: Massachusetts: Isaiah Thomas and Ebenezer Andrews. Collection of the Massachusetts Historical Society.

Page 42 *General Lafayette's Visit, 1824–1825.* John Warner Barber, *Interesting Events in the History of the United States,* New Haven: J. W. Barber, 1829, Plate 119. Courtesy of Old Sturbridge Village.

Page 44 *Kennebec Guards Militia Banner.* Portland, Maine, ca. 1825–1830. Charles Codman (ca. 1800–1842), oil on silk. Maine State Museum collections (79.120.1); Jay York photo.

Page 44 *Welcome Lafayette.* Boston, 1824–1825. Printed silk ribbon. Courtesy of Old Sturbridge Village.

Page 45 *The President's Reception at the Boston and Roxbury Lines by the Municipal Authorities, Boston, September 17, 1851.* Wood engraving. *Gleason's Pictorial Drawing Room Companion,* November 15, 1851, 372. Private collection.

Page 47 *Arch Near Baptist Church Danvers Port.* Danvers, Massachusetts, 1856. Winslow Homer (1836–1910) after Maurice C. Oby (1823–1861), J. H. Bufford's Lithograph, Boston, 1856. *Proceedings of the Reception and Dinner in Honor of George Peabody, Esq., of London, By the Citizens of the Old Town of Danvers, October 9, 1856.* Boston: Henry W. Dutton & Son, 1856. Private collection.

Page 48 *Welcome to the Prince of Wales.* Portland, Maine, October 20, 1860. Stereoview by George Stacy (1831–1897), New York: Library of Congress.

Page 49 *President U. S. Grant en route to the opening of the European and North American Railway, Bangor, Maine, October 18, 1871.* Wood engraving. *The Canadian Illustrated News,* November 4, 1871. Courtesy of William Barry.

Page 50 *Let Us Remember Our Forefathers,* Bangor, Maine, October 18, 1871. Stereoview by A. K. Dole. Maine Historic Preservation Commission.

Page 51 *Oldest Residents,* Manchester, New Hampshire, September 7, 1896. Private collection.

Funerals

Page 52 *Funeral Notice for Joshua Bailey Osgood, Esq., Biddeford, Maine, June 2, 1791. Cumberland Gazette,* Portland, Maine, June 6, 1791.

Page 53 *Funeral of Mrs. Emily Egerton.* Royalton, Vermont, 1828. *Memoir of Mrs. Emily Egerton,* assembled by Rufus Nutting, Boston, 1832. Frontispiece. Private collection.

Page 54 *Funeral Procession of the Late Hon. Daniel Webster, at Marshfield, Mass. October 1852* and *The Burial Case.* Wood engravings drawn by Manning. *Gleason's Pictorial Drawing Room Companion,* November 5, 1852, 301. Private collection.

Page 56 *Funeral Car for Three Soldiers with Masonic Procession.* Taunton, Massachusetts, February 2, 1864. Photo courtesy of the Charles E. Crowley Photographic Center at the Old Colony Historical Museum, Taunton, Massachusetts.

Page 57 *Funeral of Connecticut Governor, Thomas H. Seymour.* Hartford, Connecticut, September 7, 1868. Engraving. The Connecticut Historical Society (1972.36.28).

Monuments

Page 59 *Freemen's Quick Step. As performed on the Glorious 10th of September. Composed and dedicated to the Delegates of the Bunker Hill Whig Convention of 1840, by George Hews, Boston.* Sheet music cover (detail). William Sharp (1803–1873); tinted lithograph printed by Sharp. Michelin & Co; Published by Parker & Ditson, 135 Washington Street, Boston, 1840. Courtesy of Historic New England.

Page 60 *Ladies Fair, Quincy Hall, 1840, Remembrance of Italy, Six Waltzes for the Piano Forte Composed and dedicated to the Ladies of the Bunker Hill Fair by Giovanni Paggi.* Sheet music cover (detail). Lithograph by Thayer, successor to Moore. Published by Henry Prentiss, 1840. Courtesy, American Antiquarian Society.

Page 61 *"'76" Quick Step, As Performed by the Boston Brass Band, on the Anniversary of the Battle of Bunker Hill, and the Great Monumental Celebration, 17th June, 1843. Most Respectfully Dedicated to the Bunker Hill Monument Association, Boston.*

Sheet music cover. Lithograph by B. W. Thayer & Co.; published by Chas. H. Keith, Boston, 1843. Boston Public Library. https://ark.digitalcommonwealth.org/ark:/50959/08612s568 (accessed August 27, 2019).

Page 62 *Captain George Fishley (1760–1850).* Daguerreotype by Francis W. Ham, Portsmouth, New Hampshire, June 11, 1850. Courtesy of the Portsmouth Historical Society; on deposit at the Portsmouth Athenaeum.

Monuments to the Battles of Lexington and Concord

Page 63 *Monument at Acton.* Acton, Massachusetts, October 29, 1851. Wood engraving. *Gleason's Pictorial Drawing Room Companion,* November 22, 1851, 472. Private collection.

Page 64 *The Late Celebration at Acton, Mass.* Acton, Massachusetts, October 29, 1851. Wood engraving. *Gleason's Pictorial Drawing Room Companion,* November 22, 1851, 472. Private collection.

Civil War Veterans

Page 66 *Decoration of Soldiers Graves,* Post 4, GAR. Floral car drawn in procession. Keene, New Hampshire, May 30, 1868. Stereoview by French & Sawyer, Photographers, Keene, New Hampshire. Historical Society of Cheshire County, Keene, New Hampshire.

Page 66 *Decoration Day.* Keene, New Hampshire, *1869.* Stereoview. Historical Society of Cheshire County, Keene, New Hampshire.

Page 67 *Dedication of Monument to Civil War Soldiers.* Chester, Vermont. 1885. Courtesy of the Chester Historical Society, Chester, Vermont.

Page 68 *Decoration Day.* Peterborough, New Hampshire, 1893. Collection of the Monadnock Center for History and Culture, Peterborough, New Hampshire.

Page 70 *Dedication of the Memorial to Robert Gould Shaw and the 54th Massachusetts Regiment.* Boston, May 31, 1897. Collection of the Massachusetts Historical Society.

Page 71 *Tenting on the Old Camp Ground.* Hadley, Massachusetts, 250th Anniversary Parade, 1909. Hadley Historical Society, courtesy of Bill Hosley.

Page 72 *U. S. Grant Relief Corps.* Biddeford, Maine, September 16, 1916. McArthur Public Library, Biddeford, Maine.

Page 73 *G•A•R Yankee Boys of '61 to '65.* Bangor, Maine, ca. 1910. Collection of the Bangor Historical Society.

Page 74 *GAR Veterans.* Lexington, Massachusetts, April 19, 1930. Courtesy of the Lexington Historical Society.

CHAPTER 3—IDENTITY

Trades Pre-1845

Page 77 *Cordwainers Banner.* Boston, Massachusetts, 1789. Oil on silk. Revolutionary Spaces.

Page 78 Banners of the Maine Charitable Mechanics Association. All oil on linen. Portland, Maine 1841. Collection of Maine Historical Society.

—*Our Life Is One of Lights & Shadows.* Painters / Glaziers / and / Brushmakers Banner. William Capen, Jr. (ca. 1801–1863).

—*Strike While the Iron Is Hot.* Blacksmiths Banner. Joseph E. Hodgkins (w. 1837–1857).

—*He That Will Not Pay the Shoe-Maker Is Not Worthy of a SOLE.* Shoemakers Banner. Artist unknown.

—*United in the Bands of Temperance We Are Crowned with Honor.* Hatters Banner. Painted by William Capen, Jr. (ca. 1801–1863).

The New England Militia Prior to 1860

Page 80 *Salem Common on Training Day 1808.* Salem, Massachusetts. George Ropes, Jr. (American, 1788–1819). Oil on canvas, 35 x 52 3/4 in. (88.9 x 133.985 cm). Museum purchase made possible by William Crowninshield Endicott, Mrs. Lucy Bowdoin, Mrs. Francis Lee Higginson, Dudley P. Rogers, Henry Wycoff Belknap, George A. Peabody, Charles S. Rea, William H. Gove, George R. Lord, Arthur H. Phippen, R. Osgood, William O. Chapman, Frank Weston Benson, Henry P. Benson, John Albree, William H. Ropes, Henry Morrill Batchelder, Hardy Phippen, William M. Jelly, Arthur F. Benson, and Lawrence W. Jenkins, 1919.107924. Courtesy of the Peabody Essex Museum, Salem, Massachusetts.

Page 81 *Maine Militia Standard* (fragment). Artist unknown. Probably Boston, Massachusetts, 1822. Maine State Museum collections (2009.23.1); Jay York photo.

Page 82 *The Ancient and Honorable Artillery Company on Tremont Street in front of the newly erected Tremont House Hotel.* Boston, Massachusetts, ca. 1830. James Bennett (1777–1844). Oil on canvas. Anonymous collection.

Page 83 *Winthrop's Quick Step Dedicated to Capt: G. T. Winthrop, the Officers & Members of the Boston Independent Fusiliers.* Boston, Massachusetts, 1835. Boston: Pendleton's Lithography. (detail) Published by John Ashton & Co., 1835. Courtesy of The Lester S. Levy Sheet Music Collection, The Sheridan Libraries, Johns Hopkins University.

Page 84 *Capt.ⁿ E. G. Austin's Quick Step. As first performed by the Boston Brigade Band on the Anniversary of the Boston Light Infantry, May 31, 1837.* Boston, Massachusetts, 1837. Sheet music cover. (detail) Fitz Henry Lane (1804–1865). Lithograph; Moore's Lithog[y], Boston; published by Parker & Ditson, Boston. Courtesy, American Antiquarian Society.

Page 85"*Our Country is Safe" The Berry Street Rangers Quick Step As performed by the Boston Brigade Band, At the Volunteers' Parade of the Company Oct. 4th 1837.* Boston, Massachusetts, 1837. Sheet music cover. (detail) Lithograph; T. Moore's Lith., Boston; published by H. Prentiss, Boston. Boston Athenaeum, Special Collections.

Page 85 *North-End Forever. Hull Street Guards Quick Step, Composed & respectfully dedicated to the Officers & Members of the H. S. Guards by John Holloway. Performed for the first time by the Boston Brass Band at their parade, June 15th, 1838.* Boston, Massachusetts, 1838. Sheet music cover. (detail) Lithograph; Thos Moore's Lithog[y], Published by H. Prentiss, Boston. Courtesy of Historic New England.

Page 86 *The Stark Guards' Quick Step. Performed by the Manchester Brass Band at the presentation of an elegant standard to the Officers and Members of the Stark Guards by the ladies of Manchester September 22nd 1842. Composed and respectfully dedicated to the Officers and Members of the Stark Guards by Alonzo Bond.* Manchester, New Hampshire, September 22, 1842. Sheet music cover (detail). Lithograph: Thayer & Co's Lithog[y], Boston. Published by I. N. Metcalf, Lowell and Oliver Ditson, Boston, 1842. New Hampshire Historical Society.

Page 88 *Muster Day.* Saco, Maine, 1843. Charles Henry Granger (1812–1893). Oil on canvas. Courtesy of the National Gallery of Art.

Page 89 *The Militia Muster.* David Claypoole Johnston. (1799–1865). Watercolor, Boston, Massachusetts, 1828. Courtesy, American Antiquarian Society.

Page 90 *Col. Pluck.* Boston, Massachusetts, ca. 1824, (detail). David Claypoole Johnston (1799–1865). Lithograph by Pendleton, Boston. Courtesy, American Antiquarian Society.

Page 90 *Standing Company. Broad Grins, or Fun For the New Year.* Boston: Arthur Ashworth, 1832, 25. Courtesy of Old Sturbridge Village.

Firefighters

Page 95 *Preparing for a Muster on Middle Street in Portland, Maine.* Portland, Maine, September 30, 1846. Cabinet card of a daguerreotype by George S. Hough and Charles J. Anthony. Private collection.

Page 96 *Lexington Battle Monument, Danvers with Residence of Hon. R. S. Daniels*. Danvers, Massachusetts, 1856. Attributed to Winslow Homer after a photograph by William Snell (1817–1904). J. H. Bufford's Lithograph, Boston, 1856. *Proceedings of the Reception and Dinner in Honor of George Peabody, Esq., of London, By the Citizens of the Old Town of Danvers, October 9, 1856*. Boston: Henry W. Dutton & Son, 1856. Private collection.

Page 97 *Before the Parade*. Northampton, Massachusetts, 1879. Historic Northampton, Northampton, Massachusetts.

Page 98 *Ready for the Muster*. Chester Village, Chester, Vermont, 1905–1910. Courtesy of Chester Historical Society.

Fraternal Organizations

Page 100 *Boston Water Celebration, The Procession Passing the Boston Museum, Tremont Street*. Boston, Massachusetts, October 25, 1848. Lithograph, J. H. Bufford, Boston. Boston Public Library. https://ark.digitalcommonwealth.org/ark:/50959/xp68kr05w

Page 101 *Palanquin*. Calcutta, India, before 1803. Body 42 3/4 x 76 x 31 5/16 inches. E14329. Courtesy of the Peabody Essex Museum, Salem, Massachusetts.

Page 103 *Inauguration of the Statue of Franklin, Court Square, Boston, September 17, 1856*. Wood engraving; drawn by Charles Howland Hammatt Billings (1818–1874); engraved by John Andrew (1815–1870). *Ballou's Pictorial Drawing Room Companion*, October 11, 1856, 232–233. Courtesy of the New England Historic Genealogical Society.

Page 105 *City of Boston, Committee of Arrangements, Sept. 17, 1856*. Printed ribbon badge. Andrew, engraver. Boston, Massachusetts, 1856. Courtesy, American Antiquarian Society.

Page 105 *Franklin Statue Dedication Badge*. Boston, Massachusetts, 1856. Printed silk. Courtesy of the New England Historic Genealogical Society.

Page 105 *Banner of the New England Historic Genealogical Society*. Boston, Massachusetts, 1856. Yellow and gold lettering on silk. Courtesy of the New England Historic Genealogical Society.

Page 106 *Members of the Putnam Phalanx*. Hartford, Connecticut, 1860. As presented in *Frank Leslie's Illustrated Newspaper*, November 10, 1860. The Connecticut Historical Society. (1972.36.47)

Page 107 *Pioneers—Grange Division of the Procession*. Gorham, Maine, 1886. Collections of Maine Historical Society.

Page 108 *Ten Rod Road Float*. Rochester, New Hampshire, 1893. Courtesy of Dorothy Bean.

Page 109 *Seal of the Franklin County Agricultural Society*. Greenfield, Massachusetts, 1897. Courtesy, the Winterthur Library: Joseph Downs Collections of Manuscripts and Printed Ephemera (Doc.386-3).

Page 110 *Some Pumpkins*. Greenfield, Massachusetts, 1897. Courtesy, the Winterthur Library: Joseph Downs Collections of Manuscripts and Printed Ephemera (Doc.386-2).

Page 111 *Longshoremen's Benevolent Society*. Portland, Maine, July 4, 1894. Collections of Maine Historical Society.

Page 111 *Go Thou and Do Likewise*. Biddeford, Maine, September 14, 1905. McArthur Library, Biddeford, Maine.

Page 112 *Old Time Household Industry*. Lexington, Massachusetts, April 19, 1910. Lexington Historical Society.

Page 113 *Shawsheen Tribe I. O. O. Red Men, Old Home Week, 1912*. Bedford, Massachusetts, 1912. Courtesy of the Bedford Historical Society, Bedford, Massachusetts.

Page 114 *Indian Village*. Concord, New Hampshire, 1927. New Hampshire Historical Society.

Ethnicity

Page 116 *The Original States of the Union*. Haverhill, Massachusetts, July 3, 1890. *A Record of the Commemoration, July Second and Third, 1890 of the Two Hundred and Fiftieth Anniversary of the Settlement of Haverhill, Massachusetts.* Boston: Joseph George Cupples, 1891, opposite page 278.

Page 117 *La Grande Hermine*. Lewiston, Maine, June 24, 1897. Courtesy of Franco-American Collection, University of Southern Maine, Lewiston-Auburn College.

Page 118 *United German Societies*. Northampton, Massachusetts, June 7, 1904. Historic Northampton, Northampton, Massachusetts.

Page 119 *The Army and Navy Forever*. Norwich, Connecticut, July 6, 1909. Real photo postcard. Courtesy of the Otis Library, Norwich, Connecticut.

Page 119 *Irish Girls*. Pittsfield, Massachusetts, July 4, 1911. Pocumtuck Valley Memorial Association, Deerfield, Massachusetts.

Page 120 *Viking Ship*. Worcester, Massachusetts, July 4, 1892. From the collection of the Worcester Historical Museum, Worcester, Massachusetts.

Page 121 *Midsommar Maypole*. Worcester, Massachusetts, ca. 1917. From the collection of the Worcester Historical Museum, Worcester, Massachusetts.

Page 122 *Buy Liberty Bonds*. Haverhill, Massachusetts, 1918. Private collection.

Page 123 *Sons of Italy*. Wakefield, Massachusetts, July 4, 1922. Wakefield Historical Society.

Page 123 *Columbia*. New London, Conecticut, 1934. Mystic Seaport Museum.

Page 124 *Columbus Discovering America*. Hartford, Connecticut, October 12, 1935. The Connecticut Historical Society (1982.102.2).

Page 124 *Floral Display of the History of Bristol, 1680–1930*. Bristol, Rhode Island, September 1930. Courtesy of Bristol Historical and Preservation Society (BHPS), Bristol, Rhode Island 02809.

Page 125 *Sisterhood of Peace*. Concord, Massachusetts, April 19, 1925. Courtesy, Concord Free Public Library.

Civic Identity

Page 127 *Celebration of the Two Hundred and Fiftieth Anniversary of the Settlement of Boston, September 17, 1880*. Tableau XVI. Boston. Printed by Order of the City Council, 1880.

Page 128 *Tableau XII. Grand Allegorical Car Representing Portland*. Portland, Maine, July 6, 1886. John T. Hull, ed. *Centennial Celebration: An Account of the Municipal Celebration of the One Hundredth Anniversary of the Incorporation of the Town of Portland July 4th, 5th, and 6th, 1886.*

CHAPTER 4—PROGRESS

Page 131 *View of the Water Celebration, on Boston Common October 25th 1848. Respectfully dedicated to His Honor Josiah Quincy Jr., Mayor, the City Council and Water Commissioners*. Boston, Massachusetts, 1848. Lithograph. Drawn by Benjamin Franklin Smith (1830–1927), on stone by Samuel Worcester Rowse (1822–1901), Tappan & Bradford Lithog[y], Boston. Published by David Bigelow, 1849. *Boston Public Library*. https://ark.digitalcommonwealth.org/ark:/50959/7s75dj289 (accessed January 12, 2021).

Page 133 *Splendid Panoramic View of the Grand Procession of the Military, and Arts, Trades, Societies, and Professions on the Occasion of the Great Railroad Jubilee Celebration in Boston, September 19, 1851*. Wood engraving by Worcester & Peirce. *Gleason's Pictorial Drawing Room Companion*, October 11, 1851, 376–377. Courtesy of Historic New England.

Page 134 *Dover Street as Decorated for the Jubilee*. Boston,

Massachusetts, September 19, 1851. Wood engraving by Worcester & Peirce. *Gleason's Pictorial Drawing Room Companion*, October 11, 1851, 372. Private collection.

Page 135 *Levant Telephone Company*, Levant, Maine, ca.1910. Collections of the Bangor Historical Society.

Page 136 *Little Daisy.* Concord, New Hampshire, August 20, 1903. New Hampshire Historical Society.

Page 137 *Prototype of Modern Electric Streetcar.* Concord, New Hampshire, August 20, 1903. New Hampshire Historical Society.

Page 138 *Modern Electric Street Lights. York Power & Light Company,* Biddeford, Maine, 1916. McArthur Public Library, Biddeford, Maine.

Page 138 *The Modern Highway, Broad with Easy Grades, Opening Up New Territory and Developing the Entire State.* Portland, Maine, July 5, 1920. Collections of Maine Historical Society.

Page 139 *Crepe Paper for Floats, Automobiles, Coaches, and Carriages in Street Parades.* Framingham, Massachusetts: Dennison Manufacturing Company, 1905. Cover. Private collection.

Page 140 *Patriotic Display.* Lebanon, New Hampshire, October 13, 1919. Real photo postcard. Photograph by Alfred Pauze. Courtesy of the Lebanon Historical Society, Lebanon, New Hampshire.

CHAPTER 5—MEMORY

The Ties That Bind

Page 143 *Market St., Portsmouth, N. H. With its Triumphal Arches & Grand Procession of the Sons of Portsmouth, July 4th 1853. The Day of Jubilee Has Come. Sons of Portsmouth, Welcome Home.* Portsmouth, New Hampshire, July 4, 1853. Lithograph, Boston: J. H. Bufford, Published by Albert Gregory and Thomas Moses. Library of Congress.

Page 145 *Banners used on the Jacob Wendell House.* Portsmouth, New Hampshire, 1873 and 1893. Paint on cotton. Strawbery Banke Museum, Portsmouth, New Hampshire.

Page 146 *The Procession Forming Under the Arch at the Head of Main Street.* Gorham, Maine, May 26, 1886. *Celebration of the One Hundred and Fiftieth Anniversary of Gorham, Maine, May 26, 1886.* Portland, Maine: B. Thurston & Company, 1886, 41.

Old Home Day

Page 148 *Old Home Day.* Norwich, Connecticut, ca. 1900. The Connecticut Historical Society (1987.145.22).

Page 149 *Old Home Day.* Pittsfield, New Hampshire, 1908. Pittsfield Historical Society.

Historical Tableaux

Page 152 *Two Centuries Ago.* James Head (ca. 1830–1869). Watercolor. *The Floral Architect and Decorator's Companion, containing Designs and Rules for Projecting Forty Triumphal Arches and Monuments, Fifty Cars and Chariots for Floral, National, Horticultural, and Firemen's Processions* (unpublished manuscript). Portsmouth, New Hampshire, 1861–1865, Plate 72. Courtesy of the Portsmouth Athenaeum.

Page 152 *No Craft Ever Bore So Precious a Cargo. Landing of the Pilgrims.* James Head (ca. 1830–1869). Watercolor. *The Floral Architect and Decorator's Companion, containing Designs and Rules for Projecting Forty Triumphal Arches and Monuments, Fifty Cars and Chariots for Floral, National, Horticultural, and Firemen's Processions* (unpublished manuscript). Portsmouth, New Hampshire, 1861–1865, Plate 65. Courtesy of the Portsmouth Athenaeum.

Page 153 *Landing of the Pilgrims, 1620.* North Bennington, Vermont, 1907. Courtesy of the Fund for North Bennington Archive.

Page 154 *First Thanksgiving, 1621.* Plymouth, Massachusetts,

August 1, 1921. Photograph by Edward P. McLaughlin. Collection of the Plymouth Public Library. https://ark.digitalcommonwealth.org/ark:/50959/70795s11b (accessed August 13, 2019).

Page 155 *Speak For Yourself, John*. North Bennington, Vermont, July 4, 1914. Bennington Museum, Bennington, Vermont.

Page 157 *Hanging of Witches, Boston Common, 1630*. Boston, Massachusetts, 1930. Artist's rendering, Messmore and Damon Company records. Archives Center, National Museum of American History, Smithsonian Institution.

Page 158 *Tableau III. Cleeves & Tucker Building Ye First Log House, 1633*. Portland, Maine, July 5, 1886. John T. Hull, ed., *An Account of the Municipal celebration of the One Hundredth Anniversary of the Incorporation of the Town of Portland, July 4th, 5th, and 6th, 1886*. Portland, Maine: Owen, Strout & Company, 1886.

Page 159 *Governor John Winthrop brings the Massachusetts Bay Colony Charter and is met by John Endicott, 1630*. Newburyport, Massachusetts, 1930. Photograph by Arthur S. Adams, Boston. From the collection of the Museum of Old Newbury.

Page 160 *The Founding of Concord, 1635*. Concord, Massachusetts, April 19, 1925. Courtesy Concord Free Public Library.

Page 161 *Elizabeth Pole Making Her Purchase, 1635*. Taunton, Massachusetts, June 5, 1889. Photo courtesy of Charles E. Crowley Photographic Center at the Old Colony Historical Museum, Taunton, Massachusetts.

Page 162 *Going to Southampton to Settle, 1723*. Northampton, Massachusetts, 1904. Courtesy of Historic Northampton, Northampton, Massachusetts.

Page 163 *Jonathan Hinsdale and Family, 1750*. Lenox, Massachusetts, ca. 1921–1924. Courtesy of the Lenox Library Association. https://ark.digitalcommonwealth.org/ark:/50959/rj430r61z (accessed August 13, 2019).

Page 164 *Boston Tea Party, 1773*. Marblehead, Massachusetts, July 4, 1884. Photograph by Merrill H. Graves. Marblehead Museum Collection.

Page 165 *Isaac Davis and the Acton Minutemen*. Concord, Massachusetts, April 19, 1925. Courtesy Concord Free Public Library.

Page 166 *We Will Be Free and Independent States*. Marblehead, Massachusetts, July 4, 1884. Marblehead Museum Collection.

Page 167 *Dark Days of the American Revolution*. James Head (ca. 1830–1869), watercolor. *The Floral Architect and Decorator's Companion, containing Designs and Rules for Projecting Forty Triumphal Arches and Monuments, Fifty Cars and Chariots for Floral, National, Horticultural, and Firemen's Processions* (unpublished manuscript). Portsmouth, New Hampshire, 1861–1865, Plate 67. Courtesy of the Portsmouth Athenaeum.

Page 168 *Betsy Ross and the First American Flag*. Newport, Rhode Island, July 4, 1916. Collection of the Newport Historical Society (NDN 8182).

Page 169 *Betsy Ross and the First American Flag*. Hartford, Connecticut, October 12, 1935. Hartford Clearing House Association Banks float. Courtesy of the Connecticut Historical Society (1982.1029).

Page 169 *Design for the Betsy Ross Flag. Parade Float and Decorations*, Catalogue No. 38, Chicago Artificial Flower Company, Chicago, Illinois, 1935, 21.

Page 170 *Shays Plots Rebellion 1786*. Amherst, Massachusetts, 1930. Courtesy of the Jones Library, Inc.

Page 171 *Log Cabin, ca 1790*. Aaron B. Cole and J. L. M. Willis, ed., *History of the Centennial of the Incorporation of the Town of Eliot, Maine. August 7th–13th, 1910*. Eliot, Maine: Augustine Caldwell, 1912.

Page 172 *Early Connecticut Homestead*. Hartford, Connecticut, October 12, 1935. The Connecticut Historical Society (1982.102.6).

Then and Now: Women's Work

Page 174 *Female Accomplishments of 1776*. James Head (ca. 1830–1869). Watercolor. *The Floral Architect and Decorator's Companion, containing Designs and Rules for Projecting Forty Triumphal Arches and Monuments, Fifty Cars and Chariots for Floral, National, Horticultural, and Firemen's Processions* (unpublished manuscript). Portsmouth, New Hampshire, 1861–1865, Plate 93. Courtesy of the Portsmouth Athenaeum.

Page 175 *Female Accomplishments 1859*. James Head (ca. 1830–1869). Watercolor. *The Floral Architect and Decorator's Companion, containing Designs and Rules for Projecting Forty Triumphal Arches and Monuments, Fifty Cars and Chariots for Floral, National, Horticultural, and Firemen's Processions* (unpublished manuscript). Portsmouth, New Hampshire, 1861–1865, Plate 94. Courtesy of the Portsmouth Athenaeum.

Page 176 *This Is the Loom That Wove the Cloth for Gov. Haines First College Suit*, Levant, Maine, ca. 1913. Maine Historic Preservation Commission.

Page 176 *Days of Homespun*. Tamworth, New Hampshire, 1921. Tamworth History Center.

Page 177 *Salem Gas Light Co.* Salem, Massachusetts, 1926. Photograph by Leland O. Tilford. Peabody Essex Museum.

Page 178 *A Kitchen of 1810*. Eliot, Maine, August 11, 1910. Aaron B. Cole and J. L. M. Willis, ed., *History of the Centennial of the Incorporation of the Town of Eliot, Maine. August 7th–13th, 1910*. Eliot, Maine: Augustine Caldwell, 1912.

Commemoration

Page 179 *Fight at Old North Bridge, April 19, 1775*. Concord, Massachusetts, April 19, 1925. Courtesy Concord Free Public Library.

Page 181 *Milk St. Anniversary of Battle of Bunker Hill*. Boston, Massachusetts, June 17, 1875. Photograph by James Wallace Black (1825–1896). Boston Public Library. https://ark.digitalcommonwealth.org/ark:/50959/cf95jh542 (accessed March 5, 2021).

Page 182 *Trades Procession (Columbus Avenue looking north east* [toward] *Concord Square)*. Boston, Massachusetts, June 17, 1875. Photograph by James Wallace Black (1825–1896). Boston Public Library. https://ark.digitalcommonwealth.org/ark:/50959/cf95jh74j (accessed January 09, 2021).

Page 183 *Triumphal Arch at Charles River Avenue*. Boston, Massachusetts, June 17, 1875. Stereoview. Photographed and published by T. Lewis, Cambridgeport, Massachusetts. Boston Public Library. https://ark.digitalcommonwealth.org/ark:/50959/7p88cs73q (accessed January 09, 2021).

Page 184 *The Centennial Celebration of General Stark's Victory over the Hessians at the Battle of Bennington on August 16, 1777*. Bennington, Vermont, August 16, 1877. Wood engraving. *Frank Leslie's Illustrated Newspaper*, September 1, 1877, front page. Private collection.

Page 186 *Kearsarge–Alabama Celebration*. Portsmouth, New Hampshire, September 18, 1900. Photograph by Lafayette V. Newall (1833–1914). Courtesy of the Portsmouth Athenaeum.

Page 187 *Santa Maria*. Montpelier, Vermont, October 12, 1911. Vermont Historical Society, Barre, Vermont.

Page 188 *Lafayette and His Hoss*. Kennebunk, Maine, probably July 4, 1925. Courtesy of the Brick Store Museum, Kennebunk, Maine.

Page 189 *Company E, New Hampshire Militia*. Concord, New Hampshire, October 12, 1892. New Hampshire Historical Society.

Historical Vehicles

Page 191 *Centennial Parade*. Nantucket, Massachusetts, 1895. Nantucket Historical Association Research Library, Photographic Archives (GPN2611).

Page 192 *F. P. Reed and W. S. Brown in their 'One Hoss' Shay'.* Manchester, New Hampshire, September 10, 1896. John E. Coffin (1860–1905). *Manchester* [New Hampshire] *Union*, September 10, 1896. New Hampshire Historical Society.

Page 193 *Stagecoach Days.* Newburyport, Massachusetts, 1930. Tinted photograph. From the collections of the Museum of Old Newbury.

Page 195 *Model of Amoskeag Locomotive.* Concord, New Hampshire, August 20, 1903. New Hampshire Historical Society.

Page 196 *Locomotive* Lion*—1839.* Portland, Maine, July 4, 1898. Photograph by George Sharon. Maine State Museum collections (2013.5.2).

CHAPTER 6–ENTERTAINMENT

Page 199 *Chrysarma or Roman Chariot.* Washington, New Hampshire, 1847–1848. Solon Newman (1832–1904). Drawing, sepia and colored ink on paper. New Hampshire Historical Society.

Floral Processions

Page 203 *The Flora Testimonial.* James Head (ca. 1830–1869). Watercolor. *The Floral Architect and Decorator's Companion, containing Designs and Rules for Projecting Forty Triumphal Arches and Monuments, Fifty Cars and Chariots for Floral, National, Horticultural, and Firemen's Processions* (unpublished manuscript). Portsmouth, New Hampshire, 1861–1865, Plate 44. Courtesy of the Portsmouth Athenaeum.

Page 204 *Autumn.* James Thomson, *The Seasons.* Philadelphia: E. H. Butler, 1857. Courtesy of Old Sturbridge Village.

Page 204 *Jolly Haymaker.* Silk ribbon badge. Maker unknown, mid-nineteenth century. Courtesy, American Antiquarian Society.

Page 205 *Thomas Bailey Aldrich in Uniform of the Continentalers.* Portsmouth, New Hampshire, 1846. Daguerreotype. Strawbery Banke Museum.

Page 206 *Honor to Whom Honor is Due. Arch Erected by the Webster Club, Main St. S. Danvers, Massachusetts.* South Danvers, Massachusetts, October 9, 1856. Attributed to Winslow Homer. Lithograph by J. H. Bufford. *Proceedings of the Reception and Dinner in Honor of George Peabody, Esq., of London, By the Citizens of the Old Town of Danvers, October 9, 1856.* Boston: Henry W. Dutton & Son, 1856. Private collection.

Page 207 *Zouave.* Watercolor by John Martin (1823–1904). Bangor, Maine, July 4, 1865. Collections of Maine Historical Society and Maine State Museum.

Page 207 *Annie Martin, a Little Zephir.* Bangor, Maine, July 2, 1866. Watercolor by John Martin (1823–1904). Collections of Maine Historical Society and the Maine State Museum.

The Antiques and Horribles

Page 214, 215 *Scene Representing the Antique Procession, at the Centennial Celebration at Danvers, Mass.* Danvers, Massachusetts, June 16, 1852. Wood engraving. *Gleason's Pictorial Drawing Room Companion*, July 20, 1852, 25. Private collection.

Page 216 *Ensign Stebbings at Hingham, Feb. 15, 1855.* Hingham, Massachusetts, February 15, 1855. Parade ribbon badge. Courtesy, American Antiquarian Society.

Page 217 *4th of July.* Keene, New Hampshire, ca. 1872–1876. Stereoscopic view by J. A. French (working 1861–1898). Private collection.

Page 218 *A Company of Horribles.* Stoddard, New Hampshire, July 4, ca. 1866–1868. Historical Society of Cheshire County, Keene, New Hampshire.

Page 219 *The Fantastics.* Bryant Pond, Maine, possibly July 4, 1875. Stereoview. Maine Historic Preservation Commission.

Page 221 *Parade of the "Antiques and Horribles"in Charlestown, Massachusetts on the morning of June 17, 1875.* Wood engraving after a sketch by E. R. Morse and Harry Ogden.

Supplement to *Frank Leslie's Illustrated Newspaper*, July 3, 1875, 296. Private collection.

Page 222 *July 4, 1876*. Kilburn Brothers, Littleton, New Hampshire. Stereoview. Private collection.

Page 223 *Fourth of July Parade*. Alfred Cornelius Howland (American, 1838–1909). Oil on canvas, ca. 1886, 24 in. x 36 1/16 in. High Museum, Atlanta, Georgia. Gift of Life Insurance Company of Georgia in celebration of the Nation's Bicentennial. 75.51.

Page 225 *Roswell Blanchard (1829–1887)*. Probably Walpole, New Hampshire, 1876. Tintype. Walpole Historical Society, Walpole, New Hampshire.

Page 226 *Darktown Fire Brigade at the Conclusion of the Calithumpian and Horribles Parade*. Concord, New Hampshire, July 4, 1891. New Hampshire Historical Society.

Page 227 *The Studlefunks' Brigade Band*. J. William Fosdick, "The Studlefunks' Bonfire," *St. Nicholas, an Illustrated Magazine for Young Folks*, XXI, May–October, 1894. New York: The Century Co., p. 825. Courtesy, the Winterthur Library, Printed Book and Periodical Collection (RBR AP 201 S14).

Page 228 *The Bedford Simplex*. Bedford, Massachusetts, 1904. Courtesy of the Bedford Historical Society, Bedford., Massachusetts.

Page 229 *Calithumpian Band*. Location unknown, ca. 1900–1910. © Andover Center for History and Culture, Andover, Massachusetts.

Page 230 *Horrible Musicians*. Andover, Massachusetts, July 4, 1909–1914. © Andover Center for History and Culture, Andover, Massachusetts.

Page 231 *Columbus Day*. Barre, Vermont, October 12, 1911. Vermont Historical Society, Barre, Vermont.

Page 232 *Couple of Horribles*. Portland, Maine, July 5, 1920. Collections of Maine Historical Society/MaineToday Media.

Page 232 *Horribles at Maine Sanatorium*. Augusta, Maine, July 4, 1929. Collections of Maine Historical Society.

Page 233 *Truly Horrible*. Andover, Massachusetts, ca. 1930–1935. © Andover Center for History and Culture, Andover, Massachusetts.

Floral and Coaching Parades

Page 235 *The "Tub Parade" at Lenox, Massachusetts, September 22* [1886]. Wood engraving after Henry Sandham (1842–1910). *Harper's Weekly*, October 2, 1886, 637. Private collection.

Page 236 *A Most Beautiful Tub*, Lenox, Massachusetts, 1894. Courtesy of the Lenox Library Association. https://ark.digitalcommonwealth.org/ark:/50959/rj430t646 (accessed October 12, 2019).

Page 237 *Isabella D. Williams with her Coachman, Frank Joy, and his Two Sons*. Northampton, Massachusetts, June 7, 1904. Courtesy of Historic Northampton, Northampton, Massachusetts.

Page 239 *Coaching Parade Passing the Sinclair Hotel*. Bethlehem, New Hampshire, August 29, 1891. *White Mountain Echo*, August 29, 1891, 1. New Hampshire Historical Society.

Page 240 *A Gorgeous Oriental Vehicle*. North Conway, New Hampshire, August 9, 1894. Soule Photograph Co., Boston. Courtesy of Historic New England.

Page 241 *Empire Bridal Coach*. North Conway, New Hampshire, August 9, 1894. Soule Photograph Co., Boston. Courtesy of Historic New England.

Page 242 *Cleopatra's Barge*. North Conway, New Hampshire, August 9, 1894. Courtesy of Historic New England.

Page 243 *Queen Mab*. Greenfield, Massachusetts, 1897. Courtesy, the Winterthur Library: Joseph Downs Collection of Manuscripts and Printed Ephemera (Doc.386-1).

Page 244 *Decorated Coach with Ladies*, West Boylston, Massachusetts, July 16, 1908. Postcard, The Wohlbruck Studio. Beaman Memorial Public Library, West Boylston, Massachusetts. https://ark.digitalcommonwealth.org/ark:/50959/fb494t51x.

Winter Carnivals

Page 246 *Boston Heaters.* Concord, New Hampshire, 1891. New Hampshire Historical Society.

Page 247 *Darktown Fire Brigade.* Concord, New Hampshire, 1895. New Hampshire Historical Society.

Page 247 *The Jolly Snowman* (Manchester Traction, Light and Power Co.). Manchester, New Hampshire, 1924. Courtesy of the Manchester (NH) Historic Association.

Page 248 *Winter Carnival Float of the Amoskeag Manufacturing Company.* Manchester, New Hampshire, 1924. Courtesy of the Manchester (NH) Historic Association.

Children's Parades

Page 250 *Wigglesworth Family Parade.* Cambridge, Massachusetts, July 4, 1890. Courtesy of Historic New England.

Page 250 *Mayflower.* Location unknown, 1904. Private collection.

Page 251 *Baby Carriage Winners.* Portland, Maine, 1924. Collections of Maine Historical Society/MaineToday Media.

Page 251 *A Swan Carriage of Crepe Paper.* Design from *How to Decorate Halls—Booths and Automobiles.* Framingham, Massachusetts: Dennison Manufacturing Company, 1923, 35. Private collection.

Page 252 *Waiting to Join the Parade.* Charlestown, Massachusetts, June 17, 1937. Photograph by L. Fisher. Boston Public Library, Charlestown Branch Library. https://ark.digitalcommonwealth.org/ark:/50959/8k71p471j (accessed August 26, 2019).

Page 252 *Decorated Tricycles.* Kennebunk, Maine, 1930s. Courtesy of the Brick Store Museum, Kennebunk, Maine.

CHAPTER 7—ADVOCACY

Politics 1840–1872

Page 254 *Whig Gathering, Song and Chorus Respectively dedicated to the Whigs of the United States.* Boston, Massachusetts, 1840. Sheet music cover (detail). Drawn by Benjamin Champney (1817–1907), lithograph by B. W. Thayer & Co., published by Henry Prentiss, 1840. Courtesy of Historic New England.

Page 255 *Beneath Thy Folds We Fought and Co^{n}quered.* Kennebunk, Maine, July 4, 1840. Oil on cotton. Courtesy of the Brick Store Museum, Kennebunk, Maine.

Page 256–257 *Whig Mass Meeting on Boston Common, Sept. 19th 1844. Return of the Procession, Respectfully inscribed to the Clay Club No. 1, Boston.* Drawn by Joshua Sheldon, Jr. (1801–1890), lithograph by Thayer & Co., Boston, 1844. Boston Public Library. https://ark.digitalcommonwealth.org/ark:/50959/c821gs09x (accessed September 15, 2019).

Page 258 *No Abuse of Power.* Boston, Massachusetts, 1848. Banner of the Boston Young Men's Whig Club. Oil on silk, 1848. Courtesy of Revolutionary Spaces.

Page 259 *Honest Old Abe Is Bound to Win.* Manchester, New Hampshire, 1856, reworked 1860. Edward L. Custer (1837–1881). New Hampshire Historical Society.

Page 260 *Grant–Wilson Political Rally, Augusta Depot, Sept. 6, 1872.* Augusta, Maine, September 6, 1872. John Martin (1823–1904). Watercolor. Collections of Maine Historical Society and Maine State Museum.

Temperance and Prohibition

Page 263 *Cold Water Army Pledge.* July 4, 1842. Membership certificate (detail). The Connecticut Historical Society (MS 74141).

Page 263 *Cold Water Army Pledge.* Printed badge, published by the Massachusetts Temperance Union, ca. 1830–1840. Pocumtuck Valley Memorial Association, Deerfield, Massachusetts.

Pages 264–265 *"To Hampton 2 mi."* Hampton, New Hampshire, ca. 1841. Banner of the Cold Water Army. Artist unknown. Oil on canvas. Hampton Historical Society. Rick Hureay photo.

Page 266 *Pump and Blockmakers, Mast and Sparmakers, Rope Makers, Riggers and Sailmakers Banner.* Portland, Maine, ca. 1841. William Capen, Jr. (ca. 1801–1863). Collections of Maine Historical Society.

Page 267 *View of the Grand Mass Washingtonian Convention on Boston Common, on the 30th of May 1844.* Boston, Massachusetts, May 30, 1844. Lithograph by Thayer & Co., Boston. Published by F. Gleason. Boston Public Library. https://ark.digitalcommonwealth.org/ark:/50959/2801pn76g.

Page 268 *View of the Grand Mass Washingtonian Convention on Boston Common, on the 30th of May 1844* (detail). Boston, Massachusetts, May 30, 1844. Lithograph by Thayer & Co., Boston. Published by F. Gleason. Boston Public Library. https://ark.digitalcommonwealth.org/ark:/50959/2801pn76g.

Page 269 *Washingtonian Total Abstinence Society Banner.* Dennysville, Maine, 1841. John Regan, oil on silk. Maine State Museum collections (90.48.1).

Page 270 *Rum—Here it Goes!* Boston or Salem, Massachusetts, ca. 1836–1850. Temperance banner. Printed cotton. Courtesy, American Antiquarian Society.

Page 271 *Tableau X. The Old Oaken Bucket.* Portland, Maine, July 5, 1886. John T. Hull, ed., *An Account of the Municipal Celebration of the One Hundredth Anniversary of the Incorporation of the Town of Portland, July 4th, 5th, and 6th, 1886.* Portland, ME: Owen, Strout & Company, 1886.

Page 272 *19 Prohibition States.* Northampton, Massachusetts, June 7, 1904. Courtesy of Historic Northampton, Northampton, Massachusetts.

Page 273 *We Must Save Our Boys.* North Bennington, Vermont, July 4, 1914. Bennington Museum.

Page 273 *No Cigarettes And No Liquor For Us*, Worcester, Massachusetts, 1915. From the collection of the Worcester Historical Museum, Worcester, Massachusetts.

Page 274 *John Barleycorn's "Funeral."* Boston, Massachusetts, January 16, 1920. *Boston Globe* via Getty Images.

Page 274 *There's Still Work to Be Done.* Concord, New Hampshire, 1923. New Hampshire Historical Society.

Business and Industry

Page 276–277 *Splendid Panoramic View of the Grand Procession of the Military, and Arts, Trades, Societies, and Professions on the Occasion of the Great Railroad Jubilee Celebration in Boston, September 19, 1851.* Wood engraving by Worcester & Peirce (detail). *Gleason's Pictorial Drawing Room Companion*, October 11, 1851, 376–377. Courtesy of Historic New England.

Page 278 *Blind Hole Shoe Manufactory in 1789 in full Operation.* Danvers, Massachusetts, June 16, 1852. Detail from *Scene Representing the Antique Procession, at the Centennial Celebration at Danvers, Mass.* Published in *Gleason's Pictorial Drawing Room Companion*, July 20, 1852, 25. Private collection.

Page 279 *Two of the Thirteen Teams Displayed by Walter Corey & Co.* Portland, Maine, July 5, 1886. John T. Hull, ed., *An Account of the Municipal Celebration of the One Hundredth Anniversary of the Incorporation of the Town of Portland, July 4th, 5th, and 6th, 1886.* Portland, ME: Owen, Strout & Company, 1886, Plate F.

Page 280 *Portland Company float* (both sides). Portland, Maine, July 5, 1886. Collections of Maine Historical Society.

Page 281 *Mayflower.* Haverhill, Massachusetts, 1890. *A Record of the Commemoration, July Second and Third, 1890 of the Two Hundred and Fiftieth Anniversary of the Settlement of Haverhill, Massachusetts.* Boston: Joseph George Cupples, 1891, opposite page 264.

Page 282 *Going to the Fair.* Rochester, New Hampshire, 1899. Courtesy of Dorothy Bean.

Page 283 *Work Cattle.* Sandwich, New Hampshire, 1898. Courtesy of the Sandwich Historical Society.

Page 284 *Garden of Eden.* Manchester, New Hampshire, September 9, 1896. Courtesy of the Manchester, N. H., Historic Association.

Page 285 *Wilson's Pharmacy.* Brunswick, Maine, 1889. Wilson's Pharmacy float, *Celebration of the 150th Anniversary of Brunswick, Me. June 18, 1889.* Photograph by J. C. Higgins & Son, Bath, Maine (detail). Pejepscot Historical Society (1992.39.76).

Page 286 *Venetian Gondola.* South Framingham, Massachusetts, 1900. Framingham History Center.

Page 287 *Preston Brothers Hardware.* Norwich, Connecticut, September 4, 1901. Courtesy of the Otis Library, Norwich, Connecticut.

Page 288 *Mrs. L. E. Theoret, Milliner.* Sanford, Maine, July 4, 1903. Sanford-Springvale Historical Society.

Page 289 *Japanese Pagoda and Tea Garden.* Northampton, Massachusetts, June 7, 1904. Courtesy of Historic Northampton, Northampton, Massachusetts.

Page 290 *Mrs. Marion A. Poole as Hannah Davis, "Bandbox Maker."* Jaffrey, New Hampshire, August 12, 1923. Jaffrey Historical Society.

Page 291 *General Electric Company.* Armistice Day, Lynn, Massachusetts, November 11, 1928. Lynn Public Library, https://www.digitalcommonwealth.org/search/commonwealth-oai:tm70p640f (accessed September 7, 2019).

Page 292 *Why Pay Rent? Build A House.* Concord, New Hampshire, 1927. New Hampshire Historical Society.

Page 292 *Bedford Hardware and Plumbing Co.* Bedford, Massachusetts, 1912. Courtesy of the Bedford Historical Society, Bedford, Massachusetts.

Page 293 *The Valley Times.* Pittsfield, New Hampshire, 1908. Pittsfield Historical Society.

Page 293 *The Sanford News.* Sanford, Maine, ca. 1912–1914. Sanford-Springvale Historical Society.

Page 294 *P. H. Vose Co. Float.* Bangor, Maine, June 18, 1912. Bangor Public Library.

Page 295 *The Giant Tricycle.* Concord, New Hampshire, 1896. Postcard. New Hampshire Historical Society.

Page 296 *Moxie.* Bellows Falls, Vermont, October 1, 1912. Photograph by Russell P. Bristol (1877–1932). Vermont Historical Society, Barre, Vermont.

Page 297 *Green's Clothier.* Houlton, Maine, July 4, 1914. Aroostook County Historical and Art Museum, Houlton, Maine.

Page 297 *Seth Thomas Clock.* Hartford, Connecticut, October 12, 1935 (detail). The Connecticut Historical Society (1982.102.11).

Page 298 *Lydia Pinkham's Vegetable Compound.* Location and date unrecorded. Schlesinger Library, Radcliffe Institute, Harvard University.

Page 299 *A Merry Christmas: The "Cop" in Santason's* [sic] *Parade,* Boston, Massachusetts, Thanksgiving Day, 1938. Stereoview. Courtesy of Historic New England.

Women's Clubs and Charity

Page 301 *An Errand of Mercy, 1812.* Concord, New Hampshire, 1927. New Hampshire Historical Society.

Page 302 *Broom Brigade.* Hinesburg, Vermont, ca. 1885–1890. Vermont Historical Society, Barre, Vermont.

Page 303 *Wesley M. E. Church, Ladies'Aid.* Bath, Maine, 1907. Photograph by Otis N. E. Card. Maine Maritime Museum, courtesy of the late Charles E. Burden.

Page 304 *Southbridge Woman's Club.* Southbridge, Massachusetts, Centennial, July 4, 1916. Postcard, photograph by Arthur S. Adams, Worcester, Massachusetts. Digital reproduction provided by the Jacob Edwards Library.

Page 305 *The Bee—Workers in Four Wars.* Cambridge, Massachusetts, April 27, 1918. Longfellow House-Washington's

Headquarters National Historic Site. (Dana Collected Correspondence. Photographs not in albums).

Page 306 *The Mobilized Humanity of the World.* Portland, Maine, July 5, 1920. Collections of Maine Historical Society/MaineToday Media.

Page 307 *Prize-winning Float of the Thought and Work Club. Floral Procession of the Salem Tercentenary, 1926.* Salem, Massachusetts, July 7, 1926. Peabody Essex Museum.

Page 308 *"We Keep Clean."* Kennebunk, Maine, May 1928. Courtesy of the Brick Store Museum, Kennebunk, Maine.

Page 308 *The Greatest Mother in the World.* Bedford, Massachusetts, 1929. Courtesy of the Bedford Historical Society, Bedford, Massachusetts.

Preparedness

Page 309 *U. C. USINKEM.* Nantucket, Massachusetts, April 13, 1917. Courtesy of the Nantucket Historical Association Research Library Photograph Archives (GPN 4446).

Page 310 *Red Cross Ambulance.* Biddeford, Maine, 1917. McArthur Public Library, Biddeford, Maine.

Page 310 *Liberty and Future Generations.* Pittsfield, Massachusetts, undated (1918 or later). Courtesy of the Berkshire County Historical Society, Pittsfield, Massachusetts.

Progressivism

Page 312 *Suffrage Parade.* Boston, Massachusetts, May 2, 1914. Schlesinger Library, Radcliffe Institute, Harvard University.

Page 314 *Votes for Women.* Andover, Massachusetts, July 4, 1912. © Andover Center for History and Culture, Andover, Massachusetts.

Page 315 *Votes for Women.* Hamilton, Massachusetts, 1912. Courtesy of the Hamilton Historical Society, Hamilton, Massachusetts.

Page 316 *Still Seeking Votes for Women.* Biddeford, Maine, September 16, 1916. McArthur Library, Biddeford, Maine.

Page 316 *League of Women Voters.* Concord, New Hampshire, 1927. New Hampshire Historical Society.

Page 317 *Modern Health Crusaders.* Portland, Maine, May 1924. Collections of Maine Historical Society/MaineToday Media.

Page 318 *Brush Thoroughly Twice a Day.* Portland, Maine, May 1924. Collections of Maine Historical Society/MaineToday Media.

Page 319 *Children's Health Parade.* Kennebunk, Maine, May 1928. Courtesy of the Brick Store Museum, Kennebunk, Maine.

Page 320 *You Need Milk.* Kennebunk, Maine, May 1928. Courtesy of the Brick Store Museum, Kennebunk, Maine.

Page 320 *Farmers with a Load of Fresh Vegetables.* Kennebunk, May 1928. Courtesy of the Brick Store Museum, Kennebunk, Maine.

Page 321 *Cleanliness Is One of the Foundations of Good Government and Good Living.* Boston, Massachusetts, 1930. Messmore and Damon Company records, Archives Center, National Museum of American History, Smithsonian Institution.

Page 322 *First Parade in N. E. States of Ku Klux Klan. First Daylight Parade in U. S. A.* Milo, Maine, September 3, 1923. Maine Historic Preservation Commission.

Page 323 *The Declaration of Independence, the Constitution of the United States: the Bedrock of American Society.* Ku Klux Klan float. Portsmouth, New Hampshire, August 1923. Courtesy of the Portsmouth Athenaeum.

Page 324 *Americanization Class Ready for a Parade.* Portland, Maine 1926. Collections of Maine Historical Society/MaineToday Media.

CHAPTER 8—PATRIOTISM

Colonies and States

Page 327 *Columbia and 37 States.* Rochester, New Hampshire, July 4, 1876. Stereoview. Maine Historic Preservation Commission.

Page 328 *The Goddess of Liberty and Her Thirteen Colonies.* Nantucket, Massachusetts, 1895. Courtesy of the Nantucket Historical Association.

Page 329 *Uncle Sam and the States.* Keene, New Hampshire, September 7, 1898. Historical Society of Cheshire County, Keene, New Hampshire.

Page 330 *America.* Springvale, Maine, July 4, 1907. Courtesy of Sanford-Springvale Historical Society.

Page 331 *Miss Liberty and Her Thirteen Colonies.* Newport, Rhode Island, 1916. Collection of the Newport Historical Society (NDN 8186).

Uncle Sam

Page 332 *Uncle Sam and Lady Liberty.* Lancaster, Massachusetts, July 4, 1890. Courtesy of the Thayer Memorial Library, Lancaster, Massachusetts. https://ark.digitalcommonwealth.org/ark:/50959/02871k30b (accessed August 19, 2019).

Page 333 *Charles Bartlett Folsom.* Pittsfield, New Hampshire, 1909. Postcard. Private collection.

Page 334 *George Cousens as Uncle Sam* (two views). Kennebunk, Maine, 1920. Courtesy of the Brick Store Museum, Kennebunk, Maine.

Page 335 *Uncle Sams.* New London, Connecticut, May 6, 1934. Postcard. Mystic Seaport.

Page 336 *Uncle Sam and Sailor Boys.* Bath, Maine, ca. 1930s. Maine Maritime Museum, courtesy of the late Charles E. Burden.

Liberty Bell

Page 337 *1776 Liberty 1919.* Bennington, Vermont, July 4, 1919. Bennington Museum.

Three Cheers for the Red, White, and Blue!

Page 338 *Yankee Doodle.* Dedham, Massachusetts, possibly 1876. Dedham Historical Society.

Page 339 *Spirit of '76.* Concord, New Hampshire, June 14, 1916. New Hampshire Historical Society.

Page 340 *Stand by the President.* Brookfield, Massachusetts, June 14, 1917. Photograph by Frank Bullard. Private collection.

Page 341 *Fred Smith and His Flag Girls.* Bellows Falls, Vermont, October 1, 1912. Photograph by Russell C. Bristol (1877–1932). Vermont Historical Society, Barre, Vermont.

Page 341 *A Patriotic Neighborhood.* East Longmeadow, Massachusetts, July 4, 1923. Courtesy of the East Longmeadow Historical Commission.

Page 342 *Ruth Fairbanks, 1922.* Portland, Maine, ca. 1922. Collections of Maine Historical Society/MaineToday Media.

Page 342 *Stars and Stripes.* New Bedford, Massachusetts, perhaps November 18, 1918. Courtesy of the New Bedford Whaling Museum.

Page 343 *Old Home Day Comes Every Year.* Tamworth, New Hampshire, 1926. Courtesy of the Tamworth History Center.

Page 344 *Color Guard and Boy Scouts.* Bath, Maine, 1928 or later. Maine Martime Museum, courtesy of the late Charles E. Burden.

Page 345 *Living Flag.* Manchester, New Hampshire, November 11, 1933. Courtesy of the Manchester (NH) Historic Association.

Index